STUDIES
IN
EUROPEAN REALISM

STUDIES IN EUROPEAN REALISM

A *Sociological survey of the Writings of*
BALZAC, STENDHAL, ZOLA,
TOLSTOY, GORKI
and others

By
GEORG LUKÁCS

Translated by
Edith Bone

THE MERLIN PRESS
LONDON

© Hillway Publishing Co, 1950. Republished
by the Merlin Press, 11 Fitzroy Square
London W.1 and printed by Redwood
Press Limited, Trowbridge & London
1972

CONTENTS

PREFACE

THE ARTICLES contained in this book were written some ten years ago. Author and reader may well ask why they should be republished just now. At first sight they might seem to lack all topicality. Subject and tone alike may appear remote to a considerable section of public opinion. I believe, however, that they have some topicality in that, without entering upon any detailed polemics, they represent a point of view in opposition to certain literary and philosophical trends still very much to the fore today.

Let us begin with the general atmosphere : the clouds of mysticism which once surrounded the phenomena of literature with a poetic colour and warmth and created an intimate and "interesting" atmosphere around them, have been dispersed. Things now face us in a clear, sharp light which to many may seem cold and hard; a light shed on them by the teachings of Marx. Marxism searches for the material roots of each phenomenon, regards them in their historical connections and movement, ascertains the laws of such movement and demonstrates their development from root to flower, and in so doing lifts every phenomenon out of a merely emotional, irrational, mystic fog and brings it to the bright light of understanding.

Such a transition is at first a disillusionment to many people and it is necessary that this should be so. For it is no easy matter to look stark reality in the face and no one succeeds in achieving this at the first attempt. What is required for this is not merely a great deal of hard work, but also a serious moral effort. In the first phase of such a change of heart most people will look back regretfully to the false but "poetic" dreams of reality which they are about to relinquish. Only later does it grow clear how much more genuine humanity—and hence genuine poetry—attaches to the acceptance of truth with all its inexorable reality and to acting in accordance with it.

But there is far more than this involved in such a change of heart. I am thinking here of that philosophical pessimism which was so deeply rooted in the social conditions of the period between the two world wars. It was not by accident that everywhere there arose thinkers who deepened this pessimism and who built up their

1

Weltanschauung on some philosophical generalization of despair. The Germans, Spengler and Heidegger, and a considerable number of other influential thinkers of the last few decades embraced such views.

There is, of course, plenty of darkness around us now, just as there was between the two wars. Those who wish to despair can find cause enough and more in our everyday life. Marxism does not console anyone by playing down difficulties, or minimizing the material and moral darkness which surrounds us human beings today. The difference is only—but in this " only " lies a whole world—that Marxism has a grasp of the main lines of human development and recognizes its laws. Those who have arrived at such knowledge know, in spite of all temporary darkness, both whence we have come and where we are going. And those who know this find the world changed in their eyes : they see purposeful development where formerly only a blind, senseless confusion surrounded them. Where the philosophy of despair weeps for the collapse of a world and the destruction of culture, there Marxists watch the birth-pangs of a new world and assist in mitigating the pains of labour.

One might answer to all this—I have met with such objections myself often enough—that all this is only philosophy and sociology. What has all this to do with the theory and history of the novel? We believe that it has to do quite a lot. If we were to formulate the question in terms of literary history, it would read thus : which of the two, Balzac or Flaubert, was the greatest novelist, the typical classic of the 19th century? Such a judgment is not merely a matter of taste—it involves all the central problems of the æsthetics of the novel as an art form. The question arises whether it is the unity of the external and internal worlds or the separation between them which is the social basis of the greatness of a novel; whether the modern novel reached its culminating point in Gide, Proust and Joyce or had already reached its peak much earlier, in the works of Balzac and Tolstoy; so that today only individual great artists struggling against the current—as for instance Thomas Mann— can reach the heights already long attained.

These two aesthetic conceptions conceal the application of two opposite philosophies of history to the nature and historical development of the novel. And because the novel is the predominant art form of modern *bourgeois* culture, this contrast between the two aesthetic conceptions of the novel refers us back to the development of literature as a whole, or perhaps even culture as a whole.

2

The question asked by the philosophy of history would be : does the road of our present-day culture lead upwards or downwards? There is no denying that our culture has passed and is passing through dark periods. It is for the philosophy of history to decide whether that darkening of the horizon which was adequately expressed for the first time in Flaubert's *Education Sentimentale* is a final, fatal eclipse or only a tunnel from which, however long it may be, there is a way out to the light once more.

Bourgeois æstheticists and critics, the author of the present book among them, saw no way out of this darkness. They regarded poetry merely as a revelation of the inner life, a clear-sighted recognition of social hopelessness or at best a consolation, an outward-reflected miracle. It followed with logical necessity from this historico-philosophical conception that Flaubert's *oeuvre,* notably his *Education Sentimentale,* was regarded as the greatest achievement of the modern novel. This conception naturally extends to every sphere of literature. I quote only one instance : the real great philosophical and psychological content of the epilogue to *War and Peace* is the process which after the Napoleonic wars led the most advanced minority of the Russian aristocratic *intelligentsia*—a very small minority, of course—to the Decembrist rising, that tragically heroic prelude to the secular struggle of the Russian people for its liberation. Of all this my own old philosophy of history and aesthetics saw nothing. For me the epilogue held only the subdued colours of Flaubertian hopelessness, the frustration of the purposeless searchings and impulses of youth, their silting-up in the grey prose of *bourgeois* family life. The same applies to almost every detailed analysis of *bourgeois* aesthetics. The opposition of Marxism to the historical views of the last 50 years (the essence of which was the denial that history is a branch of learning that deals with the unbroken upward evolution of mankind) implied at the same time a sharp objective disagreement in all problems of *Weltanschauung* or aesthetics. No one can expect me to give even a skeleton outline of the Marxist philosophy of history within the limits of a preface. But we must nevertheless eliminate certain commonplace prejudices in order that author and reader may understand one another, that readers approach without bias this book with its application of Marxism to certain important problems of literary history and aesthetics and not pass judgment on it until they have compared this application with the facts. The Marxist philosophy of history is a comprehensive doctrine dealing with the necessary progress made by humanity from primitive communism

3

to our own time and the perspectives of our further advance along the same road as such it also gives us indications for the historical future. But such indications—born of the recognition of certain laws governing historical development—are not a cookery book providing recipes for each phenomenon or period; Marxism is not a Baedeker of history, but a signpost pointing the direction in which history moves forward. The final certainty it affords consists in the assurance that the development of mankind does not and cannot finally lead to nothing and nowhere.

Of course, such generalizations do not do full justice to the guidance given by Marxism, a guidance extending to every topical problem of life. Marxism combines a consistent following of an unchanging direction with incessant theoretical and practical allowances for the deviousness of the path of evolution. Its well-defined philosophy of history is based on a flexible and adaptable acceptance and analysis of historical development. This apparent duality—which is in reality the dialectic unity of the materialist worldview—is also the guiding principle of Marxist aesthetics and literary theory.

Those who do not know Marxism at all or know it only superficially or at second-hand, may be surprised by the respect for the classical heritage of mankind which one finds in the really great representatives of this doctrine and by their incessant references to that classical heritage. Without wishing to enter into too much detail, we mention as an instance, in philosophy, the heritage of Hegelian dialectics, as opposed to the various trends in the latest philosophies. "But all this is long out of date," the modernists cry. "All this is the undesirable, outworn legacy of the nineteenth century," say those who—intentionally or unintentionally, consciously or unconsciously—support the Fascist ideology and its pseudo-revolutionary rejection of the past, which is in reality a rejection of culture and humanism. Let us look without prejudice at the bankruptcy of the very latest philosophies; let us consider how most philosophers of our day are compelled to pick up the broken and scattered fragments of dialectic (falsified and distorted in this decomposition) whenever they want to say something even remotely touching its essence about present-day life; let us look at the modern attempts at a philosophical synthesis and we shall find them miserable, pitiful caricatures of the old genuine dialectic, now consigned to oblivion.

It is not by chance that the great Marxists were jealous guardians of our classical heritage in their aesthetics as well as in other

4

spheres. But they do not regard this classical heritage as a reversion to the past; it is a necessary outcome of their philosophy of history that they should regard the past as irretrievably gone and not susceptible of renewal. Respect for the classical heritage of humanity in æsthetics means that the great Marxists look for the true highroad of history, the true direction of its development, the true course of the historical curve, the formula of which they know; and because they know the formula they do not fly off at a tangent at every hump in the graph, as modern thinkers often do because of their theoretical rejection of the idea that there is any such thing as an unchanged general line of development.

For the sphere of æsthetics this classical heritage consists in the great arts which depict man as a whole in the whole of society. Again it is the general philosophy, (here : proletarian humanism) which determines the central problems posed in aesthetics. The Marxist philosophy of history analyses man as a whole, and contemplates the history of human evolution as a whole, together with the partial achievement, or non-achievement of completeness in its various periods of development. It strives to unearth the hidden laws governing all human relationships. Thus the object of proletarian humanism is to reconstruct the complete human personality and free it from the distortion and dismemberment to which it has been subjected in class society. These theoretical and practical perspectives determine the criteria by means of which Marxist æsthetics establish a bridge back to the classics and at the same time discover new classics in the thick of the literary struggles of our own time. The ancient Greeks, Dante, Shakespeare, Goethe, Balzac, Tolstoy all give adequate pictures of great periods of human development and at the same time serve as signposts in the ideological battle fought for the restoration of the unbroken human personality.

Such viewpoints enable us to see the cultural and literary evolution of the nineteenth century in its proper light. They show us that the true heirs of the French novel, so gloriously begun early in the last century, were not Flaubert and especially not Zola, but the Russian and Scandinavian writers of the second half of the century. The present volume contains my studies of French and Russian realist writers seen in this perspective.

If we translate into the language of pure æsthetics the conflict (conceived in the sense of the philosophy of history) between Balzac and the later French novel, we arrive at the conflict between realism and naturalism. Talking of a conflict here may sound a paradox to the ears of most writers and readers of our day. For most present-day writers and readers are used to literary fashions swinging to and fro between the pseudo-objectivism of the naturalist school and the mirage-subjectivism of the psychologist or abstract-formalist school. And inasmuch as they see any worth in realism at all, they regard their own false extreme as a new kind of near-realism or realism. Realism however is not some sort of middle way between false objectivity and false subjectivity, but on the contrary the true, solution-bringing third way, opposed to all the pseudo-dilemmas engendered by the wrongly-posed questions of those who wander without a chart in the labyrinth of our time. Realism is the recognition of the fact that a work of literature can rest neither on a lifeless average, as the naturalists suppose, nor on an individual principle which dissolves its own self into nothingness. The central category and criterion of realist literature is the type, a peculiar synthesis which organically binds together the general and the particular both in characters and situations. What makes a type a type is not its average quality, not its mere individual being, however profoundly conceived; what makes it a type is that in it all the humanly and socially essential determinants are present on their highest level of development, in the ultimate unfolding of the possibilities latent in them, in extreme presentation of their extremes, rendering concrete the peaks and limits of men and epochs.

True great realism thus depicts man and society as complete entities, instead of showing merely one or the other of their aspects. Measured by this criterion, artistic trends determined by either exclusive introspection or exclusive extraversion equally impoverish and distort reality. Thus realism means a three-dimensionality, an all-roundness, that endows with independent life characters and human relationships. It by no means involves a rejection of the emotional and intellectual dynamism which necessarily develops together with the modern world. All it opposes is the destruction of the completeness of the human personality and of the objective typicality of men and situations through an excessive cult of the momentary mood. The struggle against such tendencies acquired a decisive importance in the realist literature of the nineteenth century. Long before such tendencies appeared in the practice of literature, Balzac had already prophetically foreseen and outlined the entire problem in his tragi-comic story *Le Chef d'Oeuvre Inconnu*. Here experiment on the part of a painter to create a new classic three-dimensionality by means of an ecstasy of emotion and colour quite in the spirit of modern impressionism, leads to complete chaos. Fraunhofer, the tragic hero, paints a picture which is a tangled chaos of colours out of which a perfectly modelled female leg and foot protrude as an almost fortuitous fragment. Today a considerable section of modern artists has given up the Fraunhofer-like struggle and is content with finding, by means of new aesthetic theories, a justification for the emotional chaos of their works.

The central aesthetic problem of realism is the adequate presentation of the complete human personality. But as in every profound philosophy of art, here, too, the consistent following-up to the end of the aesthetic viewpoint leads us beyond pure aesthetics : for art, precisely if taken in its most perfect purity, is saturated with social and moral humanistic problems.. The demand for a realistic creation of types is in opposition both to the trends in which the biological being of man, the physiological aspects of self-preservation and procreation are dominant (Zola and his disciples) and to the trends which sublimate man into purely mental, psychological processes. But such an attitude, if it remained within the sphere of formal aesthetic judgments, would doubtless be quite arbitrary, for there is no reason why, regarded merely from the point of view of good writing, erotic conflict with its attendant moral and social conflicts should be rated higher than the elemental spontaneity of pure sex. Only if we accept the concept of the complete human personality as the social and historical task humanity has to solve; only if we regard it as the vocation of art to depict the most important turning-points of this process with all the wealth of the factors affecting it; only if aesthetics assign to art the role of explorer and guide, can the content of life be systematically divided up into spheres of greater and lesser importance; into spheres that throw light on types and paths and spheres that remain in darkness. Only then does it become evident that any description of mere biological processes—be these the sexual act or pain and sufferings, however detailed and from the literary point of view perfect it may be—results in a levelling-down of the social, historical and moral being of men and is not a means but an obstacle to such essential artistic expression as illuminating human conflicts in all their complexity and completeness. It is for this reason that the new contents and new media of expression contributed by naturalism have led not to an enrichment but to an impoverishment and narrowing-down of literature.

Apparently similar trains of thought were already put forward

7

in early polemics directed against Zola and his school.   But the psychologists, although they were more than once right in their concrete condemnation of Zola and the Zola school, opposed another no less false extreme to the false extreme of naturalism. For the inner life of man, its essential traits and essential conflicts can be truly portrayed only in organic connection with social and historical factors.   Separated from the latter and developing merely its own immanent dialectic, the psychologist trend is no less abstract, and distorts and impoverishes the portrayal of the complete human personality no less than does the naturalist biologism which it opposes.

It is true that, especially regarded from the viewpoint of modern literary fashions, the position in respect of the psychologist school is at the first glance less obvious than in the case of naturalism. Everyone will   immediately see that a description in the Zola manner of, say, an act of copulation between Dido and Aeneas or Romeo and Juliet would resemble each other very much more closely than the erotic conflicts depicted by Virgil and Shakespeare, which acquaint us with an inexhaustible wealth of cultural and human facts and types.   Pure introspection is apparently the diametrical opposite of naturalist levelling-down, for what it describes are quite individual, non-recurring traits. But such extremely individual traits are also extremely abstract, for this very reason of non-recurrence. Here, too, Chesterton's witty paradox holds good, that the inner light is the worst kind of lighting.   It is obvious to everyone that the coarse biologism of the naturalists and the rough outlines drawn by propagandist writers deform the true picture of the complete human personality.   Much fewer are those who realize that the psychologists' punctilious probing into the human soul and their transformation of human beings into a chaotic flow of ideas destroy no less surely every possibility of a literary presentation of the complete human personality. A Joyce-like shoreless torrent of associations can create living human beings just as little as Upton Sinclair's coldly calculated all-good and all-bad stereotypes.

Owing to lack of space this problem cannot be developed here in all its breadth.   Only one important and at present often neglected point is to be stressed here because it demonstrates that the live portrayal of the complete human personality is possible only if the writer attempts to create types.   The point in question is the organic, indissoluble connection between man as a private individual and man as a social being, as a member of a community. We

8

know that this is the most difficult question of modern literature today and has been so ever since modern *bourgeois* society came into being. On the surface the two seem to be sharply divided and the appearance of the autonomous, independent existence of the individual is all the more pronounced, the more completely modern *bourgeois* society is developed. It seems as if the inner life, genuine "private" life, were proceeding according to its own autonomous laws and as if its fulfilments and tragedies were growing ever more independent of the surrounding social environment. And correspondingly, on the other side, it seems as if the connection with the community could manifest itself only in high-sounding abstractions, the adequate expression for which would be either rhetoric or satire.

An unbiassed investigation of life and the setting aside of these false traditions of modern literature leads easily enough to the uncovering of the true circumstances, to the discovery which had long been made by the great realists of the beginning and middle of the nineteenth century and which Gottfried Keller expressed thus: "Everything is politics." The great Swiss writer did not intend this to mean that everything was immediately tied up with politics; on the contrary, in his view—as in Balzac's and Tolstoy's —every action, thought and emotion of human beings is inseparably bound up with the life and struggles of the community, i.e., with politics; whether the humans themselves are conscious of this, unconscious of it or even trying to escape from it, objectively their actions, thoughts and emotions nevertheless spring from and run into politics.

The true great realists not only realized and depicted this situation—they did more than that, they set it up as a demand to be made on men. They knew that this distortion of objective reality (although, of course, due to social causes), this division of the complete human personality into a public and a private sector was a mutilation of the essence of man. Hence they protested not only as painters of reality, but also as humanists, against this fiction of capitalist society however unavoidable this spontaneously formed superficial appearance. If as writers, they delved deeper in order to uncover the true types of man, they had inevitably to unearth and expose to the eyes of modern society the great tragedy of the complete human personality.

In the works of such great realists as Balzac we can again find a third solution opposed to both false extremes of modern literature, exposing as an abstraction, as a vitiation of the true poesy of life,

9

both the feeble commonplaces of the well-intentioned and honest propagandist novels and the spurious richness of a preoccupation with the details of private life.

This brings us face to face with the question of the topicality today of the great realist writers. Every great historical period is a period of transition, a contradictory unity of crisis and renewal, of destruction and rebirth; a new social order and a new type of man always come into being in the course of a unified though contradictory process. In such critical, transitional periods the tasks and responsibility of literature are exceptionally great. But only truly great realism can cope with such responsibilities; the accustomed, the fashionable media of expression, tend more and more to hamper literature in fulfilling the tasks imposed by history. It should surprise no one if from this point of view we turn against the individualistic, psychologist trends in literature. It might more legitimately surprise many that these studies express a sharp opposition to Zola and Zolaism.

Such surprise may be due in the main to the fact that Zola was a writer of the left and his literary methods were dominant chiefly, though by no means exclusively, in left-wing literature. It might appear, therefore, that we are involving ourselves in a serious contradiction, demanding on the one hand the politization of literature and on the other hand attacking insidiously the most vigorous and militant section of left-wing literature. But this contradiction is merely apparent. It is, however, well suited to throw light on the true connection between literature and *Weltanschauung*.

The problem was first raised (apart from the Russian democratic literary critics) by Engels, when he drew a comparison between Balzac and Zola. Engels showed that Balzac, although his political creed was legitimist royalism, nevertheless inexorably exposed the vices and weakness of royalist feudal France and described its death agony with magnificent poetic vigour. This phenomenon, references to which the reader will find more than once in these pages, may at the first glance again—and mistakenly—appear contradictory. It might appear that the *Weltanschauung* and political attitude of serious great realists are a matter of no consequence. To a certain extent this is true. For from the point of view of the self-recognition of the present and from the point of view of history and posterity, what matters is the picture conveyed by the work; the question to what extent this picture conforms to the views of the authors is a secondary consideration.

This, of course, brings us to a serious problem of aesthetics.

Engels, in writing about Balzac, called it "the triumph of realism"; it is a problem that goes down to the very roots of realist artistic creation. It touches the essence of true realism : the great writer's thirst for truth, his fanatic striving for reality—or expressed in terms of ethics : the writer's sincerity and probity. A great realist such as Balzac, if the intrinsic artistic development of situations and characters he has created comes into conflict with his most cherished prejudices or even his most sacred convictions, will, without an instant's hesitation, set aside these his own prejudices and convictions and describe what he really sees, not what he would prefer to see. This ruthlessness towards their own subjective world-picture is the hall-mark of all great realists, in sharp contrast to the second-raters, who nearly always succeed in bringing their own *Weltanschauung* into "harmony" with reality, that is forcing a falsified or distorted picture of reality into the shape of their own world-view. This difference in the ethical attitude of the greater and lesser writers is closely linked with the difference between genuine and spurious creation. The characters created by the great realists, once conceived in the vision of their creator, live an independent life of their own : their comings and goings, their development, their destiny is dictated by the inner dialectic of their social and individual existence. No writer is a true realist—or even a truly good writer, if he can direct the evolution of his own characters at will.

All this is however merely a description of the phenomenon. It answers the question as to the ethics of the writer : what will he do if he sees reality in such and such a light ? But this does not enlighten us at all regarding the other question : what does the writer see and how does he see it ? And yet it is here that the most important problems of the social determinants of artistic creation arise. In the course of these studies we shall point out in detail the basic differences which arise in the creative methods of writers according to the degree to which they are bound up with the life of the community, take part in the struggles going on around them or are merely passive observers of events. Such differences determine creative processes which may be diametrical opposites; even the experience which gives rise to the work will be structurally different, and in accordance with this the process of shaping the work will be different. The question whether a writer lives within the community or is a mere observer of it, is determined not by psychological, not even by typological factors; it is the evolution of society that determines (not automatically, not fatalistically, of

11

course), the line the evolution of an author will take. Many a writer of a basically contemplative type has been driven to an intense participation in the life of the community by the social conditions of his time; Zola, on the contrary, was by nature a man of action, but his epoch turned him into a mere observer and when at last he answered the call of life, it came too late to influence his development as a writer.

But even this is as yet only the formal aspect of this problem, although no longer the abstractly formal. The question grows essential and decisive only when we examine concretely the position taken up by a writer. What does he love and what does he hate ? It is thus that we arrive at a deeper interpretation of the writer's true *Weltanschauung*, at the problem of the artistic value and fertility of the writer's world-view. The conflict which previously stood before us as the conflict between the writer's world-view and the faithful protrayal of the world he sees, is now clarified as a problem within the *Weltanschauung* itself, as a conflict between a deeper and a more superficial level of the writer's own *Weltanschauung*.

Realists such as Balzac or Tolstoy in their final posing of questions always take the most important, burning problems of the community for their starting-point; their pathos as writers is always stimulated by those sufferings of the people which are the most acute at the time; it is these sufferings that determine the objects and direction of their love and hate and through these emotions determine also what they see in their poetic visions and how they see it. If, therefore, in the process of creation their conscious world-view comes into conflict with the world seen in their vision, what really emerges is that their true conception of the world is only superficially formulated in the consciously held world-view and the real depth of their *Weltanschauung*, their deep ties with the great issues of their time, their sympathy with the sufferings of the people can find adequate expression only in the being and fate of their characters.

No one experienced more deeply than Balzac the torments which the transition to the capitalist system of production inflicted on every section of the people, the profound moral and spiritual degradation which necessarily accompanied this transformation on every level of society. At the same time Balzac was also deeply aware of the fact that this transformation was not only socially inevitable, but at the same time progressive. This contradiction in his experience Balzac attempted to force into a system based on a Catholic legitimism and tricked out with Utopian conceptions of English Toryism. But this system was contradicted all the time by the social realities of his day and the Balzacian vision which mirrored them. This contradiction itself clearly expressed, however, the real truth : Balzac's profound comprehension of the contradictorily progressive character of capitalist development.

It is thus that great realism and popular humanism are merged into an organic unity. For if we regard the classics of the social development that determined the essence of our age, from Goethe and Walter Scott to Gorki and Thomas Mann, we find *mutatis mutandis* the same structure of the basic problem. Of course every great realist found a different solution for the basic problem in accordance with his time and his own artistic personality. But they all have in common that they penetrate deeply into the great universal problems of their time and inexorably depict the true essense of reality as they see it. From the French revolution onwards the development of society moved in a direction which rendered inevitable a conflict between such aspirations of men of letters and the literature and public of their time. In this whole age a writer could achieve greatness only in the struggle against the current of everyday life. And since Balzac the resistance of daily life to the deeper tendencies of literature, culture and art has grown ceaselessly stronger. Nevertheless there were always writers who in their life-work, despite all the resistance of the day, fulfilled the demand formulated by Hamlet : ' to hold the mirror up to nature,' and by means of such a reflected image aided the development of mankind and the triumph of humanist principles in a society so contradictory in its nature that it on the one hand gave birth to the ideal of the complete human personality and on the other hand destroyed it in practice.

The great realists of France found worthy heirs only in Russia. All the problems mentioned here in connection with Balzac apply in an even greater measure to Russian literary development and notably to its central figure Leo Tolstoy. It is not by chance that Lenin (without having read Engels' remarks about Balzac) formulated the Marxist view of the principles of true realism in connection with Tolstoy. Hence there is no need for us to refer to these problems again here. There is all the more need, however, to call attention to the erroneous conceptions current in respect of the historical and social foundations of Russian realism, errors which in many cases are due to deliberate distortion or concealment of facts. In Britain, as everywhere else in Europe, the newer Russian literature is well known and popular among the intelligent reading public. But as everywhere else, the reactionaries have done all they could to prevent this literature from becoming popular; they felt instinctively that Russian realism, even if each single work may not have a definite social tendency, is an antidote to all reactionary infection.

But however widespread familiarity with Russian literature may have been in the West, the picture formed in the minds of readers was nevertheless incomplete and largely false. It was incomplete because the great champions of Russian revolutionary democracy, Herzen and Bielinski, Chernyshevski and Dobrolyubov were not translated and even their names were known to very few outside the reach of the Russian language. And it is only now that the name of Saltykov-Shchedrin is getting to be known, although in him the newer Russian literature had produced a satirist unrivalled anywhere in the world since the days of Jonathan Swift.

What is more, the conception of Russian literature was not only incomplete, it was also distorted. The great Russian realist Tolstoy was claimed by reactionary ideologies for their own and the attempt was made to turn him into a mystic gazing into the past; into an " aristocrat of the spirit " far removed from the struggles of the present. This falsification of the image of Tolstoy served a second purpose as well; it helped to give a false impression of the tendencies predominant in the life of the Russian people. The result was the myth of a "holy Russia " and Russian mysticism. Later, when the Russian people in 1917 fought and won the battle for liberation, a considerable section of the *intelligentsia* saw a contradiction between the new free Russia and the older Russian literature. One of the weapons of counter-revolutionary propaganda was the untrue allegation that the new Russia had effected a complete volte-face in every sphere of culture and had rejected, in fact was persecuting, older Russian literature.

These counter-revolutionary allegations have long been refuted by the facts. The literature of the White Russian émigrés, which claimed to be the continuation of the allegedly mystical Russian literature, quickly showed its own sterility and futility, once it was cut off from the Russian soil and the real Russian problems. On the other hand, it was impossible to conceal from the intelligent reading public that in the Soviet Union the vigorous treatment of the fresh issues thrown up by the rejuvenated life of the nation was developing a rich and interesting new literature and the discerning readers of this literature could see for themselves how

14

deeply rooted were the connections between it and Russian classical realism. (It will suffice to refer here to Sholokhov, the heir to Tolstoy's realism.)

The reactionary campaign of misrepresentation directed against the Soviet Union reached its culminating point before and during the late war, and then collapsed in the course of the same war, when the liberated peoples of the Soviet Union in their struggle against German Nazi imperialism demonstrated to the world such strength and such achievements in the sphere of moral and material culture that the old-style slanders and misrepresentations ceased to be effective. On the contrary a very large number of people began to ask : what was the source of the mighty popular forces, the manifestations of which were witnessed by the whole world during the war. Such dangerous thoughts required counter-measures and now we see a fresh wave of slander and misrepresentation breaking against the rock of Soviet civilization. Nevertheless the history of the internal and external evolution of the Russian people still remains an exciting and interesting problem for the reading public of every country.

In examining the history of the liberation of the Russian people and of the consolidation of its achievements, we must not overlook the important part played by literature in these historical events, —a part greater than the usual influence exercised by literature on the rising or falling fortunes of any civilized nation. On the one hand no other literature is as public-spirited as the Russian and on the other hand there has scarcely been any society in which literary works excited so much attention and provoked such crises as in Russian society in the classical realist period of Russian literature. Hence, although a very wide public is acquainted with Russian literature, it may not be superfluous to present this freshly arising problem in a new light. The new problems imperatively demand that our analysis penetrate, both from the social and the æsthetic viewpoint, to the true roots of Russian social development.

It is for this reason that our first study attempts to fill one of the greatest gaps in our knowledge of Russian literature by giving a characterization of the little-known great Russian revolutionary-democratic critics Bielinski, Chernyshevski and Dobrolyubov. Closely linked with this question is a revaluation of the well-known classical realists, or rather a characterization and appreciation which is somewhat more in accordance with historical truth. In the past, western critics and readers in their approach to Tolstoy and others took for their guide the views on society, philosophy,

15

religion, art, and so on, which these great men had themselves expressed in articles, letters, diaries and the like. They thought to find a key to the understanding of the often unfamiliar great works of literature in these conscious opinions. In other words reactionary criticism interpreted the works of Tolstoy and Dostoyevski by deriving the alleged spiritual and artistic content of these works from certain reactionary views of the authors.

The method employed in the present studies is the exact opposite of this. It is a very simple method : it consists in first of all examining carefully the real social foundations on which say Tolstoy's existence rested and the real social forces under the influence of which the human and the literary personality of this author developed. Secondly, in close connection with the first approach, the question is asked : what do Tolstoy's works represent, what is their real spiritual and intellectual content and how does the writer build up his æsthetic forms in the struggle for the adequate expression of such contents. Only if, after an unbiassed examination, we have uncovered and understood these objective relationships, are we in a position to provide a correct interpretation of the conscious views expressed by the author and correctly evaluate his influence on literature.

The reader will see later that in applying this method a quite new picture of Tolstoy will emerge. This revaluation will be new only to the non-Russian reading public. In Russian literature itself the method of appreciation outlined in the preceding has an old tradition behind it : Bielinski and Herzen were the precursors of the method, the culminating points of which are marked by the names of Lenin and Stalin. It is this method that the author of the present book is attempting to apply to an analysis of the works of Tolstoy. That Tolstoy is followed by Gorki in this book will surprise no one; the essay on Gorki is also a polemic against reactionary literary trends, is also to some extent a revaluation; and its main theme is the close link between Gorki the great innovator and his precursors in Russian literature and an examination of the question to what extent Gorki continued and developed classical Russian realism. The uncovering of these connections is at the same time the answer to the question : where is the bridge between old and new culture, between the old and the new Russian literature?

Finally the last paper gives a short outline of Tolstoy's influence on Western literature, discusses how Tolstoy came to be a figure of international stature and attempts to define the social and artistic significance of his influence on world literature. This paper, too, is an attack on the reactionary conception of Russian realism, but an attack which also marshals allies : it shows how the finest German, French, English and American writers opposed such reactionary distortions, and fought for a correct understanding of Tolstoy and of Russian literature. The reader will see from this that the opinions put forward in this book are not the idle speculations of a solitary and isolated writer but a world-wide trend of thought constantly gaining in strength.

In the remarks about method the social tendencies underlying the essays have been strongly stressed and their significance could scarcely be exaggerated. Nevertheless the main emphasis in these papers is on the æsthetic, not the social, analysis; investigation of the social foundations is only a means to the complete grasp of the æsthetic character of Russian classical realism. This point of view is not an invention of the author. Russian literature owed its influence not only to its new social and human content but chiefly to the fact of being a really great literature. For this reason it is not enough to eradicate the old firmly-rooted false notions regarding its historical and social foundations; it is also necessary to draw the literary and æsthetic conclusions from the correct evaluation of these social and historical foundations. Only then can it be understood why great Russian realism has played a leading part in world literature for three quarters of a century and has been a beacon of progress and an effective weapon in the struggle against open and covert literary reaction and against the decadence masquerading as innovation.

Only if we have a correct æsthetic conception of the essence of Russian classical realism can we see clearly the social and even political importance of its past and future fructifying influence on literature. With the collapse and eradication of Fascism a new life has begun for every liberated people. Literature has a great part to play in solving the new tasks imposed by the new life in every country. If literature is really to fulfil this role, a role dictated by history, there must be as a natural prerequisite, a philosophical and political rebirth of the writers who produce it. But although this is an indispensible prerequisite, it is not enough. It is not only the opinions that must change, but the whole emotional world of men; and the most effective propagandists of the new, liberating, democratic feeling are the men of letters. The great lesson to be learnt from the Russian development is precisely the extent to which a great realist literature can fructifyingly educate the people and

17

transform public opinion. But such results can be achieved only by a truly great, profound and all-embracing realism. Hence, if literature is to be a potent factor of national rebirth, it must itself be reborn in its purely literary, formal, æsthetic aspects as well. It must break with reactionary, conservative traditions which hamper it and resist the seeping-in of decadent influences which lead into a blind alley.

In these respects the Russian writers' attitude to life and literature is exemplary, and for this, if for no other, reason it is most important to destroy the generally accepted reactionary evaluation of Tolstoy, and, together with the elimination of such false ideas, to understand the human roots of his literary greatness. And what is most important of all; to show how such greatness comes from the human and artistic identification of the writer with some broad popular movement. It matters little in this connection what popular movement it is in which the writer finds this link between himself and the masses; that Tolstoy sinks his roots into the mass of the Russian peasantry, and Gorki of the industrial workers and landless peasants. For both of them were to the bottom of their souls bound up with the movements seeking the liberation of the people and struggling for it. The result of such a close link in the cultural and literary sphere was then and is to-day that the writer can overcome his isolation, his relegation to the role of a mere observer, to which he would otherwise be driven by the present state of capitalist society. He thus becomes able to take up a free, unbiassed, critical attitude towards those tendencies of present-day culture which are unfavourable to art and literature. To fight against such tendencies by purely artistic methods, by the mere formal use of new forms, is a hopeless undertaking, as the tragic fate of the great writers of the West in the course of the last century clearly shows. A close link with a mass movement struggling for the emancipation of the common people does, on the other hand, provide the writer with the broader viewpoint, with the fructifying subject-matter from which a true artist can develop the effective artistic forms which are commensurate with the requirements of the age, even if they go against the superficial artistic fashions of the day.

These very sketchy remarks were required before we could express our final conclusion. Never in all its history did mankind so urgently require a realist literature as it does to-day. And perhaps never before have the traditions of great realism been so deeply buried under a rubble of social and artistic prejudice. It is for this

18

reason that we consider a revaluation of Tolstoy and Balzac so important. Not as if we wished to set them up as models to be imitated by the writers of our day. To set an example means only : to help in correctly formulating the task and studying the conditions of a successful solution. It was thus that Goethe aided Walter Scott, and Walter Scott aided Balzac. But Walter Scott was no more an imitator of Goethe than Balzac was of Scott. The practical road to a solution for the writer lies in an ardent love of the people, a deep hatred of the people's enemies and the people's own errors, the inexorable uncovering of truth and reality, together with an unshakable faith in the march of mankind and their own people towards a better future.

There is to-day in the world a general desire for a literature which could penetrate with its beam deep into the tangled jungle of our time. A great realist literature could play the leading part, hitherto always denied to it, in the democratic rebirth of nations. If in this connection we evoke Balzac in opposition to Zola and his school, we believe that we are helping to combat the sociological and æsthetical prejudices which have prevented many gifted authors from giving their best to mankind. We know the potent social forces which have held back the development of both writers and literature : a quarter-century of reactionary obscurantism which finally twisted itself into the diabolical grimace of the Fascist abomination.

Political and social liberation from these forces is already an accomplished fact, but the thinking of the great masses is still bedevilled by the fog of reactionary ideas which prevents them from seeing clearly. This difficult and dangerous situation puts a heavy responsibility on the men of letters. But it is not enough for a writer to see clearly in matters political and social. To see clearly in matters of literature is no less indispensable and it is to the solution of these problems that this book hopes to bring its contribution.

Budapest, December 1948.

George Lukács.

CHAPTER ONE

The Peasants

IN THIS novel, the most important of his maturity, Balzac wanted to write the tragedy of the doomed landed aristocracy of France. It was intended to be the keystone of the series in which Balzac described the destruction of French aristocratic culture by the growth of capitalism. The novel is indeed such a keystone, for it goes into the economic causes which brought about the ruin of the nobility. Earlier, Balzac had depicted the death-struggle of the aristocracy as it appeared in the hinterland of Paris or of some remote provincial towns, but in *The Peasants* he takes us to the theatre of war itself, to the economic battlefield on which the struggle between aristocratic landowner and peasant farmer is fought out to the bitter end.

Balzac himself considered this novel to be his most important work. He says of it : " . . . in eight years I laid aside a hundred times and then took to hand again this most important book I want to write. . . ."

Yet, for all his painstaking preparation and careful planning, what Balzac really did in this novel was the exact opposite of what he had set out to do : what he depicted was not the tragedy of the aristocratic estate but of the peasant smallholding. It is precisely this discrepancy between intention and performance, between Balzac the political thinker and Balzac the author of *La Comédie Humaine* that constitutes Balzac's historical greatness.

The ideological roots of *The Peasants* strike back much farther and deeper than the immediate preparatory work Balzac himself mentions as such. He was still in his early youth when he already wrote a pamphlet arguing against the dispersal of the large estates and advocating the maintenance of the right of entail in favour of the eldest son; and long before he completed *The Peasants* (in 1844) he had already put forward in the two Utopian novels *The Country Doctor* and *The Village Priest* his views on the social function of the large estate and the social duties of the great land-owner. But having written these two Utopias he crowned the work

21

by showing in *The Peasants* how social realities destroyed all such Utopias, how every Utopian dream evaporated at the touch of economic reality.

What makes Balzac a great man is the inexorable veracity with which he depicted reality even if that reality ran counter to his own personal opinions, hopes and wishes. Had he succeeded in deceiving himself, had he been able to take his own Utopian fantasies for facts, had he presented as reality what was merely his own wishful thinking, he would now be of interest to none and would be as deservedly forgotten as the innumerable legitimist pamphleteers and glorifiers of feudalism who had been his contemporaries.

Of course even as a political thinker Balzac had never been a commonplace, empty-headed legitimist; nor is his Utopia the fruit of any wish to return to the feudalism of the Middle Ages. On the contrary: what Balzac wanted was that French capitalist development should follow the English pattern, especially in the sphere of agriculture. His social ideal was that compromise between aristocratic landowner and bourgeois capitalist which was achieved in England by the " glorious revolution " of 1688 and which was to become the basis of social evolution in England and determine its specific form. When Balzac (in a paper dealing with the tasks facing the royalists after the July revolution and written in 1840, just when he was about to begin *The Peasants*) severely censured the attitude of the French aristocracy, he based his criticism on an idealized conception of the English Tory nobility,

Balzac blamed the French aristocrats for having in the past (in 1789) " contrived petty intrigues against a great revolution," instead of saving the monarchy by wise reforms, and for having in the present, even after the bitter lessons of the revolution, failed to transform themselves into Tories, introduce self-government on the English model and put themselves as leaders at the head of the peasantry. It was to this that he ascribed the ill-will existing between the nobility and the mass of the peasants and believed that the revolution had triumphed in Paris for similar reasons. He says : " In order that men should rise in arms, as the workmen of Paris have done, they must believe that their interests are at stake."

This Utopia, this dream of transplanting English social relationships to France was shared by many others beside Balzac. Guizot, for instance, in a pamphlet published immediately after the revolution of 1848, followed similar lines of thought and was scathingly critized by Karl Marx. Marx ridiculed the "great enigma" which had baffled Guizot and " could be solved only by the superior intelligence of the English," and then proceeded to solve the "enigma" by pointing out the difference between the bourgeois revolutions in England and in France. He wrote :

"This class of large landowners was linked with the bourgeoisie . . . they were not, as the French feudal landowners had been in 1789, in conflict with the vital interests of the bourgeoisie, but in perfect harmony with them. Their tenure of land was in fact not feudal holding at all, but bourgeois property. On the one hand they supplied the industrial bourgeoisie with the manpower their manufacturers required; on the other hand they were able to develop agriculture in the direction the needs of industry and trade demanded. Hence the community of interest between them and the bourgeoisie, hence the alliance with the bourgeoisie."

Balzac's English Utopia was based on the illusion that a traditional but nevertheless progressive leadership could mitigate the evils of capitalism and the class antagonisms resulting from them. Such leadership could in his opinion be given by none save throne and altar. The English land-owning nobility was the most important intermediate link in such a system. Balzac saw with merciless clarity the class antagonisms engendered by capitalism in France. He saw that the period of revolutions had by no means come to an end in July, 1830. His Utopia, his idealization of English conditions, his romantic conception of the supposed harmony existing between the great English landowners and their tenants, together with other ideas of a similar nature, all had their origin in the fact that Balzac despaired of the future of capitalist society because he saw with pitiless clarity the direction in which social evolution was moving.

It was this conviction—that a consistent development of capitalism and the concomitant consistent development of democracy would inevitably lead to revolutions which must sooner or later destroy *bourgeois* society itself—that induced him to extol every historical figure who attempted to halt this revolutionary process and deflect it into " orderly " channels. Thus Balzac's admiration for Napoleon Bonaparte is quite out of keeping with his English Utopia and yet, precisely in its contradictory quality, it is a necessary complement of that Utopia in Balzac's historical conception of the world.

In the two Utopian novels that preceded *The Peasants* Balzac intended above all to demonstrate the economic superiority of the large estate as compared with the peasant smallholding. He noted quite correctly certain aspects of the economic advantages of rationalized large-scale husbandry, such as a systematic policy of investment, large-scale stockbreeding, rational forest conservation, proper irrigation schemes, etc. What he did not see—and in the two novels mentioned did not wish to see—was that *mutatis mutandis* the limits imposed by capitalism applied just as much to large-scale agriculture as they did to the peasant smallholding. In *The Village Priest* he had to resort to artificial, non-typical conditions in order to prove by an apparently realistic experiment the feasibility and excellence of his Utopia. Balzac was rarely guilty of distorting into non-typicality the essential features of economic reality, and the fact that he had recourse to such distortion more than once in connection with this particular point reveals that it was the crucial point, the point which caused him to despair about the future of bourgeois society and that it was this problem that he regarded as decisive for the survival of " culture."

For in Balzac's eyes the question of large-scale land-ownership was not merely a question of evolution or revolution; it was also the question of culture or barbarism. He feared the destructive effect the revolutionary mass movement might have on culture; in this respect he saw eye to eye with Heine, although the latter held far more radical political views; yet he never failed to stress also the deep-seated barbarism of the capitalist system whenever he depicted conditions in the France of his time.

Caught in the meshes of these contradictions, Balzac was driven to idealize the disappearing culture of the aristocracy. Engels said of him that " his great work was one long elegy deploring the inevitable decline of " good society " ' !

When in his quality of political thinker he nevertheless sought a way out, he looked for it in the preservation of the large estates as the basis of those aristocratic material resources and that undisturbed leisure which from the Middle Ages to the French revolution had created the aristocratic culture of France. In the long introductory letter written by Emile Blondet, the royalist writer in *The Peasants,* this conception can be very clearly discerned.

As we have seen by now, the theoretical basis of Balzac's Utopia is contradictory enough. But however greatly he may distort reality in these novels by a propagandist, exhortatory, non-typical bias, the great realist and incorruptibly faithful observer breaks through everywhere, rendering even sharper the already existing contradictions. Balzac always maintained that religion—and specifically the Roman Catholic religion—was the only ideological foundation on which society could be saved, and he did so with particular emphasis in the two Utopian novels mentioned in the preceding. At the same time he admitted, however, that the only economic basis on which society could build was capitalism with all that it involved. " Industry can be based only on competition " says Dr. Benassis, Utopian hero of *The Country Doctor,* and it is from this acceptance of capitalism that he derives his ideological conclusions :

" At present we have no other means of supporting society except egoism. The individual has faith only in himself, . . . The great man who will save us from the great shipwreck towards which we are being driven will doubtless make use of egoism to rebuild the nation."

But no sooner has he laid this down, than he brings faith and interest into sharp conflict with each other :

" But to-day we have no more faith, we now know only interest alone. If everyone thinks only of himself, from where do you want to derive civic virtue, particularly if such virtue can only be achieved by renouncing self ? "

This irreconcilable contradiction which Dr. Benassis (who voices Balzac's own Utopian views) blurts out so uncouthly, is manifested in the whole structure of both novels. For who are those who put Balzac's Utopia into practice? It would be quite in order for them to be exceptionally intelligent individuals, for Balzac lived in the era of Utopian socialism and we might concede a wise millionaire to him as willingly as to his older contemporary Fourier. But there is a decisive difference between these two : Fourier's socialist Utopias were conceived in a period when the working-class movement was as yet scarcely born, while Balzac laid down his Utopian way of saving capitalism at a time when the working class was already vigorously surging forward.

But apart from this Balzac was a poet and had to present his millionaires in literary form. The way he chose is most characteristic of the contradictions inherent in the Balzacian Utopia. The heroes of both novels, Dr. Benassis in *The Country Doctor* and Veronique Glaslin in *The Village Priest,* are penitents. They have each committed a great crime and thereby ruined their personal life and individual happiness. They both regard their personal life as ended and do their work as a religious penance—on no other basis could the realist Balzac conceive people willing and able to turn his Utopia into reality.

This conception of the principal characters is in itself an unconscious but not the less cruel condemnation of its reality. Only those who give up everything, only those who renounce all thought of individual happiness can serve the common good sincerely and unselfishly in a capitalist society : such is the unspoken but implied lesson of Balzac's Utopian novels. With this mood of renunciation Balzac does not stand alone among the great bourgeois writers of the first half of the nineteenth century. The aged Goethe also regarded renunciation as the great fundamental rule for all noble, high-minded men who wished to serve the community. The sub-title of his last great novel, *Wilhelm Meister's Wanderings,* is " The Renouncers." But Balzac goes even further in the tacit condemnation of his own Utopian conceptions. In *The Village Priest* a young engineer employed by Veronique Graslin tells of his experiences in the days of the July revolution. He says :

" Patriotism now survives only under a dirty shirt and that spells the doom of France. The July revolution was the voluntary defeat of those who, through their name, their wealth and their talents, belong to the upper ten thousand. The self-sacrificing masses defeated the rich and educated few who disliked making sacrifices."

Balzac here reveals his own despairing conviction that his Utopias run contrary to the economically determined instincts of the ruling classes and hence cannot become the typical norm governing their behaviour.

That he himself did not really believe in the social feasibility of his dreams, is shown by the whole structure of these novels. Too much attention is focussed on the non-typical heroes and their non-typical behaviour, often obscuring the actual purpose of the novels, which is to depict the blessings of rationalized large-scale agriculture. But even the passages relating to these blessings are sketched in with a superficiality rarely encountered in Balzac's writings; he skates over details and picks out isolated non-typical episodes as a means of throwing light on wide issues.

In other words, what Balzac does in these novels is not to describe a social process, the mutual social impact on each other of large-scale landowners, land-hungry peasants and agricultural labourers, but to give an almost exclusively technical description of the great advantages offered by his economic ideas. But these advantages—again quite unlike Balzac's usual practice—operate in a complete vacuum. He does not show the people at all. We know only by hearsay of the general poverty which had existed before the experiment and then, when the experiment has been carried out, we again only hear that everyone is now better off and contented. In the same way the commercial success of the ventures is taken for granted and shown only as an accomplished fact.

That Balzac thus deviates from his usual methods shows how little inner confidence he felt in these Utopias, although he consistently remained true to them throughout his life in every sphere save in his work as a writer.

It was in *The Peasants* that Balzac, after long preparation, depicted for the first time the actual impact on each other of the social classes of the countryside. Here the rural population is shown realistically in a rich variety of types, now no longer as the abstract and passive object of Utopian experiments but as the acting and suffering hero of the novel.

When Balzac, in the fulness of his creative powers, approached this problem with his own most personal method, he provided in his quality of writer a devastating criticism of the opinions which he in his quality of political thinker stubbornly held to the end of his life. For even in this novel his own point of view is the defence of the large estate. " Les Aigues," the Comte de Montcornet's aristocratic seat, is the focal point of an ancient traditional culture—which in Balzac's eyes is the only possible culture.

The struggle for the preservation of this cultural base occupies the central position in the story. It ends with the utter defeat of the large estate and its carving up into peasant smallholdings. This is a further stage of the revolution which was begun in 1789, and which in Balzac's view was destined to end with the destruction of culture.

This perspective determines the tragic, elegiac, pessimistic keynote of the whole novel. What Balzac intended to write was the tragedy of the aristocratic large estate and with it the tragedy of culture. At the end of the novel he relates with deep melancholy that the old chateau has been demolished, that the park has disappeared, and that only a small pavilion is left of all the former splendour. This small pavilion dominates the landscape, or rather the smallholdings that have taken the place of the landscape. After the demolition of the real castle, the pavilion seems a castle, so miserable are the cottages scattered all round it, built " as peasants are accustomed to build." But the probity of the realist Balzac as a writer finds expression even in this mournful final chord. Although he says with aristocratic hatred that : "the land was like the sample sheet of a tailor," he adds that "the land was taken by the peasants as victors and conquerors. It was by now divided into more than a thousand smallholdings and the population living between Conches and Blangy had tripled."

Balzac painted this tragedy of the aristocratic large estate with all the richness of his literary genius . Although he depicts the land-hungry peasants with the greatest political hostility (" a Robespierre with one head and twenty million arms "), yet, as the great realist that he is, he gives a monumental and perfectly balanced picture of the forces locked in struggle on both sides.

He himself says in the novel about the writer's duty :

" A story-teller must never forget that it is his business to do justice to every party; the unfortunate and the rich are equals before his pen; for him the misery of the peasant has its grandeur and the meanness of the rich its ridicule; finally, while the rich man has passions, the peasant has only needs, hence he is twice poor and although his destructive tendencies must be mercilessly suppressed for reasons of state, he has a human and divine right to our respect."

From the outset Balzac presents the struggle raging around the aristocratic large estate not merely as a duel between landowner and peasant, but as a three-cornered fight between three parties all pitted against each other; the small-town and village usurper-capitalist takes the field against both landowner and peasant. A great variety of types are introduced to represent each warring camp and they bring into play every economic, political, ideological and other weapon in support of their cause. Montcornet the nobleman-landowner has connections reaching from the provincial *préfecture* to the upper ranks of the judicature and the ministries in Paris; he is naturally supported by the military and ideologically assisted by the church in the person of Father Brossette and the Royalist press in the person of Emile Blondet.

Even richer and more varied is the presentation of the usurer-capitalist camp.

We see the peasant usurer who skins the poorer peasants by means of small loans and makes them his dependents for life (Rigou); with him is his ally, the small-town timber-dealer, formerly bailiff on the Montcornet estate (Gaubertin). Around these two characters Balzac's brilliant imagination groups all the corruption of provincial nepotism and graft.

Gaubertin and Rigou hold the whole world of the lower administrative officials and of provincial finance in the hollow of their hands. By shrewd marriages of their sons and daughters, by well-timed financial aid to their followers, they have created a web of connections which not only enables them to get all they want from the local authorities, but also to dominate the markets of the entire province.

Montcornet, for instance, cannot sell the timber felled in his forests if he wants to do so outside the Rigou-Gaubertin clan. The power of the clan is so great that when the Comte de Montcornet discharges his bailiff Gaubertin for dishonesty, they can smuggle another bailiff of their own choosing into his employment, a bailiff who is their agent and spy. The clan thrives on robbing the peasants by means of mortgages and small usurious loans, by rigging the market, and by rendering trifling services, such as helping young men to avoid military service, etc.

The power of the Gaubertin-Rigou class is so great that they care nothing for Montcornet's good connections in high but distant places. Rigou says : " . . . as for the Minister of Justice—ministers of justice come and go, but we will always be here." Thus on the actual battlefield of the struggle between two sets of exploiters the group of provincial usurers is the more powerful of the two. Balzac was profoundly incensed at this, but nevertheless depicted the true interplay of forces with the greatest accuracy, showing the real balance of power and every phase of the struggle for it with absolute fidelity.

The third group, the peasants, fights against both other groups. In his quality of political partisan, Balzac would have liked to see the great estate and the peasants join forces against the usurer-capitalists; but what he could not avoid showing here, concretely and with realistic power, was that the peasants had to ally themselves with the usurers they hated and fight together with them against the great estate. The struggle of the peasants against the remnants of feudal exploitation, for a bit of land, for a smallholding of their own, necessarily makes them accessories of the usurer-capitalists on whom they are dependent. The tragedy of the dying aristocratic estate is transformed into the tragedy of the peasant smallholding; the liberation of the peasants from feudal exploitation is tragically nullified by the advent of capitalist exploitation.

This triangle, in which each party fights the two others, forms the basis of Balzac's composition and the inevitability of this double-fronted struggle of each of the three parties, in every phase of which one aspect of the struggle necessarily predominates in accordance with the immediate economic compulsions acting on each party, gives the composition its richness and complexity. The action swings to and fro from the nobleman's castle to the peasant tavern, the bourgeois apartment and the small-town café, and this restless shifting of the scene and characters give Balzac the opportunity of showing up the basic factors of the class struggle fought out in the French countryside.

Balzac's own personal sympathies are with the nobility, but as a writer he gives a meticulously complete picture of all the participants in the struggle. He shows in all its ramifications the dependence of the peasants on the Gaubertin-Rigou clique; he draws the usurer-capitalists, the deadly enemies of the nobility, with all the hatred of which his heart is capable, and although his hatred springs from the wrong source and is rooted in a wrong political conception, he yet penetrates to the very core of the tragedy that overtook the peasant smallholding in the forties of the nineteenth century.

Balzac thought that the revolution of 1789 had caused all these evils, the dispersal of the great estates as well as the rapid growth of capitalism which he conceived mainly as usurious money-lending —a conception quite justified in the France of his time. For Balzac the central problem of French social history was the way in which, amidst the storms of the revolution, bourgeois wealth was born out of the expropriation of the aristocratic estates, speculation with the depreciated currency, exploitation of hunger and scarcities of all kinds and more or less fraudulent army contracting. We need only recall the origins of the Goriot, Rouget or Nucingen fortunes.

The central characters in *The Peasants,* Rigou the village usurer, and Gaubertin, the small-town trader, have both acquired their great fortunes by exploiting the opportunities that offered during the revolution and the Empire. In particular when he describes the origins of the Gaubertin fortune, Balzac shows with great subtlety how the old-fashioned frauds practised by the noble landowner develop in the hands of the capitalist estate-bailiff into new forms of fraudulent and usurious speculation and how the nobleman's dishonest, abjectly servile lackey acquires a fortune, develops into an independent speculator and finally gets the better of his former master.

Balzac describes with bitter irony, and hence with all the more lifelike accuracy, the corruption and pseudo-culture of the owners of these new fortunes. But at the same time he also describes with perfect truthfulness the real economic and social factors which make the victory of the bourgeois group over the Montcornet group inevitable.

As in all other works of Balzac, what is described in *The Peasants* is not merely the defeat of the nobility, but also the inevitability of this defeat. The struggle is waged around the question whether Montcornet will be able to retain his land or the Gaubertin-Rigou speculation in real estate be successful. The latter are bound to win because the nobility is concerned only with retaining, increasing, and enjoying in peace its revenues, while the bourgeoisie is engaged in a stormy accumulation of capital. Needless to say, the basis of such accumulation is the usurious exploitation of the peasantry. The increasing indebtedness of the already existing peasant smallholdings (Rigou invests 150,000 francs in such mortgages), the manœuvres directed towards the future exploitation of the parcelled Montcornet estate, the inevitably inflated prices asked for small holdings—all this from the very beginning put the smallholders completely at the mercy of the Rigou-Gaubertin clique.

Thus the peasants are caught between two fires. Balzac the politician would have liked to represent this struggle as though the peasants had been seduced by the intrigues and demagogy of the Gaubertin-Rigou group, as though the " bad elements " among the peasants themselves (Tonsard, Fourchon) had " incited " the peasants. But in fact the novel shows all the dialectic of the situation : the peasants are necessarily dependent on the small-town or village usurers, and although the peasants hate these usurers, economic necessity nevertheless drives them to serve their ends. For instance, Balzac thus describes a peasant who has obtained a smallholding with the " aid " of Rigou :

" In fact, Courtecuisse, when he bought the Bâchelerie estate, had wanted to rise to be a *bourgeois* and had boasted as much. His wife went out to gather manure ! She and Courtecuisse got up before daybreak to hoe their abundantly manured garden, made it bear several crops one after the other, and yet never managed to pay more than the interest due to Rigou on the balance of the purchase-money. . . . The good fellow had improved and fertilized the three acres of land sold to him by Rigou and was yet living in fear of being turned out ! The garden adjoining the house was beginning to bear. . . . This gnawing work made the formerly so cheerful fat little man gloomy and dazed to such an extent that he seemed like a victim of poison or of some incurable disease."

This dependence of the peasant on the usurer—the economic basis of which is precisely the " independence " of the smallholding, the desire of the landless peasant to turn owner—manifests itself among other things in the compulsion for the peasant to work for the usurer without being paid for it. Marx says about this : " At this point Balzac aptly shows how the small peasant, in order to win favour with his usurer, does all sorts of work for him without pay, because such work does not require any cash outlay. The usurer thus kills two birds with one stone : he saves paying wages and drives the peasant—who by working on another man's land is thereby prevented from tilling his own—further along the road to ruin and hence ever further in to the web of the usurer-spider."

Naturally enough, the peasants harbour a savage hatred for their plunderers. But this hatred is impotent, not only because of the peasant's economic dependence, but also because of their land-hunger and because of the immediate pressure of exploitation through the stranglehold kept on them by the great estate. Thus it is in vain that the peasants hate the village usurers; they are never-theless forced to become their servants and allies in the struggle against the great estate. Balzac gives the following interesting dialogue on this subject :

" So you think that Les Aigues will be sold in lots for the sake of your ugly mug? " replied Fourchon. " What, old Rigou has been sucking the marrow from your bones for the last thirty years and you still don't see that the *bourgeois* will be worse than the *seigneurs* ? . . . A peasant will always be a peasant ! Can't you see (but of course you know nothing about politics) that the govern-ment has put such high taxes on the wine simply to get our money out of our pockets and keep us poor? The *bourgeois* and the government are one and the same. What would become of them if we were all rich? Would *they* labour in the fields? Would *they* do the harvesting? They must have poor folk for that. . . .

" But we must hunt with them for all that," said Tonsard, " be-cause they are out to break up the big estates. We can turn against the Rigou afterwards ! "

In the given class position in France Tonsard is right, and in real life it is his attitude that must prevail

Of course, there are a few peasants who think of a revolution, of re-enacting, more radically, the partition of the land which was carried out by the revolution in 1793. Tonsard's son expresses such revolutionary views :

" You are playing the *bourgeois* game, I tell you. To frighten the gentry at Les Aigues so as to maintain your rights, well and good. But to drive them from the district and make them sell Les Aigues, as the *bourgeois* of the valley want to do, is against our interests. If you help to break up the big estates, where are the lands to come from for us to buy in the next revolution? Then you would get the land for a song, as old Rigou did; but if you let the *bourgeois* gobble it up, it will be much poorer and much dearer when they bring it up again; and then you will have to work for the *bourgeois,* just like those others who work for Rigou. Look at Courtecuisse ! "

The tragedy of these peasants was that a generation of Rigous and Gaubertins had already issued from the revolutionary *bourgeoisie* of 1789, at a time when the French working class was as yet insufficiently developed to be able to stage a revolution in alliance with the peasants. This social isolation of the rebellious peasantry is reflected in their sectarian confusion and pseudo-radical tactics.

The real play of economic forces in this period drives the peasants, however unwilling they may be, to pull Rigou's chestnuts out of the fire. The various political consequences of this economic situation turn " Rigou, whom the peasants hated and cursed for his usurious machinations . . . into the champion of their political and financial interests. . . . For him, as for certain bankers in Paris, politics cloaked with the purple of popularity a series of infamous frauds." Rigou is now the economic and political representative of the land-hungry peasants, although not so long ago he would not have ventured abroad after nightfall for fear of running into some ambush in which he would have met with a fatal " accident."

But a tragedy is always the clash of two necessities, and for the peasants a smallholding obtained from Rigou, however heavily mortgaged, was better than no holding at all, and merely a labourer's job on the Montcornet estate.

Just as Balzac persuaded himself that the peasants had been " incited " against the big estate, so he also attempted to persuade himself that a patriarchal, " beneficent " relationship between the great landowners and the peasants was possible. What the truth is in respect of the first of these beliefs we have already shown. The second illusion is dispelled by Balzac himself no less cruelly.

Although he mentions once that the Countess of Montcornet was the " benefactress " of the whole district, he does not specify in what these good works consisted, and with Balzac this is always an indication that he has a bad conscience and does not himself really believe what he is saying. In a conversation between Father Brossette and the Countess, when the priest calls the attention of the Countess to the duties towards the poor which devolve on the rich, the Countess answered with that fatal " We shall see ! " which is just enough of a promise for the rich to evade an appeal to their purse and which permits them later to remain passive spectators in the face of every misfortune, on the plea that it was "no use crying over spilt milk."

Father Brossette, like the other priests in Balzac's Utopian novels, is a representative of the "social Christianity" of the Lamennais school, but with the difference that here, where Balzac, instead of merely preaching, creates characters, the priest himself is made to sense the hopelessness of this ideology :

" ' Is Belshazzar's feast to be the eternal symbol of the last days of a doomed caste, oligarchy or power? ' . . . he said to himself when he was ten paces away. " ' O God, if it be your holy will to loose the poor like a torrent to transform the social order, then I can understand that you abandon the rich to their blindness.' "

What the benefactions of the landowners really amount to is shown by Balzac in a few concrete instances. The former owner of the Montcornet estate—who had been a famous actress in the golden age of the ancien régime so greatly praised by Balzac—on one occasion granted the request of a peasant in this fashion :

"The worthy lady, accustomed to making others happy, presented him with an acre of vineyard—in return for one hundred days of labour."

And Balzac, in his quality of politician, adds to this :

" This generous action was not sufficiently appreciated."

But he also tells us what the peasant who received the " gift " thought of the lady's generosity :

" Dammit, I've bought it and paid for it. Do the *bourgeois* ever give you anything for nothing? Are a hundred days of work nothing? This has cost me three hundred francs and it is nothing but stones ! "

And Balzac adds :

" This point of view was generally shared." .

But Montcornet is not just an ordinary old-fashioned aristocrat. Formerly a general in the army of Napoleon, he took part with the Imperial army in the looting of Europe. He is therefore an expert in squeezing the peasantry. Balzac stresses this trait in him, when he relates the quarrel between Montcornet and Gaubertin, which ends with the dismissal of the dishonest bailiff.

" After mature consideration the Emperor permitted Montcornet to play in Pomerania the same part that Gaubertin played on the Montcornet estate. Hence the general knew all about army contracting."

It is not only in this passage that Balzac points out the deep—and capitalist—community of interests between Montcornet and

Gaubertin, and he not only shows that Gaubertin and Montcornet are merely two warring factions of the same capitalism, that the object of their struggle is merely the sharing-out of the surplus value squeezed out of the peasantry—he also shows the capitalist character of the Montcornet estate. It is a particularly deep irony on the part of the great realist Balzac that Father Brossette absolutely approves of these measures of capitalist exploitation.

Montcornet wants to do away with all the traditional rights of the poor : the right to gather brushwood in the forest, the right to glean in the fields after the harvest. The abolition of these rights is a necessary concomitant of the capitalist transformation of the large estates. A few years before Balzac's novel was published, Karl Marx, then a young man, put up a bitter fight in the columns of the *Rheinische Zeitung* against the Wood Theft Bill which was before the Rhenish Diet and which proposed to abolish similar ancient rights.

In this question Balzac definitely takes sides with Montcornet. In order to defend Montcornet's attitude, he picks on cases in which the brushwood-gatherers cut down or deliberately injured growing trees. But it is clear that Montcornet's action is directed not against abuses of these rights, but against the ancient rights themselves. Montcornet gives orders that only those peasants be permitted to glean who are provided with a certificate of indigence by the authorities; he also sees to it that the results of the gleaning should be as meagre as possible. This shows that Montcornet, well trained in Pomerania, is quite determined to do away with these remnants of feudalism. The peasants on the Montcornet estate are in a position in which " all the brutality of primitive forms of society is combined with all the torments and miseries of civilized countries." (Marx.)

The peasants are driven to despair, and this despair must lead to terrorist outbursts which in their turn contribute to the victory of Rigou's speculation in real estate.

Balzac here gives us a masterly picture of the tragedy of the peasant smallholding. He presents in literary form the same essential development of the post-revolutionary smallholding that Marx described in *The Eighteenth Brumaire*.

" But in the course of the nineteenth century the urban usurer takes the place of the feudal lords, the mortgage the place of the feudal obligations attached to the land, and *bourgeois* capital the place of the aristocratic estate."

Later Engels stated more concretely the tragic part played by the peasantry in the establishment and development of the capitalist social order. He says :

" . . . The urban *bourgeoisie* set it in motion and the yeomanry of the country districts carried it to victory. It is strange enough that in each of the three great bourgeois revolutions the peasants provided the army for the onslaught, although the peasants were the class which, once the victory won, were the most certain to be ruined by the economic consequences of this same victory. A hundred years after Cromwell the yeomanry of England had practically disappeared."

Naturally Balzac, the pro-aristocrat royalist, could not have had a correct conception of this process. But several of his characters express a vague, confused uneasiness which reflects, however indistinctly, a similar evolution of the peasantry.

Old Fourchon says :

" I have seen the old times and I see the new, my dear learned sir. True, the sign has changed but the wine is the same as ever. To-day is only younger brother to yesterday. There ! Go and put that in your paper ! Liberated, are we? We are still in the same village and the *seigneur* is there just the same; I call him ' hard work.' . . The hoe, our only property, has not left our hands. Whether it is the *seigneur* or the tax-collector who takes the best part of our substance, we still have to sweat our guts out. . . ."

We have already dealt with Balzac's idealized Tory Utopia, by means of which, as he imagined, the disastrous consequences of the French revolution could be eliminated. But in depicting the evolution of French society from 1789 to 1848, he penetrates very much deeper. He repeatedly demonstrates not only the inevitability of the French revolution, but also the inevitability of the general capitalist transformation of France as a result of that revolution.

Thus in *The Peasants* Father Brossette says :

" Historically speaking, the peasants are still where they were the morning after the Jacquerie; that defeat has remained deeply engraved on their minds. They no longer remember the facts—but the facts have now become an instinctive idea and this idea is in the very blood of the peasants just as the idea of superiority was once in the blood of the nobles. The revolution of 1789 was the revenge of the vanquished. The peasants have taken possession of the soil from which the feudal laws had barred them for twelve hundred years. Hence their love of the land, which they divide up among themselves until even a single furrow is cut in half. . . ."

Balzac saw clearly enough that Napoleon's still unabated and even increasing popularity with the peasants was due to the fact that Napoleon had completed and defended the division of the land brought about by the French revolution.

Father Brossette goes on :

" In the eyes of the people, Napoleon, united with his people through a million of common soldiers, is still the king sprung from the loins of the revolution, the man who guaranteed their possession of the confiscated lands of the aristocracy. This idea was the balm with which he was anointed at his coronation. . . ."

Perhaps the only really live scene in the Utopian novel, *The Country Doctor,* is the one in which Balzac shows how closely the peasants, old soldiers of Napoleon, are still linked with their former leader. For Napoleon's political ideas—which were later so scurrilously parodied by the Second Empire, " were the ideas of the undeveloped, virginal smallholding " (Marx).

But the insight of Balzac the creative historian goes deeper than a mere understanding of the Napoleonic era. For all his Royalist hostility to the French revolution, he never loses sight of the human and moral uplift which the revolution brought into French society. The simple human greatness and magnificent heroism he attributes to the Republican officers and soldiers is quite striking already in his early novel, *Les Chouans.* Nor has Balzac in any of his other novels failed to show the Republicans as models of honesty and steadfast courage (e.g., Pillerault in *César Birotteau*).

In portraying such honest, heroic Republicans Balzac reached his highest level when he drew the picture of Michel Chrestien, one of the heroes who died on the steps of St. Merry. It is characteristic that Balzac himself was not pleased with this figure—he found that it was unsatisfactory, that it did less than justice to the great original on which it was modelled. In reviewing Stendhal's *Chartreuse de Parme,* Balzac spoke warmly of the revolutionary republican character Ferrante Palla; pointed out that Stendhal had intended to draw the same type which he himself had attempted in Michel Chrestien, and found that Stendhal had surpassed him in depicting the greatness of this figure.

In *The Peasants* this type appears in the person of old Niseron, an honest and intrepid fighter in the revolution, who not only did not acquire any worldly goods, but stoically renounced even the privileges which were his due, living in honourable and courageous poverty. In this character Balzac shows of course something more : the hopelessness of the Jacobean tradition in a capitalistically developing France. Niseron hates the rich, and therefore the peasants look upon him as one of themselves; but Niseron hates growing capitalism and the ruthless chase after profits just as much, although he can see no way out of the situation, which he regards as hopeless.

It is interesting to observe how deeply and truly Balzac understood the human implications of capitalist development in France, from its basic trends down to its subtlest details, irrespective of his own politically reactionary attitude towards these tendencies of development. Thus he can draw a correct picture of the Jacobin republican in all that character's later incarnations, even though he, Balzac, can see no connection between the antique ideals of Jacobinism on the one hand and the free smallholding on the other.

Marx, in his economic analysis of the smallholding, states that "the smallholding was the economic basis of society in the best periods of classical antiquity," i.e., in the epochs which Rousseau and the Jacobins had taken for their ideological model.

Marx, of course, clearly saw the difference between the *polis* democracy of antiquity and the Jacobin dream of its revival, that heroic self-deception of the Jacobins.   In his historical writings dealing with the French revolution of 1848, and later in *Capital,* he brilliantly analysed from every aspect all the forces within capitalism which drive the smallholder into slavery, into the clutches of the usurer, and the tax-collector, "which compel the peasant to be both merchant and artisan, without the conditions which would make it possible for him to turn his products into commodities. . . . The disadvantages of the capitalist system of production with its dependence of the producers on the money-price of their product, coincide here with the disadvantages arising from the incomplete development of the capitalist system of production." Marx shows on this basis that the conditions of the peasantry in the revolutionary processes of the first half of the nineteenth century are of necessity full of contradictions; he shows how the social basis for the rule of Napoleon III emerged from the despair of the peasantry and the inevitable illusions which it created.

Balzac did not see this dialectic of objective economic evolution and, as the legitimist extoller of the aristocratic large estate that he was, he could not possibly have seen it. But as the inexorable observer of the social history of France he did see a great deal of the social movements and evolutionary trends produced by this economic dialectic of the smallholding. Balzac's greatness lies precisely in the fact that in spite of all his political and ideological prejudices he yet observed with incorruptible eyes all contradictions as they arose, and faithfully described them. It is true that he regarded them as destructive of " culture " and " civilization," as the prelude to the extinction of his world; but he nevertheless saw and depicted them —and is so doing achieved a depth of vision reaching far into the future. He revealed against his will the economic tragedy of the smallholding—and showed at the same time, incarnated in living characters, the social conditions which necessarily led, first to the miserable caricature of Jacobinism in 1848, and immediately afterwards to the Second Empire—that caricature of the Napoleonic era.

This vision of an imminent cataclysm, of the imminent destruction of culture and of the world, is the idealistically inflated form which a presentiment of class extinction always takes. In this novel, as in all his other novels, Balzac mourns the decline of the French aristocracy, and this elegiac form determines the composition of the novel. It starts with a description, by the journalist Blondet, of the aristocratic perfection of the Montcornet *chateau*. It ends with a melancholy picture of all this past beauty swept away by the parcelling of the estate into smallholdings. But the melancholy end of the novel dips into even deeper melancholy. Blondet, the Royalist newspaperman who appears at the beginning of the novel as a guest at the *chateau* and lover of the Countess of Montcornet (the Countess, unlike her husband, is the scion of an ancient noble house) suffers complete shipwreck in his career, is ruined materially and morally and is on the point of committing suicide when he is saved by the death of General Montcornet and by his marriage to the general's wealthy widow.

Blondet's catastrophe deserves special attention because he, as the mouthpiece for Balzac's own views, plays a very important and positive part in the whole *Human Comedy*—only Daniel d'Arthez, Balzac's poetic self-portrait, is more positive than he. The fact that Balzac makes Blondet meet disaster is an indication of how hopeless legitimist royalism appeared to a writer so meticulously careful of detail. And it is again characteristic of Balzac that he saw and depicted with merciless accuracy not only Blondet's catastrophe in itself, but also the wretched form which it took. While Michel Chrestien, the republican, heroically perishes on the barricades, Blondet, the royalist, escapes into the parasitic existence of a rich wife's husband, rendered presentable by an appointment to a préfetship obtained by backstairs influence. This parasitism finds ironical expression in the epilogue to the novel, when Blondet, gazing at the smallholdings which occupy the site of the vanished *chateau,* utters a few royalist sentiments about how wrong Rousseau was and about the fate of the monarchy.

" You love me, we are together. . . . I find the present very beautiful and care nothing about the distant future," his wife replies.

" Then hurrah for the present, together with you ! To hell with the future ! " cries Blondet, very much in love.

The greatness of Balzac's art rests, says Marx, "on a deep understanding of real conditions," i.e., of the conditions governing the development of French capitalism. We have shown how faithfully Balzac depicted the specific traits of the three warring factions and how well he understood the peculiarities in the development of all classes of society in France since the revolution of 1789. But such a statement would be incomplete if it disregarded the other side of the dialectic of class evolution, i.e., the continuity of the evolutionary trends from the French revolution onwards, or rather from the emergence of a *bourgeois* class in France and the beginning of the struggle between feudalism and absolute monarchy. The deep comprehension of this continuity of development was the foundation on which the great edifice of the *Human Comedy* was built. Revolution, Empire, restoration and July monarchy were in Balzac's eyes merely stages in the great, continuous and contradictory process of French evolution towards capitalism, a process in which the irresistible and the atrocious are inseparably linked together.

The destruction of the nobility—Balzac's ideological and political starting-point—was only one aspect of this total process, and however biassed Balzac may have been in favour of the nobility, he saw quite clearly the inevitability of its extinction, nor did he fail to see the internal decadence, the moral deterioration of the nobility in the course of this process. In several historical studies he uncovered the origins of this eclipse of the nobility. He rightly regarded the transformation of the feudal nobility into a court nobility, its transformation into a parasitic group with dwindling socially necessary functions, as the basic cause of its extinction. The French revolution and the capitalistic development it unleashed were merely the final stage of this process. The more intelligent among the nobility themselves knew well enough that their end was inevitable. Thus in Balzac's *Cabinet of Antiques* the cynical and corrupt but clever Duchesse de Maufrigneuse says to those who put forward the old conception of nobility : " Are you all crazy ? Do you want to live to-day as your ancestors lived in the fifteenth century? But we are in the nineteenth century now, my dears, and to-day there is no liberty, only an aristocracy ! "

Balzac pursues this theme of the historical continuity of capitalist development in his portrayal of every class of French society. He traces not only the specific differences between the merchants and manufacturers of the pre-revolutionary period and of the period of growing capitalism under the restoration and the July monarchy (Ragon, Birotteau, Popinot, Crével, etc.) but does the same in respect of all other classes of society, everywhere showing up the domination of life by the mechanics of capitalism, Hegel's " spiritual animal kingdom " of capitalism, the capitalist world of " dog eat dog." In this Balzac is as cynical as Ricardo, but with him too, as Marx said " the cynicism lies in the thing itself and not in the words that express it."

This overall conception of the process of capitalist evolution enabled Balzac to uncover the great social and economic forces which govern historical development, although he never does so in direct fashion.

In Balzac's writings social forces never appear as romantic and fantastic monsters, as superhuman symbols (as e.g. later in Zola). On the contrary Balzac dissolves all social relationships into a network of personal clashes of interests, objective conflicts between individuals, webs of intrigue, etc. He never, for instance, depicts justice or the courts of law as institutions independent of society and standing above it. Only certain petty bourgeois characters in his novels imagine the law courts to be that. A law court is always presented by Balzac as consisting of individual judges whose social origins, ambitions and prospects the author describes in great detail. Every participant in the proceedings is shown enmeshed in the real conflicts of interest around which the lawsuit in question is being fought; every position taken up by any member of the judiciary depends on the position he occupies in this jungle of conflicting interests. An instance of this are the judicial intrigues in *The Harlot's Progress* or in the *Cabinet of Antiques*.

It is against such a background that Balzac shows the workings of all the great social forces. Each participant in these conflicts of interest is, inseparably from his own purely personal interests, the representative of a certain class, but it is in these purely personal interests and indivisibly from them, that the social cause, the class basis, of these interests finds expression. Thus, precisely by stripping the social institutions of their apparent objectivity and seemingly dissolving them into personal relationships, the author contrives to express what is truly objective in them, what is really their social *raison d'être* : their functions as bearers of class interests and as the instruments of enforcing them. The essence of Balzac's realism is that he always reveals social beings as the basis of social consciousness, precisely through and in the contradictions between social being and social consciousness which must necessarily manifest themselves in every class of society. This is why Balzac is right when he says in *The Peasants*:

"Tell me what you possess and I will tell you what you think."

This profound realism permeates Balzac's creative method down to the smallest detail. We can here indicate only a few main points in connection with this.

For one thing Balzac never confines himself to a trivial photographic naturalism, although on every essential point he is always absolutely true to life. In other words he never makes his characters say, think, feel or do anything that does not necessarily arise from their social being and is not in complete conformity with both its abstract and its specific determinants. But in expressing some such intrinsically correct thought or feeling, he always refuses to keep within the limits of the average power of expression of the average representative of a certain class. In order to express some socially correct and deeply conceived content, he always seeks and finds the most clear-cut, the most trenchant expression, such as would be quite impossible within the limits set by naturalism.

In the course of this analysis we have already seen a few instances of this method of expression. As a further instance of Balzac's way of putting things we quote a few fragments of dialogue between the peasant Fourchon and Father Brossette. The priest asks the peasant whether he is bringing up his grandchild in the fear of God.

"Oh no, your reverence, I don't tell him to fear God, but to fear men .... I tell him: 'Mouche, beware of prison, it's from prison that you go to the gallows. Don't steal; get people to give you things! Stealing leads to murder and murder brings you up against human justice. Beware of the razor of justice that protects the sleep of the rich from the sleeplessness of the poor. Learn to read. With education you'll find a way to make money and still keep within the law, like that fine M. Gaubertin ... The thing to do is to side with the rich, there are crumbs under their tables. That is what I call a sound education. So the young limb always keeps on the right side of the law ... He'll turn out all right and will look after me some day.' "

It is obvious that an old French peasant in 1844 would not have used such words as these. And yet, the whole character and every-thing Balzac puts into his mouth are absolutely true to life, pre-cisely because they go beyond the limits of a pedestrian copying of reality. All that Balzac does is to express on its potentially highest level what a peasant of the Fourchon type would dimly feel but would not be able to express clearly. Balzac speaks for those who are mute and who fight their battles in silence. He ful-fils the vocation of the poet in the Goetheian sense of that vocation :

Und wenn der Mensch in seiner Qual verstummt
Gab mir ein Gott zu sagen was ich leide ...

but he gives expression only to the things which really struggle to manifest themselves as social and individual necessities. This ex-pression, transcending the limits of the trivial, but ever true in social content, is the hall-mark of the old great realists, of Diderot and Balzac, in contrast with the realism of their modern epigones whose stature dwindles more and more as time goes by. It would have been impossible to give a complete picture of French capitalist society even by means of the innumerable characters and human destinies which figure in *The Human Comedy,* had not Balzac always sought and found the essentially right expres-sion, on the highest plane, for all their multiple interconnections.

The realism of Balzac rests on a uniformly complete rendering of the particular individual traits of each of his characters on the one hand and the traits which are typical of them as representa-tives of a class on the other. But Balzac goes even further than this; he also throws light on the traits which different people be-longing to different groups within *bourgeois* society have in com-mon from the capitalist viewpoint. By stressing these common traits—which he does very sparingly and only on crucial points—Balzac clearly demonstrates the intrinsic unity of the social evo-lutionary process, the objective social bond between apparently quite dissimilar types. We have already seen how Balzac under-lines the common, only quantitatively differing, traits in the char-acters of Montcornet and Gaubertin; how he shows as being of equal importance both what they have in common as products of post-Thermidorian French capitalism and what is quantitatively different in them, the latter serving as a foil for the demonstra-tion of their qualitative differences. For however much they may have in common, one of them is a gallant general of the Empire, a nobleman and a great landowner while the other is a little pro-vincial rogue, even though he is already on his way up the social ladder. The concrete presentation of social interconnections is rendered possible only by raising them to so high a level of abstraction that from it the concrete can be sought and found as a "unity of diversity," as Marx says. The modern realists who as a result of the decline in *bourgeois* ideology have lost their deep understanding of social interconnections and with it their capacity for abstraction, vainly attempt by concretizing details to render concrete the social totality and its real, objectively decisive determinants.

It is this quality of Balzacian realism, the fact that it is solidly based on a correctly interpreted social existence, that makes Balzac an unsurpassed master in depicting the great intellectual and spiritual forces which form all human ideologies. He does so by tracing them back to their social origins and making them function in the direction determined by these social origins.

Through this method of presentation ideologies lose their seeming independence of the material life-processes of society and appear as part, as an element of that process. To quote an instance : Balzac brings up Bentham's name and his theory of usury during a business negotiation conducted by old Grandet, the provincial usurer and speculator. The greed with which the old usurer Grandet swallows, as if it were a glass of good wine, those parts of Bentham's theory which happen to suit his book and the instant advantage he derives from absorbing the ideological expression (until then unknown to him) of his own social situation, suddenly put life into Bentham's theory, not as an abstract theory but as an ideological component of capitalist development in the beginning of the nineteenth century.

Of course this ideological effect is not always an adequate one. But often it is precisely the ironical inadequacy of the effect that mirrors the fate which may overtake ideologies in the course of historical development. Thus Balzac in *The Peasants* calls Rigou the provincial usurer a "Thélèmite" i.e. says of him that he is (quite unconsciously, of course) an adherent of the *bourgeois* Utopia outlined by Rabelais with its monastry of Thélème, the gates of which bear the inscription "Do as you please !" On the one hand one could not show the decline of *bourgeois* ideology more vividly than by the fact that the great revolutionary slogan proclaimed in the struggle for the liberation of humanity from the yoke of feudalism had become the guiding maxim of a village usurer. On the other hand the ironical emphasis on this decline and deterioration express precisely the continuity of *bourgeois* development: Rigou is in fact the product of the same struggle for liberty which overthrew feudalism and on the eve of which the great writers and thinkers of the *Renaissance* created their immortal works as the ideological weapons in the struggle for just this development.

Balzac uses these forms of characterization to indicate, concretize and deepen, both on the personal and on the social plane, the diversities existing between individuals of the same social type. In Rigou, for instance, Balzac creates a most interesting addition to the great gallery of misers and usurers to which Gobseck, Grandet, Rouget and others belong; he is the type of the Epicurean miser and usurer, who is concerned with scraping and saving, hoarding and swindling, like those others, but who at the same time creates an extremely comfortable life for himself. Thus he marries an old wife for her money, the latter to enmesh the whole village in a web of usurious debt and the former to provide himself with young and beautiful mistresses without incurring any expense. Again and again he picks out the prettiest girl in the village, engages her as a servant, seduces her by promising to marry her as soon as his old wife is dead, and when he tires of her, discards her and gets himself another.

The basic rule which Balzac follows is to focus attention on the principal factors of the social process in their historical development and to show them in the specific forms in which they manifest themselves in different individuals. That is why he can demonstrate concretely, in any detached episode of the social process, the great forces that govern its course. In *The Peasants* he describes the struggle for the breaking-up of the great estate without ever going beyond the narrow limits of the estate itself and the neighbouring small town.

But when he shows the decisive social essence of the men and groups fighting for and against the parcelling of the Montcornet estate, when he draws a picture of this basic feature of provincial capitalism, then within this narrow framework, he manages to show us the whole development of French capitalism after the revolution, the decline of the nobility, and above all the tragedy of a peasantry once liberated and then for a second time enslaved by the revolution—the tragedy of the peasant smallholding.

Balzac did not see all the implications of this development; we have shown that he could not possibly have seen it, and why he could not have done so.

Showing the revolutionary working-class was quite beyond the range of Balzac's vision. Hence he could depict the despair of the peasantry but not the only possible way out of it. Balzac could not foresee the results arising from the disappointment of the peasant smallholder, i.e. that as a consequence of this disappointment " the whole edifice of the state, built up on these same smallholdings, collapses and the chorus is taken up by the proletarian revolution without which its solo part would turn into a song of death in every peasant nation " (Marx). Balzac's genius showed itself in that he depicted this despair and disillusionment realistically as an inevitable necessity.

CHAPTER TWO

Balzac: Lost Illusions

BALZAC WROTE this novel in the fullness of his maturity as a writer; with it he created a new type of novel which was destined to influence decisively the literary development of the nineteenth century. This new type of novel was the novel of disillusionment, which shows how the conception of life of those living in a *bourgeois* society—a conception which although false, is yet necessarily what it is—is shattered by the brute forces of capitalism.

It was not, of course, in the works of Balzac that the shipwreck of illusions made its first appearance in the modern novel.

The first great novel, Cervantes' *Don Quixote* is also a story of lost illusions. But in *Don Quixote* it is the nascent *bourgeois* world which destroys the still lingering feudal illusions; in Balzac's novel it is the conceptions of mankind, human society, art, etc., necessarily engendered by *bourgeois* development itself—i.e. the highest ideological products of the revolutionary development of the *bourgeoisie*—which are shown to be empty illusions when measured by the standards set by the realities of capitalist economy.

The eighteenth-century novel also dealt with the destruction of certain illusions, but these illusions were feudal survivals still lingering in the sphere of thoughts and emotions; or else certain groundless, pedestrian conceptions imperfectly anchored in reality were dispelled by another more complete conception of the same reality viewed from the same angle.

But it is in this novel of Balzac that the bitter laughter of derision at the highest ideological products of *bourgeois* development itself is heard for the first time—it is here that we see for the first time, shown in its totality, the tragic self-dissolution of *bourgeois* ideals by their own economic basis, by the forces of capitalism. Diderot's immortal masterpiece *The Nephew Of Rameau* is the only work that can be regarded as the ideological precursor of this Balzac novel.

Of course Balzac was by no means the only writer of the time

47

who chose this theme. Stendhal's *Scarlet And Black* and Musset's *Confessions Of A Child Of The Century* even preceded *Lost Illusions* in time. The theme was in the air, not because of some literary fashion but because it was thrown up by social evolution in France, the country that provided the pattern for the political growth of the *bourgeoisie* everywhere. The heroic epochs of the French revolution and the First Empire had awakened, mobilized and developed all the dormant energies of the *bourgeois* class. This heroic epoch gave the best elements of the *bourgeoisie* the opportunity for the immediate translation into reality of their heroic ideals, the opportunity to live and to die heroically in accordance with those ideals. This heroic period came to an end with the fall of Napoleon, the return of the Bourbons and the July revolution. The ideals became superfluous ornaments and frills on the sober reality of everyday life and the path of capitalism, opened up by the revolution and by Napoleon, broadened into a convenient, universally accessible highway of development. The heroic pioneers had to disappear and make way for the humanly inferior exploiters of the new development, the speculators and racketeers.

" *Bourgeois* society in its sober reality had produced its true interpreters and spokesmen in the Says, the Cousins, the Royer-Collards, the Benjamin Constants, the Guizots; its real generals sat at the counting-house desks and their political head was the fat-head Louis XVIII." (Marx).

The drive of ideals, a necessary product of the previous necessarily heroic period was now no longer wanted; its representatives, the young generation schooled in the traditions of the heroic period, was inevitably doomed to deteriorate.

This inevitable degradation and frustration of the energies born of the revolution and the Napoleonic era was a theme common to all novels of disillusionment of the period, an indictment common to them all of the prosaic scurviness of the Bourbon restoration and the July monarchy. Balzac, although politically a royalist and legitimist, yet saw this character of the restoration with merciless clarity. He writes in *Lost Illusions*:

" Nothing is such a condemnation of the slavery to which the restoration has condemned our youth. The young men who did not know what to do with their strength, have harnessed only to journalism, political conspiracies and the arts, but in strange excesses as well ... If they worked, they demanded power and pleasure; as artists, they desired treasures, as idlers passionate excitement—but be that as it may, they demanded a place for themselves and politics refused it to them . . ."

It was the tragedy of a whole generation and the recognition of this fact and the portrayal of it is common to Balzac and his contemporaries both great and small; but in spite of this common trait, *Lost Illusions* in its portrayal of the time rises to a solitary height far above any other French literary work of the period. For Balzac did not content himself with the recognition and description of this tragic or tragi-comic social situation. He saw farther and delved deeper.

He saw that the end of the heroic period of French *bourgeois* evolution was at the same time the beginning of the rapid development of French capitalism. In almost every one of his novels Balzac depicts this capitalist development, the transformation of traditional handicrafts into modern capitalist production; he shows how stormily accumulating money-capital usuriously exploits town and countryside and how the old social formations and ideologies must yield before its triumphant onslaught.

Lost Illusions is a tragi-comic epic showing how, within this general process, the spirit of man is drawn into the orbit of capitalism. The theme of the novel is the transformation of literature (and with it of every ideology) into a commodity and this complete " capitalization " of every sphere of intellectual, literary and artistic activity fits the general tragedy of the post-Napoleonic generation into a much more profoundly conceived social pattern than can be found in the writings even of Stendhal, Balzac's greatest contemporary.

The transformation of literature into a commodity is painted by Balzac in great detail. From the writer's ideas, emotions and convictions to the paper on which he writes them down, everything is turned into a commodity that can be bought and sold. Nor is Balzac content merely to register in general terms the ideological consequences of the rule of capitalism—he uncovers every stage in the concrete process of " capitalization " in every sphere (the periodical press, the theatre, the publishing business, etc.) together with all the factors governing the process.

" What is fame ? " asks Dauriat, the publisher, and answers himself : " Twelve thousand francs' worth of newspaper articles and three thousand francs' worth of dinners..." Then he expounds : " I haven't the slightest intention of risking two thousand francs on a book merely in order to make the same amount by it. I speculate in literature; I publish forty volumes in an edition of ten thousand copies each.—My power and the newspaper articles which I get published thus, bring me in business to the value of three hundred thousand francs, instead of a measly two thousand. A manuscript which I buy for a hundred thousand francs is cheaper than the manuscript of an unknown author which I can get for a mere 600 francs."

The writers think as the publishers do.

"Do you really believe what you write?" Vernon asks sarcastically. "But surely we are word-merchants and are talking shop. . . The articles that the public reads today and has forgotten by tomorrow have no other meaning for us save that we get paid for them."

With all this, the writers and journalists are exploited, their talent has become a commodity, an object of profiteering by the capitalist speculators who deal in literature. They are exploited but they are also prostitutes; their ambition is to become exploiters themselves or at least overseers over other exploited colleagues. Before Lucien de Rubempré turns journalist, his colleague and mentor Lousteau explains the situation to him in these terms:

"Mark this, my boy: in literature the secret of success is not work, but the exploitation of the work done by others. The newspaper-owners are the building contractors and we are the bricklayers. The more mediocre a man is, the sooner he will reach his goal, for he will at need be willing to swallow a frog, and do anything else to flatter the passions of the little literary sultans. Today you are still severe and have a conscience, but to-morrow your conscience will bow to the ground before those who can tear success from your grasp and those who could give you life by a single word and yet refuse to speak that word, for believe me, a fashionable author is haughtier and harsher towards the new generation than the most leech-like of publishers. Where the publisher sees only a loss of money, the fashionable author fears a rival; the publisher merely rejects the beginner, the fashionable author annihilates him."

This breadth of the theme—the capitalization of literature, embracing everything from the manufacturing of paper to the lyrical sensibility of a poet, determines the artistic form of the composition in this as in all other works of Balzac. The friendship between David Séchard and Lucien de Rubempré, the shattered illusions of their enthusiastic youth and their mutually complementary contrasting characters are the elements that provide the general outline of the story. Balzac's genius manifests itself even in this basic lay-out of the composition. The objective tensions inherent in the theme are expressed through the human passions and individual aspirations of the characters : David Séchard, the inventor who discovers a cheaper method of making paper but is swindled by the capitalists, and Lucien de Rubempré, the poet who carries the purest and most delicate lyrical poems to the capitalist market of Paris. On the other hand, the contrast between the two characters demonstrates the extremely different ways in which men can react to the abominations accompanying the transition to capitalism. David Séchard is a puritan stoic while Lucien de Rubempré incarnates perfectly the sensual love of pleasure and the rootless, over-refined epicureanism of the post-revolutionary generation.

Balzac's composition is never pedantic; unlike his later successors he never affects a dry "scientific" attitude. In his writings the unfolding of material problems is always indissolubly bound up with the consequences arising from the personal passions of his characters. This method of composition—although it seems to take the individual alone for its starting-point—contains a deeper understanding of social interconnections and implications, a more correct evaluation of the trends of social development than does the pedantic, "scientific" method of the later realists.

In *Lost Illusions* Balzac focuses his story on Lucien de Rubempré's fate and with it the transformation of literature into a commodity; the capitalization of the material basis of literature, the capitalist exploitation of technical progress is only an episodic final chord. This method of composition, which apparently reverses the logical and objective connection between the material basis and the superstructure, is extremely skilful both from the artistic point of view and from the angle of social criticism. It is artistically skilful because the rich diversity of Lucien's changing destinies, unfolded before our eyes in the course of his struggle for fame, provides a much more colourful, lively and complete picture than the pettily infamous intrigues of the provincial capitalists out to swindle David Séchard. It is skilful from the point of view of social criticism because Lucien's fate involves in its entirety the question of the destruction of culture by capitalism. Séchard in resigning himself to his fate, quite correctly feels that what is really essential is that his invention should be put to good use; the fact that he has been swindled is merely his personal bad luck. But Lucien's catastrophe represents at the same time the capitalist debasement and prostitution of literature itself.

The contrast between the two principal characters illustrates most vividly the two main types of personal reaction to the transformation of ideology into a commodity. Séchard's reaction is to resign himself to the inevitable.

Resignation plays a very important part in the *bourgeois* literature of the nineteenth century. The aged Goethe was one of the first to strike this note of resignation. It was the symptom of a new period in the evolution of the *bourgeoisie*. Balzac in his utopian novels follows in Goethe's footsteps : only those who have given up or who must give up their personal happiness can pursue social, non-selfish aims. Séchard's resignation is, of course, of a somewhat different nature. He gives up the struggle, abandons the pursuit of any aim and wants only to live for his personal happiness in peace and seclusion. Those who wish to remain pure must withdraw from all capitalist business—it is in this, not ironical, not in the least Voltairean sense that David Séchard withdraws to " cultivate his own garden."

Lucien for his part plunges into life in Paris; he is determined to win through and establish the rights and power of " pure poetry." This struggle makes him one of those post-Napoleonic young men who either perished with polluted souls during the restoration or adapted themselves to the filth of an age turned unheroic and in it carved a career for themselves, like Julien Sorel, Rastignac, de Marsay, Blondet and others of the same kidney. Lucien belongs to the latter group but occupies an entirely independent position in this company. With admirable daring and sensitivity Balzac created a new, specifically *bourgeois* type of poet : the poet as an Aeolian harp sounding to the veering winds and tempests of society, the poet as a rootless, aimlessly drifting, oversensitive bundle of nerves,—a type of poet as yet very rare in this period, but most characteristic for the subsequent evolution of *bourgeois* poetry from Verlaine to Rilke. This type is diametrically opposed to what Balzac himself wanted the poet to be; he portrayed his ideal poet in the person of Daniel D'Arthez, a character in this novel who is intended for a self-portrait.

The characterization of Lucien is not only true to type, it also provides the opportunity for unfolding all the contradictions engendered by the penetration of capitalism into literature. The intrinsic contradiction between Lucien's poetic talent and his human weakness and rootlessness makes him a plaything of the political and literary trends exploited by the capitalists. It is this mixture of instability and ambition, the combination of a hankering for a pure and honourable life with a boundless but erratic ambition, which make possible the brilliant rise of Lucien, his rapid prostitution and his final ignominious disaster. Balzac never serves up his heroes with a sauce of morality; he shows the objective dialectic of their rise or fall, always motivating both by the total sum of their own natures and the mutual interaction of this their nature with the total sum of objective circumstances, never by any isolated value-judgment of their "good" and "bad" qualities.

Rastignac, the climber, is no worse than Lucien, but in him a different mixture of talent and demoralization is at work, which enables him adroitly to turn to his own advantage the same reality on which Lucien, for all his naive Machiavellianism, is shipwrecked both materially and morally.

Balzac's sour remark in *Melmoth Reconciled* that men are either cashiers or embezzlers, i.e. either honest fools or clever rogues, is proved true in endless variety in this tragi-comic epic of the capitalization of the spirit.

Thus the ultimate integrating principle of this novel is the social process itself and its real subject is the advance and victory of capitalism. Lucien's personal catastrophe is the typical fate of the poet and of true poetic talent in the world of fully developed capitalism.

Nevertheless Balzac's composition is not abstractly objective and this novel is not a novel with a theme, not a novel relating, in the manner of the later novelists, to one sphere of society alone. although Balzac by a most subtle weaving of his story introduces every feature of the capitalization of literature and brings onto the scene none but these features of capitalism. But here as in all other works of Balzac the general social fabric is never directly shown on the surface. His characters are never mere lay figures expressing certain aspects of the social reality he wants to present. The aggregate of social determinants is expressed in an uneven, intricate, confused and contradictory pattern, in a labyrinth of personal passions and chance happenings. The characters and situations are always determined by the totality of the socially decisive forces, but never simply and never directly. For this reason this so completely universal novel is at the same time the story of one particular individual, an individual different from all others. Lucien de Rubempré, on the stage, seems to react independently to the internal and external forces which hamper his rise and which help or hinder him as a result of apparently fortuitous personal circumstances or passions, but which, whatever form they take, always spring from the same social environment which determines his aspirations and ambition.

This unity of the multifarious is a feature peculiar to Balzac; it is the poetic form in which he expresses his conception of the working of social forces. Unlike many other great novelists he does not resort to any machinery such as, for instance, the tower in *Wilhelm Meister's Apprenticeship;* every cog in the mechanism of a Balzacian plot is a complete, living human being with specific personal interests, passions, tragedies and comedies. The bond which links each character with the whole of the story is provided by some element in the make-up of the character itself, always in full accordance with the tendencies inherent to it. As this link always develops organically out of the interests, passions etc. of the character, it appears necessary and vital. But it is the broader inner urges and compulsions of the characters themselves which give them fulness of life and render them non-mechanical, no mere components of the plot. Such a conception of the characters necessarily causes them to burst out of the story. Broad and spacious as Balzac's plots are, the stage is crowded by so many actors living such richly varied lives that only a few of them can be fully developed within one story.

This seems a deficiency of Balzac's method of composition; in reality it is what gives his novels their full-blooded vitality and it is also what made the cyclic form a necessity for him. His remarkable and nevertheless typical characters cannot unfold their personality fully within a single novel, but only certain features of it and that only episodically; they protrude beyond the framework of one novel and demand another, the plot and theme of which permit them to occupy the centre of the stage and develop to the full all their qualities and possibilities. The characters who remain in the background in *Lost Illusions,* Blondet, Rastignac, Nathan, Michel Chrestien, play leading parts in other novels. The cyclical interdependence of Balzac's novels derives from his urge to develop every one of his characters to the full and hence is never dry and pedantic as cyclic novels of other, even very good writers, so often are. For the several parts of the cycle are never determined by circumstances external to the characters, i.e. by chronological or objective limits.

The general is thus always concrete and real because it is based on a profound understanding of what is typical in each of the characters figuring in it—an understanding so deep that the particular is not eclipsed but on the contrary emphasized and concretized by the typical, and on the other hand the relationship between the individual and the social setting of which it is the product and in which—or against which—it acts, is always clearly discernible, however intricate this relationship may be. The Balzac characters, complete within themselves, live and act within a concrete, complexly stratified social reality and it is always the totality of the social process that is linked with the totality of the character. The power of Balzac's imagination manifests itself in his ability to select and manipulate his characters in such a way that the centre of the stage is always occupied by the figure whose personal, individual qualities are the most suitable for the demonstration, as extensively as possible and in transparent connection with the whole, of some important single aspect of the social process. The several parts of a Balzacian cycle have their own independent life because each of them deals with individual destinies. But these individual destinies are always a radiation of the socially typical, of the socially universal, which can be separated from the individual only by an analysis *a posteriori*. In the novels themselves the individual and the general are inseparably united, like a fire with the heat it radiates. Thus, in *Lost Illusions* the development of Lucien's character is inseparably bound up with the capitalist penetration of literature.

Such a method of composition demands an extremely broad basis for characterization and plot. Breadth is also required to exclude the element of chance from that accidental intertwinement of persons and events which Balzac, like every other great epic poet, uses with such sovereign superiority. Only a great wealth of multiple interconnections affords sufficient elbow-room in which chance can become artistically productive and ultimately lose its fortuitous character.

" In Paris only people who have many connections can count on chance to favour them; the more connections one has, the greater the prospect of success; for chance, too, is on the side of the bigger battalions."

Balzac's method of sublimating chance is thus still " old-fashioned " and differs in principle from the method used by modern authors. In his review of John Dos Passos' *Manhattan Transfer* Sinclair Lewis criticizes the " old " method of plot-building. Although he talks mostly of Dickens, the gist of his criticism applies to Balzac just as much. He says that the classical method was clumsily contrived; by an unhappy chance Mr. Jones had to travel in the same mail coach as Mr. Smith, in order that something very unpleasant and very entertaining might happen. He points out that there is nothing of this in *Manhattan Transfer,* where the characters either do not meet at all, or do so in a perfectly natural way.

What lies at the core of this modern conception is a non-dialectical approach to causality and chance, although of course most writers are entirely unaware of this. They contrast chance with causality and believe that chance ceases to be chance if its immediate cause is revealed. But poetic motivation gains little, if anything, by such a device. Introduce an accident, however well-founded causally, into any tragic conflict and it is merely grotesque; no chain of cause and effect could ever turn such an accident into a necessity. The most thorough and accurate description of the state of the ground which would cause Achilles to sprain his ankle while pursuing Hector or the most brilliant medico-pathological explanation why Antony lost his voice through a throat infection just before he was due to make his great speech over Caesar's body in the forum could ever make such things appear as anything but grotesque accidents; on the other hand, in the catastrophe of Romeo and Juliet the rough-hewn, scarcely motivated accidents do not appear as mere chance.

Why?

For no other reason, of course, than that the necessity which nullifies chance consists of an intricate network of causal connections and because only the aggregate necessity of an entire trend of developments constitutes a *poetic* necessity. Romeo's and Juliet's love *must* end in tragedy and only this necessity nullifies the accidental character of all the happenings which are the immediate causes that bring about, stage by stage, this inevitable development of the plot. It is of secondary importance whether such happenings taken by themselves, are motivated or not, and if the former, to what extent. One happening is not more a matter of chance than another and the poet has a perfect right to choose, among several equally accidental occurrences, the one he regards as best suited to his purpose. Balzac makes sovereign use of this freedom, and so did Shakespeare.

The poetic presentation of necessity by Balzac rests on his profound grasp of the line of development concretely incarnated in the theme in hand. By means of a broad and deep conception of his characters, a broad and deep portrayal of society and of the subtle and multiple interconnections between his characters and the social basis and setting of their actions, Balzac creates a wide space within which hundreds of accidents may intersect each other and yet in their aggregate produce fateful necessities.

The true necessity in *Lost Illusions* is that Lucien must perish in Paris. Every step, every phase in the rise and decline of his fortunes provide ever more profound social and psychological links in this chain of necessity. The novel is so conceived that every incident is a step towards the same end, although each single happening, while helping to reveal the underlying necessity, is in itself accidental. The uncovering of such deep-seated social necessities is always effected by means of some action, by the forceful concentration of events all moving towards the catastrophe. The extensive and sometimes most circumstantial descriptions of a town, a dwelling or an inn are never mere descriptions; by means of them Balzac creates again and again the wide and varied space required for the explosion of the catastrophe. The catastrophe itself is mostly sudden, but its suddenness is only apparent, for the traits brightly illuminated by the catastrophe are the same traits we have long been able to observe, even though at a much lower intensity.

It is most characteristic of Balzac's methods that in *Lost Illusions* two great turning-points in the story occur within a few days or even within a few hours of each other. A few days suffice for Lucien de Rubempré and Louise Bargeton to discover of each other that they are both provincials—a discovery that causes each of them to turn from the other. The catastrophe occurs during an evening spent together at the theatre. Even more sudden is Lucien's journalistic success. One afternoon, in despair, he reads his poem to the journalist Lousteau; Lousteau invites him to his office, introduces him to his publisher, takes him to the theatre; Lucien writes his first review as a dramatic critic and awakes next morning to find himself a famous journalist. The truth of such catastrophes is of a social nature; it lies in the truth of the social categories which in the final count determine such sudden turns of fortune. The catastrophe produces a concentration of essential determinants and prevents the intrusion of inessential details.

The problem of the essential and inessential is another aspect of the problem of chance. From the point of view of the writer every quality of every human being is an accident and every object merely a piece of stage property, until their decisive interconnections are expressed in poetic form, by means of some action. Hence there is no contradiction between the broad foundations on which Balzac's novels are built up and their pointed, explosive action which moves from catastrophe 'o catastrophe. On the contrary, the Balzacian plots require just such broad foundations, because their intricacy and tension, while revealing ever new traits in each character, never introduce anything radically new, but merely give explicit expression in action to things already implicitly contained in the broad foundation. Hence Balzac's characters never possess any traits which are in this sense accidental. For the characters have not a single quality, not even a single external attribute which does not acquire a decisive significance at some point in the plot. Precisely for this reason Balzac's descriptions never create a setting in the sense in which the word was later used in positivist sociology and it is for the same reason that for instance Balzac's very detailed descriptions of people's houses never appear as mere stage settings.

Consider for instance, the part played in Lucien's first disaster in Paris by his four suits of clothes. Two of these he has brought with him from Angoulême and even the better of the two proves quite impossible during the very first walk Lucien takes in Paris. His first Paris-made suit also turns out to be an armour with too many chinks in the first battle with Parisian society which he has to fight in Madame d'Espard's box at the Opera. The second Parisian suit is delivered too late to play a part in this first phase of the story and is put away in a cupboard during the ascetic, poetic period—to emerge again later for a short time in connection with the journalistic episode. All other objects described by Balzac play a similar dramatic part and embody similar essential factors.

Balzac builds his plots on broader foundations than any other author before or after him, but nevertheless there is nothing in them not germane to the story. The many-sided influence of multifariously determined factors in them is in perfect conformity with the structure of objective reality whose wealth we can never adequately grasp and reflect with our ever all too abstract, all too rigid, all too direct, all too unilateral thinking.

Balzac's many-sided, many-tiered world approaches reality much more closely than any other method of presentation.

But the more closely the Balzacian method approaches objective reality, the more it diverges from the accustomed, the average, the direct and immediate manner of reflecting this objective reality. Balzac's method transcends the narrow, habitual, accepted limits of this immediacy and because it thus runs counter to the comfortable, familiar, usual way of looking at things, it is regarded by many as "exaggerated" or "cumbersome." It is the wide sweep, the greatness itself of Balzac's realism which forms the sharpest contrast to the habits of thought and the experience of an age which is to an increasing degree turning away from objective reality and is content to regard either immediate experience, or experience inflated into a myth as the utmost that we can grasp of reality.

But it is, of course, not only in the breadth, depth and multifariousness of his reproduction of reality that Balzac transcends the immediate. He goes beyond the boundaries of average reality in his mode of expression as well. D'Arthez (who is meant for a portrait of Balzac himself) says in this novel : "And what is art? Nothing more than concentrated nature. But this concentration is never formal; on the contrary, it is the greatest possible intensification of the content, the social and human essence of a situation."

Balzac is one of the wittiest writers who ever lived. But his wit is not confined to brilliant and striking formulations; it consists rather in his ability strikingly to present some essential point at the maximum tension of its inner contradictions. At the outset of his career as a journalist, Lucien de Rubempré must write an unfavourable review of Nathan's novel which he greatly admires. A few days later he has to write a second article refuting his own unfavourable review. Lucien, the novice journalist, is at first completely at a loss when faced with such a task. But first Lousteau and then Blondet enlighten him. In both cases Balzac gives us a brilliant discourse, perfect in its reasoning. Lucien is amazed and dismayed by Lousteau's arguments. " But what you are saying now," he exclaims, "is perfectly correct and reasonable." "Well, could you tear Nathan's book to pieces, if it were not ?" asks Lousteau. Many writers after Balzac have described the unprincipled nature of journalism and shown how men wrote articles against their own convictions and better knowledge; but only Balzac penetrated to the very core of the journalistic sophism when he made his journalists playfully and brilliantly marshal the arguments for and against any issue according to the requirements of those who paid them and turn the ability to do this into a trade in which they are highly skilled, quite without relation to their own convictions.

On this level of expression the Balzacian "stock-exchange of the spirit" is revealed as a profound tragi-comedy of the spirit of the *bourgeois* class. Later realist writers described the already completed capitalist corruption of bourgeois ethics; but Balzac paints its earlier stage, its primitive accumulation in all the sombre splendour of its atrocity. In *Lost Illusions* the fact that the spirit has become a commodity to be bought and sold is not yet accepted as a matter of course and the spirit is not yet reduced to the dreary greyness of a machine-made article. The spirit turns into a commodity here before our very eyes; it is something just happening, a new event loaded with dramatic tension. Lousteau and Blondet were yesterday what Lucien turns into in the course of the novel : writers who have been forced to allow their gifts and convictions to become a commodity. It is the cream of the post-war *intelligentsia* which is here driven to take the best of their thoughts and feelings to market, offering for sale the finest, if belated, flowering of the ideas and emotions produced by the *bourgeois intellectuals* since the days of the Renaissance. And this late flowering is not merely an aftermath of epigones. Balzac endows his characters with an agility, scope and depth of mind, with a freedom from all provincial narrowmindedness, such as had never before been seen in France in this form, even though its dialectic is constantly twisted into a sophistic toying with the contradictions of existence. It is because this fine flowering of the spirit is at the same time a swamp of self-prostitution, corruption and depravity that the tragicomedy enacted before us in this novel achieves a depth never before attained in *bourgeois* literature.

Thus it is the very depth of Balzac's realism which removes his art so completely beyond the photographic reproduction of "average" reality. For the great concentration of the content lends the picture, even without the addition of any romantic ingredients, a sombre, gruesome and fantastic quality. Only in this sense does Balzac at his best submit to some extent to romantic influences, without himself becoming a romanticist. The fantastic element in Balzac derives merely from the fact that he radically thinks through to the end the necessities of social reality, beyond their normal limits, beyond even their feasibility. An instance of this is the story *Melmoth Reconciled,* in which Balzac turns the soul's salvation into a commodity which is quoted on the produce exchange and the price of which begins to fall rapidly from its initial height owing to excessive supplies.

The figure of Vautrin is the incarnation of this fantastic quality in Balzac. It is certainly not by chance that this " Cromwell of the hulks" figures in those novels of Balzac in which the typical figures of the young post-war revolutionary generation turn from ideals to reality. Thus Vautrin appears in the shabby little boarding-house in which Rastignac experiences his personal ideological crisis; thus he turns up again at the end of *Lost Illusions* when Lucien de Rubempré, hopelessly ruined both materially and moral-

ly, is about to commit suicide. Vautrin takes the stage with the
same motivated-unmotivated suddenness as Mephistopheles in
Goethe's *Faust* or Lucifer in Byron's *Cain*. Vautrin's function in
Balzac's *Human Comedy* is the same as that of Mephistopheles
and Lucifer in Goethe's and Byron's mystery-plays. But the
changed times have not only deprived the devil—the principle of
negation—of his superhuman greatness and glory, have not only
sobered him and brought him down to earth—the nature and
method of his temptation have also changed. Although Goethe's
old age reached well into the post-revolutionary epoch and although he gave the most profound expression to its deepest problems, he still regarded the great transformation of the world since
the Renaissance as something positive and valuable and his Mephistopheles was ' a part of the force that ever wills the evil but ever
creates the good.' In Balzac this ' good ' no longer exists save in
the shape of fantastic dreams. Vautrin's Mephistophelian criticism
of the world is only the brutal and cynical expression of what
everyone does in this world and of what everyone who wants to
survive *must* do. Vautrin says to Lucien : " You have nothing.
You are in the position in which the Medicis, Richelieu, Napoleon
were at the outset of their careers. They all bought their future
with ingratitude, betrayals and sharp contradictions. He who
wants everything must risk all. Consider : when you sit down to
the gaming-table, do you argue about the rules of the game? The
rules are cut and dried. You accept them." In this conception of
society it is not only the content that is cynical. Such conceptions
had already been put forward long before Balzac. But the point
in the words of temptation spoken by Vautrin is that they express
nakedly, without illusions and without spiritual frills, the wordly
wisdom which is common to all intelligent men. The ' temptation '
lies in the fact that Vautrin's wisdom is identical with the wisdom
of the purest, saintliest characters of Balzac's world.

In the famous letter which the ' saintly ' Mme. de Mortsauf
writes to Felix de Vandenesse, she says about society :

" For me the existence of society is not in question. As soon as
you accept society instead of living outside it, you must accept as
excellent its basic principles and to-morrow you will, in a manner
of speaking, sign a contract with it."

This is expressed in a rather vague and poetic form, but the
naked meaning of the words is the same as what Vautrin tells Lucien—just as Rastignac noted with amazement that Vautrin's
cynical wisdom was identical in its content with the dazzlingly

witty aphorisms of the Vicomtesse de Beauséant . . . This profound
conformity in the assessment of what is essential in capitalist reality,
this conformity of opinion between the escaped convict and the
flower of the aristocratic *intelligentsia* takes the place of the theatri-
cally mystic appearance of a Mephistopheles. Not for nothing is
Vautrin nicknamed ' Cheat-Death ' in the language of the hulks
and of the police narks. Vautrin stands in truth in the graveyard
of all illusions developed during several centuries, on his face the
satanic grin of the bitter Balzacian wisdom that all men are either
fools or knaves.

But this sombre picture does not signify pessimism in the later-
nineteenth-century sense of the word. The great poets and thinkers
of this phase of *bourgeois* development fearlessly rejected the dull
apologetics of capitalist progress, the myth of a contradictionless,
smoothly evolutionary advance. It was precisely this depth and
many-sidedness that forced them into a contradictory position :
their proud, critical recognition, their intellectual and poetic grasp
of the contradictions of capitalist development is necessarily
coupled with groundless illusions. In *Lost Illusions* the circle around
Daniel D'Arthez is the poetic manifestation of these illusions, just
as in *The Nephew of Rameau* Diderot himself is the incarnation
of these illusions. In all these cases the existence of another and a
better truth is poetically opposed to. the squalid reality. In his
analysis of Diderot's masterpiece Hegel already pointed out the
weakness of this poetic argumentation. Hegel saw clearly, in connection with Diderot, that the voice of historical evolution is heard,
not in the isolated portrayal of what is good, but in the negative,
in what is evil and perverse. According to Hegel, the perverse
consciousness sees the connection—or at least the contradictory
nature of the connection—while the illusory good has to be content with incidental and isolated details. ' The content of what the
spirit says of and about itself is thus a complete inversion of all
concepts and realities, a general deception of itself and all others
and hence the shamelessness with which the deception is proclaimed is the greatest truth.'

But in spite of all illusions, the Diderot of the Rameau dialogue
or the D'Arthez-Balzac of *Lost Illusions* should not, of course, be
rigidly set against the poetically represented negative world. The
basic contradiction lies precisely in the fact that in spite of all the
illusions of D'Arthez, Balzac did write *Lost Illusions*. Diderot's
and Balzac's consciousness did embrace both the positive and the
negative of the worlds they described, both the illusions and their

refutation by capitalist reality. By thus creatively expressing the true nature of the capitalist world, these writers rose not only above the illusory opinions put forward in their writings by the characters who are their mouthpieces, but also above the sophistic cynicism of the genuine representatives of capitalism which they portray. To express ' that-which-is ' is the highest level of cognizance which a *bourgeois* thinker or poet can attain before social evolution has reached the stage at which he can altogether jettison the *bourgeois* class basis. Naturally a core of idealist illusions inevitably still persists even in such expressions of ' that-which-is.' Hegel, at the end of his analysis of Diderot, sums up these illusions by saying that the clear recognition of these contradictions signifies that the spirit has in reality already overcome them.

It is of course an obvious and typical idealist illusion when Hegel believes that the perfect intellectual grasp of the contradictions of reality is equivalent to overcoming them in fact; for even this intellectual grasp of contradictions which cannot as yet be overcome in fact, will itself always prove illusory. The form is different but the essence of the illusion remains the same.

Nevertheless these illusions contributed to the continuation of the great struggle of mankind for freedom, however mistaken a motivation may have been Balzac's desperately earnest searching for truth and justice is an important and tragic phase in the history of humanism. In the twilight of a traditional period when the sun of the revolutionary humanism of the *bourgeoisie* had already set and the light of the rising new democratic and proletarian humanism was not yet visible over the horizon, such a criticism of capitalism as Balzac's was the surest way to preserve the great heritage of *bourgeois* humanism and save what was best in it for the future benefit of mankind.

In *Lost Illusions* Balzac created a new type of novel of disillusionment, but his novel far outgrew the forms which this type of novel took later in the nineteenth century. The difference between the latter and the former, which makes this novel and Balzac's whole *oeuvre* unique in the literature of the world, is a historical difference. Balzac depicted the original accumulation of capital in the ideological sphere, while his successors, even Flaubert, the greatest of them, already accepted as an accomplished fact that all human values were included in the commodity structure of capitalism. In Balzac we see the tumultuous tragedy of birth; his successors give us the lifeless fact of consummation and lyrically or ironically mourn the dead. Balzac depicts the last great struggle against the capitalist degradation of man, while his successors paint an already degraded capitalist world. Romanticism—which for Balzac was only one feature of his total conception, a feature which he overcame and developed further—was not overcome by his successors, but lyrically and ironically transmuted into reality which it overgrew, blanketing the great motive forces of evolution and providing only elegiac or ironical moods and impressions instead of an active and objective presentation of things in themselves.   The militant participation in the great human struggle for liberation slackens into mourning over the slavery that capitalism has brought on mankind and the militant anger at this degradation dies down to an impotently arrogant passive irony. Thus Balzac not only created the novel of disillusionment but also exhausted the highest possibilities of this type of novel. His successors who continued in his footsteps, moved on a downward slope, however great their literary achievements may have been. Their artistic decline was socially and historically unavoidable.

CHAPTER THREE

Balzac and Stendhal

IN SEPTEMBER 1840, Balzac, then at the zenith of his glory published an enthusiastic and most profound review of *The Monastery of Parma* by Stendhal, an as yet quite unknown author. In October Stendhal replied to this review in a long and detailed letter, in which he listed the points on which he accepted Balzac's criticism and those in reference to which he wished to defend his own creative method in opposition to Balzac. This encounter, which brought the two greatest writers of the XIXth century face to face in the arena of literature, is of the greatest importance, although—as we will show later—Stendhal's letter was more guarded and less candid in expressing his objections than Balzac's review. Nevertheless it is clear from the review and the letter that the two great men were essentially in agreement as to their view of the central problems of realism and also of the diverging paths which each of them pursued in search of realism.

Balzac's review is a model for the concrete analysis of a great work of art. In the whole field of literary criticism there are few other examples of such a detailed, sympathetic and sensitive revelation of the beauty of a work of art. It is a model of criticism by a great and thinking artist who knows his own craft inside out. The significance of this criticism is not in the least diminished by the fact—which we propose to show in the course of our argument—that despite the admirable intuition with which Balzac understood and interpreted Stendhal's intentions, he yet remained blind to Stendhal's chief aim and attempted to foist on the latter his own creative method.

These limitations, however, are not limitations of Balzac's own personality. The reason why the comments of great artists on their own works and the works of others are so instructive is precisely because such comments are always based on the inevitable and productive single-mindedness. But we can really benefit by such criticisms only if we do not regard them as abstract canons but uncover the specific point of view from which they spring. For the single-mindedness of so great an artist as Balzac, is as we have already said, both inevitable and productive; it is precisely this single-mindedness which enables him to conjure up before us life in all its fullness.

The urge to clarify his attitude to the only contemporary writer he regarded as his equal caused Balzac to define at the very beginning of his review with more than his accustomed precision, his own position in reference to the development of the novel, i.e. his own place in the history of literature. In the introduction to *The Human Comedy* he confined himself in the main to establishing his own position in relation to Sir Walter Scott, mentioning only the features he regarded as a continuation of Scott's life-work and those which transcended it. But in his review of *The Monastery of Parma* he gives a most profound analysis of all the trends of style existing in the novel of his time. The concrete depth of this analysis of style will not be diminished in the eyes of the intelligent reader by the fact that Balzac's terminology is rather loose and sometimes misleading.

The essential content of this analysis could be summed up as follows : Balzac distinguishes three principal trends of style in the novel. These trends are : the "literature of ideas" by which he means chiefly the literature of the French enlightenment. Voltaire and Le Sage among the old and Stendhal and Mérimée among the new writers are in his view the greatest representatives of this trend. Another trend is the "literature of images," represented mainly by the romantics Chateaubriand, Lamartine, Victor Hugo and others. The third trend, to which he himself adheres, strives for a synthesis of both the other trends. Balzac—rather unfortunately—calls this trend "literary eclecticism." (The source of this unfortunate term is probably his over-estimation of the idealist philosophers of his time, such as Royer-Collard). Balzac enumerates Sir Walter Scott, Mme. de Stael, Fennimore Cooper and George Sand as representing this trend. The list shows clearly how lonely Balzac felt in his own time. What he has to say about these writers —for instance his most interesting review of Fennimore Cooper's works which he published in the *Revue Parisienne,* show that his agreement with them regarding the deeper problems of creative methods did not go very far. But in the Stendhal review, when he wanted to justify his own creative method, as a great historical trend, in the eyes of the only contemporary writer whom he regarded as his equal, he felt compelled to point to a galaxy of precursors, of writers striving towards similar goals.

Balzac works out the contrast between his own trend and the "literature of ideas" most pointedly and this is understandable enough because his opposition to Stendhal shows itself here more clearly than anywhere else. Balzac says: "I don't believe that it is possible to depict modern society by the methods of seventeenth-century and eighteenth-century literature. I think pictures, images, descriptions, the use of dramatic elements of dialogue are indispensable to the modern writers. Let us admit frankly that the form of Gil Blas is tiring and that there is something infertile in the piling up of events and ideas." When immediately after this he extols Stendhal's novel as a masterpiece of the "literature of ideas," he stresses at the same time that Stendhal has made certain concessions to the other two schools of literature. We shall see in the following that Balzac understood with exceptional sensitivity that it was impossible for Stendhal to make concessions in artistic detail either to romanticism or to the trend represented by Balzac himself; on the other hand we shall also see that when discussing the final problems of composition, the problems which already almost touch on basic problems of *Weltanschauung,* he censured Stendhal precisely for his failure to make concessions.

What is at issue here is the central problem of the nineteenth-century world-view and style: the attitude to romanticism. No great writer living after the French revolution could avoid this issue. Its discussion began already in the Weimar period of Goethe and Schiller and reached its culminating point in Heine's critique of romanticism. The basic problem in dealing with this issue was that romanticism was by no means a purely literary trend; it was the expression of a deep and spontaneous revolt against rapidly developing capitalism, although, naturally in very contradictory forms. The extreme romanticists soon turned into feudalist reactionaries and obscurantists. But the background of the whole movement is nevertheless a spontaneous revolt against capitalism. All this provided a strange dilemma for the great writers of the age, who, while they were unable to rise above the *bourgeois* horizon, yet strove to create a world-picture that would be both comprehensive and real. They could not be romanticists in the strict sense of the word; had they been that, they could not have understood and followed the forward movement of their age. On the other hand they could not disregard the criticism levelled by the romanticists at capitalism and capitalist culture, without exposing themselves to the danger of becoming blind extollers of *bourgeois* society, and apologists of capitalism. They therefore had to at-

tempt to overcome romanticism (in the Hegelian sense), i.e. to
fight against it, preserve it and raise it to a higher level all at the
same time. (This was a general tendency of the time and by no
means required acquaintance with Hegel's philosophy, which Balzac himself lacked.) We must add that this synthesis was not
achieved completely and without contradictions by any of the
great writers of the age. Their greatest virtues as writers rested on
contradictions in their social and intellectual position, contradictions which they boldly followed through to their logical conclusion,
but which they could not objectively solve.

Balzac may also be counted among the writers who while accepting romanticism, at the same time consciously and vigorously
strove to overcome it. Stendhal's attitude to romanticism is on the
contrary a complete rejection. He is a true disciple of the philosophers of the Enlightenment. This difference between the two
writers is of course manifest in their creative methods. Stendhal
for instance advises a novice author not to read modern authors;
if he wanted to learn to write good French he should study, if
possible, books written before 1700; if he wanted to learn to think
correctly, he should read Helvetius' " De l'esprit " and Jeremy
Bentham.

Balzac on the contrary admired such outstanding romanticists
as Chénier and Chateaubriand, although not uncritically. We shall
see later that it is this divergence of opinion that lies at the root
of the decisive controversy between them.

We must stress this divergence from the start, for unless we are
clear on this point we cannot assess the true significance of the
praise Balzac gave to Stendhal's book. For the feeling, the wealth
of thought and the perfect absence of envy with which Balzac
championed his only real rival is admirable not only as a personal
attitude,—although the history of *bourgeois* literature knows very
few examples of a similar objective tribute. Balzac's review and his
enthusiasm are so admirable because by them he strove to ensure
the success of a work which was in diametrical opposition to his own
most cherished aims. Again and again Balzac stresses the stream-
lined, concentrated structure of Stendhal's novel. He describes
this structure with some justification as dramatic, and claims that
in this incorporation of a dramatic element Stendhal's style is related to his own. Following this train of thought he praises
Stendhal for not embellishing his novel with " hors d'oeuvres ",
with insertions. " No, the persons act, reflect and feel and the
drama goes forward all the time. The poet, a dramatist in his

thoughts, does not stray from his path to pick any little flower; everything has a dithyrambic speed." All along Balzac stresses the absence of episode, the directness, and frugality of Stendhal's composition. In this praise a certain community of tendencies inherent in both writers is made manifest. Superficially it would be precisely in this sphere that the contrast in style between Stendhal's " enlightenist " severity and Balzac's romantically many-coloured and almost inextricably rich and chaotic mode of composition is greatest. Yet this contrast conceals a deep affinity as well; in his better novels Balzac also does not stoop to pick a flower by the roadside; he, too, depicts the essential and nothing but the essential. The difference and the contrast is in what Balzac and Stendhal, each for his part, consider essential. Balzac's conception of the essential is far more intricate and far less concentrated into a few great moments than Stendhal's.

This passionate striving for the essential, this passionate contempt for all trivial realism is the artistic link that unites these two great writers in spite of the polar divergence of their philosophies and creative methods. That is why Balzac, in his analysis of Stendhal's novel, could not refrain from touching upon the deepest problems of form—problems which are highly topical to this day. Balzac the artist sees quite clearly the indissoluble connection between a felicitous choice of subject and successful composition. He therefore considers it most important to explain in detail the consummate artistry shown by Stendhal in setting the scene of his novel in a little Italian court. Balzac, quite rightly, stresses the point that Stendhal's picture grows far beyond the framework of petty court intrigues in a small Italian duchy. What he shows in his novel is the typical structure of modern autocracy. He brings before us in their most characteristic manifestation the eternal types produced by this form of social existence. "He has written the modern *Il Principe*," says Balzac, "the novel that Macchiavelli would have written had he been exiled to nineteenth-century Italy. *The Monastery of Parma* is a typical book in the best sense of the word. Finally it brilliantly lays before the reader all the sufferings inflicted on Richelieu by the *camarilla of* Louis XIII."

In Balzac's view Stendhal's novel achieves its comprehensive typicality precisely because its scene is laid in Parma, on a stage ot trivial interests and petty intrigues. For—Balzac continues to present such vast interests as those which occupied the cabinets of Louis XIV or Napoleon would necessarily require so wide a stage, so much objective explanation, as would greatly impede the smooth continuity of the action. In contrast, the stage of Parma can be taken in at a glance and Stendhal's Parma, small as it is, yet demonstrates the characteristic inner structure of the court of any autocratic ruler." In saying this, Balzac reveals an essential structural quality of the great realistic *bourgeois* novel. The writer. the 'historian of private life' as Fielding put it, must describe the hidden fluctuations of society, the intrinsic laws governing its movements, its incipient trends, its invisible growth and its revolutionary upheavals. But great historical events, and the great figures of history can very rarely be adapted to the demonstration of the development of society in the form of concrete types. It is not by accident that in Balzac's writings Napoleon appears very rarely and always only episodically, although the Napoleonic ideals and the intellectual content of the Napoleonic empire play a dominant part in many novels of Balzac. Balzac considers that a writer does not know his craft if he chooses for his subject the external glitter of great historical events instead of the internal riches found in the characteristic development of social elements. In another of his reviews, (also published by the *Revue Parisienne*) dealing with Eugéne Sue, Balzac quotes the example of Sir Walter Scott. He says: "The novel tolerates the appearance of great historical figures only as secondary characters. Cromwell, Charles II, Mary Queen of Scots, Louis XI, Elizabeth of England, Richard Cœur-de-Lion—all these great figures take the stage for short moments only, when the dramatic plot woven by the creator of this literary form requires their presence on the scene, but not before the reader has already made the acquaintance of a host of secondary characters and has shared their reaction to the imminent appearance of the great historical figure. When the latter does appear the reader already sees such a figure through the eyes of the minor characters in the story. Scott never chose great events as subjects for his pen, but he always carefully develops the causes which led to them, by depicting the spirit and morals of the age, and presenting a whole social *milieu* instead of moving in the rarified atmosphere of great political events."

On this point Balzac regards Stendhal as an ally, as a comrade-in-arms of equal rank, as a writer who despises petty realism, the trivially detailed painting of local colour or an empty historical monumentality and who, just like Balzac himself, by conscientiously uncovering the true driving forces of the social process, strives to present to the reader the most typical and essential traits in every social phenomenon. In this analysis the two greatest realists of the past century meet and join hands; they are at one in their rejection of all attempts to drag realism down from this height of the essential.

Balzac admires in Stendhal's novel above all the remarkable characters which come to life in it. In this respect, too, the final objectives of the two great realists are closely related. Both regard the portrayal of the great types of social evolution as their main task, but their conception of what is typical has nothing in common with that of the later Western realists who wrote after 1848 and who confuse the typical with the average. Balzac and Stendhal regard as typical only figures of exceptional qualities, who mirror all the essential aspects of some definite stage of development, evolutionary tendency or social group. In Balzac's view Vautrin is the typical criminal and not some ordinary average citizen who by chance gets drunk, and kills a man—as the later naturalists would in this case have handled the problem of typicality. What Balzac admires is precisely the energy with which Stendhal has kneaded the two princes of Parma, their minister Count Mosca, the Duchess of Sanseverina and the revolutionary Ferrante Palla into such typical figures. Balzac's unbiassed enthusiasm for Ferrante Palla is especially interesting and deeply characteristic of the objectivity with which he sets aside his own interests and concerns himself with nothing but the problems of the evolution of realism. He stresses that in creating the character of Michel Chrestien he had himself created something similar to Stendhal's Ferrante Palla; but adds most emphatically that in the shaping of such a type he has been far surpassed by Stendhal.

Nevertheless, the deeper Balzac probes into the composition problems of Stendhal's, the more evident the difference between their modes of composition must become. We have seen with what reasoned enthusiasm Balzac followed, step by step, the form and content of Stendhal's portrayal of the court at Parma. But it is this his delighted admiration that finally leads Balzac to his greatest and most important objection to the Stendhal novel. He says that this part is the real novel and the story of Fabrice del Dongo's youth that precedes it should have been only briefly touched upon. The portrayal of the de Dongo family; the antagonism between the pro-Austrian aristocratic family and the Napoleon-admirer Fabrice and his aunt, the future Duchess of Sanseverina; the description of Eugene Beauharnais' court at Milan and many other things do not, in Balzac's view, belong in this novel at all, nor does the whole Stendhalian building-up of the

end,—the period following upon the return of Count Mosca and
the Duchess of Sanseverina to Parma, the story of the love between
Fabrice and Clelia and Fabrice's withdrawal to the monastery.

Here Balzac would like to impose his own method of composition
on Stendhal. Most of the Balzac novels have a much rounder plot
and their predominant atmosphere is much more of one piece than is
found in Stendhal or in the novels of the eighteenth century. Balzac
mostly depicts some catastrophe tensely concentrated both in time
and space or else shows us a chain of catastrophes, and tints the
picture with the magic of a mood that is never inconsistent or out
of tune. Thus does he seek artistic escape from the flabby shapeless-
ness of modern bourgeois life by embodying certain compositional
features of the Shakespearean drama and of the classical *novella*
in the structure of his novels. A necessary result of this mode of
composition is that many characters in such a novel cannot fulfil
their destinies within its limits. The Balzacian principle of cyclic
structure rests on the assumption that such unfinished and incomplete characters will reappear as the central figures of some other
story in which the mood and atmosphere are appropriate to their
occupying a central position. This principle has nothing in common
with later forms of the cyclic novel, such as we find in the works of
Zola. One should think of how Balzac makes Vautrin, Rastignac,
Nucingen, Maxime de Trailles and others appear as episodic figures
in " Le Pere Goriot," but find their true fulfilment in other novels.
Balzac's world is, like Hegel's, a circle consisting entirely of circles.

Stendhal's principle of composition is diametrically opposed to
Balzac's. He too, like Balzac, strives to present a totality, but
always tries to crowd the essential features of a whole epoch into
the personal biography of some individual type (the period
of the Bourbon restoration in *Le Rouge et le Noir,* the
absolutism of the small Italian states in *The Monastery of
Parma* and the July monarchy on *Lucien Leuwen*). In adopting
this biographical form Stendhal followed his predecessors, but
endowed it with a different, quite specific meaning. Throughout
his career as a writer he always presented a certain type of man and
all representatives of this type, despite their clear-cut individuality,
and the wide divergences in their class position and circumstances,
are at the core of their being and in their attitude to Stendhal's
whole epoch are very closely related to each other (Julien Sorel,
Fabrice del Dongo, Lucien Leuwen). The fate of these characters is
intended to reflect the vileness, the squalid loathsomeness of the
whole epoch—an epoch in which there is no longer room for the

great, noble-minded descendants of the heroic phase of *bourgeois* history, the age of the revolution and Napoleon. All Stendhal heroes save their mental and moral integrity from the taint of their time by escaping from life. Stendhal deliberately represents the death of Julien Sorel on the scaffold as a form of suicide and Fabrice and Lucien withdraw from life in a similar way, if less dramatically and with less pathos.

Balzac entirely failed to notice this decisive point in Stendhal's world-view when he suggested that *The Monastery of Parma* ought to be concentrated around and restricted to the struggles at the court of Parma. But all that Balzac considered superfluous from the viewpoint of his own method of composition were for Stendhal matters of primary importance. Thus, to begin with, the opening of *The Monastery of Parma*—the Napoleonic age, Eugene Beauharnais' glittering, colourful viceregal court, as the decisive influence determining Fabrice's whole mentality and development, and in contrast to it the vivid satirical description of the vile, contemptible Austrian tyranny and the portrayal of the Del Dongos, the rich Italian aristocrats demeaning themselves to act as spies of the hated Austrian enemy—all these things were absolute essentials to Stendhal, and for the same reason the same applies to the end of the novel, Fabrice's final evolution.

True to his own principles of composition, Balzac suggests that Fabrice might be made the hero of a further novel under the title : " Fabrice or the Italian of the Nineteenth Century." " But if this young man is made the principal figure of the drama," says Balzac, " then the author is under the obligation to inspire him with some great idea, give him some quality which ensures his superiority over the great figures surrounding him—and such a quality is lacking here." Balzac failed to see that according to Stendhal's conception of the world and his method of composition, Fabrice did possess the quality which entitled him to be the principal hero of the novel. Mosca and Ferrante Palla are far more characteristic representatives of the type Balzac wanted to see, i.e. of the nineteenth-century Italian, than is Fabrice. The reason why Fabrice is nevertheless the hero of Stendhal's novel is that, despite his constant adaptation of himself to realities in his external way of life, he nevertheless represents that final refusal to accept a compromise, to formulate which was Stendhal's essential poetic objective. (I mention only *en passant* Balzac's almost comic misunderstanding of Fabrice's withdrawal to a monastery which he, Balzac, would have liked to see motivated on a religious, preferably Catholic basis. Such a possibility, quite feasible in the case of Balzac—we need only to recall the conversion of Mlle. de la Touche in *Beatrix* —is quite foreign to the world created by Stendhal.)

Things being thus, one may well understand that Balzac's criticism roused very conflicting emotions in Stendhal. As an artist unrecognised or misunderstood in his own time and hoping for recognition and understanding only in a distant future, he was naturally deeply moved by the passionate enthusiasm with which the greatest living writer had acclaimed his book. He realised, too, that Balzac was the only man who had on many points recognized his own deepest creative aspirations and paid tribute to them in a brilliant analysis. He was especially gratified by the part of Balzac's analysis which dealt with his choice of subject and the setting of the scene in a little Italian court. But in spite of the sincere pleasure he felt at Balzac's review, he yet voiced objectively his very sharp opposition, although in a very polite and diplomatic form, especially to Balzac's strictures on his style. Balzac, at the end of his review, criticized Stendhal's style rather severely, although he again showed his deep appreciation of Stendhal's great literary qualities, especially his ability to characterize people and bring out their essential traits by very few words. " Few words suffice M. Beyle; he characterizes his figures by action and dialogue; he does not fatigue the reader with descriptions but hurries forward towards the dramatic climax —and achieves it by a word, a single remark." In this sphere, therefore, Balzac accepted Stendhal as his equal, although—specifically in respect of characterization—he often mercilessly criticized other authors, even those whom he regarded as belonging to his own trend of thought. Thus he frequently criticizes Sir Walter Scott's dialogue and, in the *Revue Parisienne,* deplored Cooper's proneness to characterize his personages by a few constantly recurring phrases. He pointed out that examples of this can be found in Scott's writings too, " but the great Scotsman never abused this device which indicates an aridity, an infertility of the mind. Genius consists in throwing light on every situation by words which reveal the character of the figures, and not in muffling the personages in phrases which might apply to anything." (This remark is still most pertinent, for since the days of naturalism and through the influence of Richard Wagner and others, the leitmotiv-like stereotyped characterization of figures is still in vogue. Balzac rightly stresses that this is merely a means of concealing the inability to create lifelike characters in their movement and evolution.)

But although Balzac greatly appreciates Stendhal's capacity **for** characterizing his figures succinctly and yet profoundly by the words he puts in their mouths, he yet expresses considerable dissatisfaction with the style of his novel. He quotes a number of lapses of style and even grammar. But his criticism goes further than this. He demands that Stendhal should subject his novel to very extensive editing, and argues that Chateaubriand and De Maistre often rewrote some of their works. He concludes with the hope that Stendhal's novel, thus rewritten, " would be enriched by that ineffable beauty with which Chateaubriand and De Maistre endowed their favourite books."

Stendhal's every artistic instinct and conviction revolted against this conception of style. He readily admitted slovenliness of style. Many pages of the novel were dictated and sent to the publisher without revision. " I say what children say : ' I won't do it again '." But his acquiescence in the criticism of his style is almost entirely limited to this one point. He heartily despises the models of style quoted by Balzac. He writes : "Never, not even in 1802 . . . could I read even twenty pages of Chateaubriand. . . . I find M. De Maistre unbearable. The reason why I write badly is probably that I am too fond of logic." In defence of his style he adds the further remark : " If Mme. Sand had translated the *Monastery* into French, it would have been a great success. But in order to express all that is contained in the present two volumes, she would have needed three or four. Please consider this." The style of Chateaubriand and his companions he characterizes in these terms : " 1. Very many small pleasant things which it was quite superfluous to say. . . . 2. Very many small lies which are pleasant to hear."

As we see, Stendhal's criticism of the romantic style is very severe indeed, although he by no means said all that he thought about Balzac as a stylist and as a critic of style. He seizes the opportunity of hinting, when he makes these polemical remarks, that he has the greatest admiration for certain writings of Balzac (*The Lily in theValley, Old Goriot*), and naturally this was not mere politeness. But at the same time he passes over in silence, with understandable diplomacy, the fact that he despises the romantic traits in Balzac's style just as much as the style of the romanticists proper. Thus he once said about Balzac : " I can quite believe that he writes his novels twice. First he writes them sensibly and the second time he decorates them in a nice neologistic style with ' *pâtiments de l'âme*,' ' *il neige dans son cœur* ' and similar charming things." Nor does he mention how deeply he despises himself for every concession he makes to the neologistic style. Once he wrote of Fabrice : " He went for a walk, listening to the silence." On the margin of his own copy he apologised for this phrase to " the reader of 1880 " in these terms : 'In order that an author should find readers in 1838 he had to write such things as " listening to the silence." ' This shows that Stendhal had no intention of concealing his dislikes, he merely refrained from expressing them and drawing conclusions from them as radically and explicitly as he felt them.

To this negative criticism he appends a positive admission : "Sometimes I consider for a quarter of an hour whether I should put the adjective before or after the noun. I try to relate clearly and truthfully what is in my heart. I know only one rule : to express myself clearly. If I cannot speak clearly, my whole world is annihilated." From this point of view he condemns the greatest French writers, such as Voltaire, Racine and others, for filling their lines with empty words for the sake of a rhyme. ' These verses,' says Stendhal, ' fill up all the spaces that rightly belong to the true little facts.' This ideal of style he finds realized in his positive models. ' The memoirs of Gouvion-St.-Cyr are my Homer. Montesquieu and Fénelon's *Dialogues of the Dead* are I believe very well written. . . . I often read Ariosto, I like his narrative style.'

It is thus obvious that in matters of style Balzac and Stendhal represent two diametrically opposed trends, and this conflict manifests itself sharply on every individual issue. Balzac, in criticizing Stendhal's style, says of him : " His long sentences are ill-constructed, his short sentences are not rounded off. He writes approximately in Diderot's manner, who was not a writer." (Here Balzac's sharp opposition to Stendhal's style drives him into an absurd paradox; in other reviews he judges Diderot with far more justice.) It is true, however, that even this paradoxical utterance expresses a trend of style really existing in Balzac. To it, Stendhal replies : " As for the beauty, roundness, and rhythm of sentences (as in the funeral oration in *Jaques the Fatalist*) I often consider that a fault."

What is revealed in these problems is a conflict of style between the two great trends in French realism. During the subsequent evolution of French realism the principles of Stendhal fall ever more into disuse.

Flaubert, the greatest figure among the post-1848 French realists, is an even more enthusiastic admirer of Chateaubriand's beauties of style than was Balzac. And Flaubert no longer had any understanding at all of Stendhal's greatness as a writer. The Goncourts relate in their diary that Flaubert flew into fits of rage every time ' M.

Beyle' was described as a writer. And it is obvious without any special analysis that the style of the greater representatives of later French realism, of Zola, Daudet, the Goncourts, etc. was determined by their acceptance of the romanticist ideals and not at all by a Stendhal-like rejection of the romantic 'neologisms.' Zola, of course, thought his teacher Flaubert's worship of Chateaubriand a fad, but this did not prevent him from modelling his own style on that of another great romanticist, Victor Hugo.

The reason for the contrast in style between Balzac and Stendhal is at core one of world-view. We recapitulate : the attitude to romanticism of the great realists of the period, the attempt to turn it into a sublimated element of a greater realism is, as we have already said, no mere question of style. Romanticism, in the more general sense of the word, is no mere literary or artistic trend, but the expression of the attitude taken up towards the post-revolutionary development of *bourgeois* society. The capitalist forces liberated by the revolution and the Napoleonic empire are deployed on an ever widening scale and their deployment gives birth to a working class of ever more decidedly developing class-consciousness. Balzac's and Stendhal's careers as writers extend to the period of the first great movements of the working class (e.g. the rising in Lyons). This is also the time when the Socialist world-view was born, the time of the first Socialist critics of *bourgeois* society, the time of the great Utopians St. Simon and Fourier. It is also the time when, parallel with the Utopian-Socialist criticism of capitalism, its romanticist criticism also reaches its theoretical culminating point (Sismondi). This is the age of religious-feudalist Socialist theories (Lamennais). And it is this period which reveals the pre-history of *bourgeois* society as a permanent class war (Thiers, Guizot, etc.).

The deepest disagreement between Balzac and Stendhal rests on the fact that Balzac's world-view was essentially influenced by all these newer trends, while Stendhal's world-view was at bottom an interesting and consistent extension of the ideology of pre-revolutionary Enlightenment. Thus Stendhal's world-view is much clearer and more progressive than that of Balzac, who was influenced both by romantic, mystic Catholicism and a feudalist Socialism and strove in vain to reconcile these trends with a political monarchism based on English models and with a poetic interpretation of Geoffroy de Saint Hilaire's dialectic of spontaneous evolution.

This difference of world-view is quite in keeping with the fact that Balzac's last novels were full of a profound pessimism about society and apocalyptic forebodings regarding culture, while Stendhal, who was very pessimistic regarding the present and criticized it so wittily and with such profound contempt, optimistically expected his hopes regarding *bourgeois* culture to be realized around 1880. Stendhal's hopes were no mere wistful dreams of a poet unappreciated by his own time; they were pregnant with a definite conception of the evolution of *bourgeois* society, although of course an illusory conception. In Stendhal's view, in pre-revolutionary times there had been a culture and a section of society able to appreciate and judge cultural products. But after the revolution, the aristocracy goes in eternal fear of another 1793 and has hence lost all its capacity for sound judgment. The new rich, on the other hand, are a mob of self-seeking and ignorant upstarts indifferent to cultural values. Not until 1880 did Stendhal expect *bourgeois* society to have reached the stage again permitting a revival of culture—a culture conceived in the spirit of enlightenment, as a continuation of the philosophy of enlightenment.

It is a curious result of this strange dialectic of history and of the unequal growth of ideologies, that Balzac—with his confused and often quite reactionary world-view—mirrored the period between 1789 and 1848 much more completely and profoundly than his much more clear-thinking and progressive rival. True, Balzac criticized capitalism from the right, from the feudal, romantic viewpoint, and his clairvoyant hatred of the nascent capitalist world order has its source in that viewpoint. But nevertheless this hatred itself becomes the source of such eternal types of capitalist society as Nucingen and Crevel. One need only contrast these characters with old Leuwen, the only capitalist ever portrayed by Stendhal, in order to see how much less profound and comprehensive Stendhal is in this sphere. The figure itself, the embodiment of a superior spirit and superior culture, with an adventurous gift for finance, is a very lifelike transposition of the pre-revolutionary traits of the Enlightenment into the world of the July monarchy. But however delicately portrayed and lifelike the figure is, Leuwen is an exception among capitalists and hence greatly inferior to Nucingen as a type.

We can observe the same contrast in the portrayal of the main types of the restoration period. Stendhal hates the restoration and regards it as the era of petty baseness, which has unworthily supplanted the heroic epoch of the revolution and Napoleon. Balzac in contrast, is personally an adherent of the restoration, and although he flays the policy of the nobility, he does so only because he thinks it was not the policy by means of which the nobility could have prevented the July revolution. But matters stand quite otherwise when we turn to the worlds created by the pens of the two great writers. Balzac the writer understands that the restoration is merely a backdrop for the increasing capitalisation of France and that this process of capitalisation is carrying the nobility along with it with irresistible force. So he proceeds to put before us all the grotesque, tragic, comic and tragicomic types engendered by this capitalist development. He shows how the demoralising effect of this process must of necessity involve the whole of society and corrupt it to the core. Balzac the monarchist can find decent and sincere adherents of the ancient regime only among *borné* and outdated provincials, such as old d'Esgrignon in the *Cabinet of Antiques* and old Du Guenic in *Beatrix*. The ruling aristocrats, who keep up with the times, have only smiles for the honourably narrow-minded backwardness of these types. They themselves are concerned only with making the best use of their rank and privileges in order to derive the greatest possible personal advantages from this capitalist development. Balzac the monarchist depicts his beloved nobles as a gang of gifted or ungifted careerists and climbers, empty-headed nitwits, aristocratic harlots, etc.

Stendhal's restoration novel, *Le Rouge et le Noir,* exhales a fierce hatred of this period. And yet Balzac has never created so positive a type of romantic monarchist youth as Stendhal's Mathilde de la Mole. Mathilde de la Mole is a sincere convinced monarchist who is passionately devoted to romantic monarchist ideals and who despises her own class because it lacks the devoted and passionate faith which burns in her own soul. She prefers the plebeian Julien Sorel, the passionate Jacobin and Napoleon-admirer, to the men of her own station. In a passage, most characteristic of Stendhal, she explains her enthusiasm for the romantic monarchist ideals. ' "The time of League wars was the most heroic period of French history " she said to him (Julien Sorel) one day, her eyes flashing with passion and enthusiasm. " In those days everyone fought for a cause they chose for themselves. They fought to help their own party to win, not just in order to collect decorations, as in the days of your precious Emperor. Admit that there was less self-seeking and pettiness then. I love the cinquecento." ' This Mathilde de la Mole counters Julien's enthusiasm for the heroic Napoleonic epoch with a reference to another, in her eyes even more heroic, period of history. The whole story of Mathilde's and Julien's love is painted with the greatest possible authenticity and accuracy. Nevertheless Mathilde de la Mole as a representative of the young aristocrats of the restoration period is by no means as truly typical as is Balzac's Diane de Maufrigneuse.

Here we come back again to the central problem of Balzac's criticism of Stendhal : to the question of characterization and in connection with it to the ultimate principles of composition applied by the two great writers to their novels. Both Balzac and Stendhal chose as central characters that generation of gifted young people on whose thoughts and emotions the storms of the heroic period have left deep traces and who at first felt out of place in the sordid baseness of the restoration world.

The qualification " at first " really applies only to Balzac. For he depicts precisely the catastrophe, the material, moral and intellectual crises in the course of which his young men do finally find their bearings in a French society rapidly evolving towards capitalism and who then conquer or attempt to conquer a place for themselves (Rastignac, Lucien de Rubempré, etc.). Balzac knew perfectly well the price that had to be paid for finding a niche in the society of the restoration period. It is not by accident that the almost superhuman figure of Vautrin appears twice, like another Mephistopheles, to tempt the heroes struggling in a desperate crisis onto the path of "reality," or, in other words, the path of capitalist corruption and unprincipled careerism. Nor is it by accident that Vautrin succeeds in this on both occasions. What Balzac painted here is how the rise of capitalism to the undisputed economic domination of society carries the human and moral degradation and debasement of men into the innermost depths of their hearts.

Stendhal's composition is quite different. As a great realist, he of course sees all the essential phenomena of his time no less clearly than Balzac. It is certainly no accident and probably not due to Balzac's influences that Count Mosca, in his advice to Fabrice, says much the same about the part played by ethics in society as Vautrin does in his advice to Lucien de Rubempré when he compares life with a card game, in which he who wants to play cannot first investigate the rules of the game as to their rightness, their moral and other values. Stendhal saw all this very clearly, sometimes with even greater contempt and cynicism (in the Ricardian sense) than Balzac. And as the great realist that he is, he allows his hero to take part in the game of corruption and careerism, to wade through all the filth of growing capitalism, to learn, and apply, sometimes even skilfully, the rules of the game as expounded by Mosca and Vautrin. But it is interesting to note that none of his principal characters is at heart sullied or corrupted by this participation in the " game." A pure and passionate ardour, an inexorable search for truth preserves from contamination the souls of these men as they wade through the mire, and helps them to shake off the dirt at the end of their career (but still in the prime of their youth), although it is true that by so doing they cease to be participants in the life of their time and withdraw from it in one way or another.

This is the deeply romantic element in the world-view of Stendhal the enlightened atheist and bitter opponent of romanticism. (The term ' romanticism ' is of course used here in the widest, least dogmatic sense). It is in the last instance due to Stendhal's refusal to accept the fact that the heroic period of the *bourgeoisie* was ended and that the ' antediluvian colossi '—to us a Marxian phrase—had perished for ever. Every slightest trace of such heroic trends as he can find in the present (although mostly only in his own heroic, uncompromising soul) he exaggerates into proud reality and contrasts it satirico-elegiacally with the wretched dishonesty of his time.

Thus the Stendhalian conception comes into being; a gallery of heroes who idealistically and romantically exaggerate mere tendencies and dawnings into realities and hence can never attain the social typicality which so superbly permeates *The Human Comedy*. It would be quite wrong, however, to overlook the great historical typicality of Stendhal's heroes because of this romantic trait. The mourning for the disappearance of the heroic age is present throughout the whole of French romanticism. The romantic cult of passion, the romantic worship of the Renaissance all spring from this grief, from this desperate search for inspiring examples of great passions which could be opposed to the paltry, mercenary present. But the only true fulfiller of this romantic longing is Stendhal himself, precisely because he nevertheless always remained faithful to realism. He translates into reality all that Victor Hugo tried to express in many of his plays and novels. But Victor Hugo gave us only abstract skeletons dressed in the purple mantle of rhetoric, while Stendhal created flesh and blood, the destinies of real men and women. What makes these men and women typical —although regarded superficially they are all extreme individual cases—is that these extreme cases incarnate the deepest longings of the best sons of the post-revolutionary *bourgeois* class. Stendhal differs sharply from all romanticists in two respects : firstly, in that he is quite aware of the exceptional, extreme character of his personages and renders this very exceptionality with incomparable realism by the aura of loneliness with which he surrounds his heroes; secondly, in that he depicts with admirable realism the inevitable catastrophe of these types, their inevitable defeat in the struggle against the dominating forces of the age, their necessary withdrawal from life or more accurately their necessary rejection by the world of their time.

These characters possess so great a historical typicality that a similar conception of human destinies was put forward in postrevolutionary Europe quite independently by many writers who knew nothing of each other. We find this conception in Schiller's *Wallenstein,* when Max Piccolomini rides to his death. Hoelderlin's Hyperion and Empedocles abandon life in the same way. Such, too, is the fate of more than one of Byron's heroes. It is therefore not a chase after literary paradoxes, but merely an intellectual expression of the dialectic of class evolution itself, if we here set Stendhal the great realist side by side with such writers as Schiller and Hoelderlin. However profound are the differences between them in all points relating to creative method (the reason for which is the difference in French and German social evolution) the affinity of basic conception is no less profound. The accents of Schiller's elegiac ' such is the fate of beauty upon earth ' are echoed in the accents with which Stendhal accompanies his Julien Sorel to the scaffold and his Fabrice del Dongo to the monastery. Finally it must be said that not all these accents were purely romantic, even in Schiller. The affinity of the conception of hero and destiny in all these writers derives from the general affinity of their conception of the evolution of their own class, from a humanism that despairs of the present, from a steadfast adherence to the great ideals of the rising *bourgeoisie* and from the hope that a time would come when these ideals would be realized after all (Stendhals hopes of the year 1880).

Stendhal differs from Schiller and Hoelderlin in that his dissatisfaction with the present does not manifest itself in lyrical elegiac forms (like Hoelderlin's) nor limit itself to an abstract-philosophical judgment on the present (like Schiller's) but provides the foundation for his portrayal of the present with a magnificent, profound and sharply satirical realism.

The reason for this is that Stendhal's France had recently experienced revolution and the Napoleonic empire and live revolutionary forces had actually taken the field in opposition to the Restoration, while Schiller and Hoelderlin, living in a Germany as yet socially and economically unchanged. a Germany that had not yet had its *bourgeois* revolution, could only dream of developments, the real motive forces of which necessarily remained unknown to them. Hence Stendhal's satirical realism, hence the elegiac lyricality of the Germans. What nevertheless lends Stendhal's writings a wonderful depth and richness, is that despite all pessimism in regard to the present he never abandoned his humanist ideals. The hopes Stendhal harboured in conjunction with *bourgeois* society as it would be in 1880, was a pure illusion, but because it was an historically legitimate, basically progressive illusion, it could become the source of his literary fertility. One should not forget that Stendhal was also a contemporary of Blanqui's risings, by which that heroic revolutionary attempted merely to renew a plebeian-Jacobin dictatorship. But Stendhal did not live to see the distortion of *bourgeois* Jacobinism into a travesty of itself, the transformation which turned the best revolutionaries from citizens into proletarians. His attitude to the working-class unrest of his time (see *Lucien Leuwen*) was democratic-revolutionary; he condemned the July monarchy for its ruthless bludgeoning of the workers; but did not and could not see the part the proletariat was to play in the creation of a new society, nor the perspectives opened up by socialism and by a new type of democracy.

As we have already seen, Balzac's illusions, his incorrect conception of social evolution, were of a totally different nature. That is why he does not conjure up, and oppose to the present, the ' antediluvian ' monsters of a past heroic age. What he did was to depict the typical characters of his own time, while enlarging them to dimensions so gigantic as in the reality of a capitalist world can never pertain to single human beings, only to social forces.

Because of his attitude to life Balzac is the greater realist of the two and, despite the wider acceptance of romantic elements in his world-view and style, he is in the final count the less romantic too.

In their attitude to the development of *bourgeois* society in the period between 1789 and 1848, Balzac and Stendhal represent two important extremes in the gamut of possible attitudes. Each of them built a whole world of characters, an extensive and animated reflection of the whole of social evolution, and each of them did so from his own distinct angle. Where their point of contact lies is in their deep understanding and their contempt of the trivial tricks of mere naturalistic realism and of the mere rhetorical treatment of man and destiny. A further point of contact is that they both regard realism as transcending the trivial and average, because for both of them realism is a search for that deeper essence of reality that is hidden under the surface. Where they diverge widely is in their conception of what this essence is. They represent two diametrically opposed, although historically equally legitimate, attitudes towards the stage of human development reached in their time. Hence, in their literary activities—with the one exception of the general problem of the essence of reality—they must of necessity follow diametrically opposite paths.

Thus the profound understanding and appreciation of Stendhal shown by Balzac in spite of all divergencies, is more than a mere piece of fine literary criticism. The meeting of these two great realists is one of the outstanding events of literary history. We might compare it with the meeting of Goethe and Schiller, even though it did not lead to so fruitful a co-operation as that of those two other great men.

CHAPTER FOUR

The Zola Centenary

E M I L E Z O L A the novelist is the 'historian of private life' under the Second Empire in France in the same way as Balzac was the historian of private life under the restoration and the July monarchy. Zola himself never disclaimed this heritage. He always protested against the assumption that he had invented a new art form and always regarded himself as the heir and follower of Balzac and Stendhal, the two great realists of the beginning of the nineteenth century. Of the two, he regarded Stendhal as the connecting link with the literature of the eighteenth century. Of course so remarkable and original a writer as Zola could not regard his literary predecessors as mere models to copy; he admired Balzac and Stendhal but vigorously criticized them none the less; he tried to eliminate what he considered dead and antiquated in them and to work out the principles of a creative method which could have a fertilizing influence on the further evolution of realism. (It should be said here that Zola never speaks of realism, but always of naturalism.)

But the further development of realism in Zola's hands took a far more intricate course than Zola himself imagined. Between Balzac and Zola lies the year 1848 and the bloody days of June, the first independent action of the working class, which left so indelible an impression on the ideology of the French *bourgeoisie,* that after it *bourgeois* ideology ceased to play a progressive part in France for a long time. Ideology grew adaptable and developed into mere apologetics on behalf of the *bourgeoisie.*

Zola himself, however, never stooped to be an apologist of the *bourgeois* social order. On the contrary, he fought a courageous battle against the reactionary evolution of French capitalism, first in the literary sphere and later openly in the political. In the course of his life he gradually came ever closer to socialism, although he never got beyond a paler version of Fourier's Utopianism, a version lacking, however, Fourier's brilliantly dialectical social criticism. But the ideology of his own class was too deeply ingrained in his thinking, his principles and his creative method, although the conscious sharpness of his criticism of society was never dulled; on the contrary, it was much more vigorous and progressive than that of the Catholic Royalist Balzac.

Balzac and Stendhal, who had described the ghastly transformation of bourgeois France from the heroic period of the revolution and Napoleon to the romantically hypocritical corruption of the restoration and the no longer even hypocritical philistine filth of the July monarchy, had lived in a society in which the antagonism of bourgeoisie and working-class was not as yet the plainly visible hub around which social evolution moved forward. Hence Balzac and Stendhal could dig down to the very roots of the sharpest contradictions inherent in bourgeois society while the writers who lived after 1848 could not do so : such merciless candour, such sharp criticism would have necessarily driven them to break the link with their own class.

Even the sincerely progressive Zola was incapable of such a rupture.

It is this attitude which is reflected in his methodological conception, in his rejection, as romantic and ' unscientific,' of Balzac's bred-in-the-bone dialectic and prophetic fervour in the exposure of the contradictions of capitalism, for which he, Zola, substitutes a 'scientific' method in which society is conceived as a harmonious entity and the criticism applied to society formulated as a struggle against the diseases attacking its organic unity, a struggle against the 'undesirable features' of capitalism.

Zola says : "The social cycle is identical with the life-cycle : in society as in the human body, there is a solidarity linking the various organs with each other in such a way that if one organ putrefies, the rot spreads to the other organs and results in a very complicated disease."

This 'scientific' conception led Zola to identify mechanically the human body and human society, and he is quite consistent when he criticizes Balzac's great preface to *The Human Comedy* from this angle. In this preface Balzac, as a true dialectician, raises the same question : he asks to what extent the dialectic of race evolution as developed by Geoffroy de Saint Hilaire applies to human society; but at the same time he sharply stresses the new categories created by the specific dialectic of society. Zola thinks that such a conception destroys the 'scientific unity' of the method and that the conception itself is due to the 'romantic confusion' of Balzac's mind.. What he then puts in the place of Balzac's ideas, as a 'scientific' result, is the undialectic conception of the organic unity ot nature and society; the elimination of antagonisms is regarded as the motive power of social movement and the principle of 'harmony' as the essence of social being. Thus Zola's subjectively most sincere and courageous criticism of society is locked into the magic circle of progressive *bourgeois* narrow-mindedness. On this basis of principle, Zola carries on the tradition established by the creative methods of Balzac and Stendhal with great consistence. It is not by accident nor a result of some personal bias in favour of his older friend and comrade-in-arms Flaubert that Zola found in the latter the true realization of all that in Balzac was merely a beginning or an intent.

Zola wrote about *Madame Bovary* : ' It seems that the formula of the modern novel, scattered all over Balzac's colossal *oeuvre,* is here clearly worked out in a book of 400 pages. And with it the code of the modern novel has now been written.'

Zola stresses as the elements of Flaubert's greatness : above all the elimination of romantic traits. ' The composition of the novel lies only in the way in which incidents are chosen and made to follow each other in a certain harmonic order of evolution. The incidents themselves are absolutely average. . . All out-of-the-ordinary inventions have been excluded. . The story is unfolded by relating all that happens from day to day without ever springing any surprises.' According to Zola, Balzac, too, had in his greatest works sometimes achieved this realistic presentation of everyday life. ' But before he could reach the point of concerning himself only with accurate description, he revelled for a long time in inventions and lost himself in the search for false thrills and false magnificence '

He continues : ' The novelist, if he accepts the basic principle of showing the ordinary course of average lives, must kill the "hero." By "hero" I mean inordinately magnified characters, puppets inflated into giants. Inflated "heroes" of this sort drag down Balzac's novels, because he always believes that he has not made them gigantic enough.' In the naturalist method ' this exaggeration by the artist and this whimsicality of composition are done away with' and 'all heads are brought down to the same level, for the opportunities permitting us to depict a truly superior human being are very rare.'

Here we already see quite clearly the principles on the basis of which Zola criticizes the heritage left by the great realists.. Zola repeatedly discusses the great realists, particularly Balzac and Stendhal and constantly reiterates the same basic idea that Balzac and Stendhal were great because, in many details and episodes of

their works, they described human passions faithfully and contributed very interesting documents to our knowledge of human
passions.   But according to Zola both of them, and particularly
Stendhal, suffered from a mistaken romanticism.   He writes, about
the end of *Le Rouge et le Noir* and Julien Sorel : 'This goes absolutely beyond everyday truth, the truth we strive for; the psychologist Stendhal, no less than the story-teller Alexander Dumas,
plunges us up to our necks in the unusual and extraordinary.   Seen
from the viewpoint of exact truth, Julien Sorel provides me with
as many surprises as d'Artagnan.'   Zola applies the same criticism
to Mathilde de la Mole, all the characters in *The Monastery of
Parma*, Balzac's Vautrin and many other Balzac characters.

Zola regards the whole relationship between Julien and Mathilde
as mere brain-gymnastics and hair-splitting and both characters as
unusual and artificial.   He entirely fails to realize that Stendhal
could not raise to the highest level of typicality the great conflict
which he wanted to depict unless he invented these two absolutely
above-average and quite extraordinary characters; only thus could
he bring in his criticism of the hypocrisy, duplicity and baseness
of the restoration period, and show up the infamously greedy and
mean capitalist essence of its feudal-romantic ideology.   Only by
creating the figure of Mathilde, in whom the romantic ideology of
reaction grows into a genuine passion, even though in heroically
exaggerated form, could Stendhal raise the plot and the concrete
situations to a level on which the contrast between these ideologies
and their social basis on the one hand, and the plebeian Jacobinism
of the Napoleon-admirer Julien Sorel on the other, could be fully
developed.   Similarly, Zola failed to realize that Balzac could not
possibly dispense with Vautrin's larger-than-life figure if he wanted
the otherwise merely personal and individual catastrophe of Lucien
de Rubempré's ambitions to become the tragedy of the whole
ruling class of the restoration period; it was only by this device
that Balzac was enabled to weave into this tragicomedy the entire
tissue of the moribund society of the restoration, from the king
meditating a *coup d'état* to the bureaucrat carving a career for
himself.

But Zola could not see this.   He says of Balzac : " His imagination, that unruly imagination which drove him to exaggeration
and with which he wanted to re-create the world in his own image,
irritates me more than it attracts me.   If the great novelist had
had nothing but this his imagination. he would now be merely a
pathological case. a curiosity of our literature."

According to Zola, Balzac's greatness and his claim to immortality lay in the fact that he was one of the first who ' possessed a sense of reality.' But Zola arrived at this ' sense of reality ' by first cutting out of Balzac's life-work the great contradictions of capitalist society and accepting only the presentation of everyday life which was for Balzac merely a means of throwing the contradictions into bolder relief and giving a total picture of society in motion, complete with all its determinants and antagonisms.

It is most characteristic that Zola (and with him Hyppolite Taine) should speak with the greatest admiration of General Hulot, a character in the novel *La Cousine Bette*. But both of them see in him only a masterly portrait of an oversexed man. Neither Zola nor Taine say a word about the artistry with which Balzac traces Hulot's passions to the conditions of life in the Napoleonic era; and yet it would not have been difficult to notice this, for Balzac uses Crével—a character also painted with no less consummate mastery —as a counterfoil to show up the difference between the eroticism of the Napoleonic era and that of the reign of Louis Philippe. Neither Zola, nor Taine mention the doubtful operations with which Hulot tries to make money, although in describing them, Balzac gives an admirable picture of the infamies and horrors of incipient French colonial policy.

In other words both Zola and Taine insulate Hulot's erotic passion from its social basis and thus turn a socially pathological figure into a psychopathological one. It is natural that looking at it from this angle he could see only ' exaggeration ' (i.e. romanticism) in the great, socially typical characters created by Balzac and Stendhal.

" Life is simpler than that " Zola says at the end of one of his criticisms of Stendhal. He thus completes the transition from the old realism to the new, from realism proper to naturalism. The decisive social basis of this change is to be found in the fact that the social evolution of the *bourgeoisie* has changed the way of life of writers. The writer no longer participates in the great struggles of his time, but is reduced to a mere spectator and chronicler of public life. Zola understood clearly enough that Balzac himself had to go bankrupt in order to be able to depict Cesar Birotteau; that he had to know from his own experience the whole underworld of Paris in order to create such characters as Rastignac and old Goriot.

In contrast, Zola—and to an even greater extent Flaubert, the true founder of the new realism,—were solitary observers and critical commentators of the social life of their own day. (The courageous public fight put up by Zola in connection with the Dreyfus affair came too late and was too much a mere episode in Zola's life to effect any radical change in his creative method.) Zola's naturalist ' experimental ' novels were therefore merely attempts to find a method by which the writer, now reduced to a mere spectator, could again realistically master reality. Naturally Zola never became conscious of this social degradation of the writer; his theory and practice grew out of this social existence without his ever becoming aware of it. On the contrary, inasmuch as he had some inkling of the change in the writer's position in capitalist society, he, as the liberal positivist that he was, regarded it as an advantage, as a step forward, and therefore praised Flaubert's impartiality (which in reality did not exist) as a new trait in the writer's make-up. Lafargue who, in accordance with the traditions of Marx and Engels, severely criticized Zola's creative method and contrasted it with that of Balzac, saw very clearly that Zola was isolated from the social life of his time. Lafargue described Zola's attitude to reality as similar to that of a newspaper reporter and this is perfectly in accordance with Zola's own programmatic statements about the correct creative method in literature.

Of these statements we quote only one, in which he gives his opinion on the proper conception of a good novel : " A naturalist writer wants to write a novel about the stage. Starting from this point without characters or data, his first concern will be to collect material, to find out what he can about this world he wishes to describe. He may have known a few actors and seen a few performances . . Then he will talk to the people best informed on the subject, will collect statements, anecdotes, portraits. But this is not all. He will also read the written documents available. *Finally* he will visit the locations, *spend a few days* in a theatre in order to acquaint himself with the smallest details, pass an evening in an actress' dressing-room and absorb the atmosphere as much as possible. When all this material has been gathered, the novel will take shape of its own accord. All the novelist has to do is to group the facts in a logical sequence . . . *Interest will no longer be focussed on the* peculiarities of the story—on the contrary, the more general and commonplace the story is, the more typical it will be."

Here we have the new realism, *recte* naturalism, in concentrated essence and in sharp opposition to the traditions of the old realism;

a mechanical average takes the place of the dialectic unity of type and individual; description and analysis is substituted for epic situations and epic plots. The tension of the old-type story, the co-operation and clashing of human beings who are both individuals and at the same time representatives of important class tendencies—all these are eliminated and their place is taken by 'average' characters whose individual traits are accidents from the artistic point of view (or in other words have no decisive influence on what happens in the story) and these 'average' characters act without a pattern, either merely side by side or else in completely chaotic fashion.

It was only because he could not always consistently adhere to his own programme that Zola could ever come to be a great writer.

But we must not assume that Zola represents the same 'triumph of realism' of which Engels speaks in connection with Balzac. The analogy is merely formal and the assumption would therefore be wrong. Balzac boldly exposed the contradictions of nascent capitalist society and hence his observation of reality constantly clashed with his political prejudices. But as an honest artist he always depicted only what he himself saw, learned and underwent, concerning himself not at all whether his true-to-life description of the things he saw contradicted his pet ideas. It was out of this conflict that the 'triumph of reality', was born, but then Balzac's *artistic* objectives did not preclude the extensive and penetrating presentation of social reality.

Zola's position was totally different. There is no such wide gap between Zola's social and political views and the social-critical tendencies of his work as there is in Balzac's. True, his observation of facts and of historical evolution did slowly radicalize Zola and bring him closer to Utopian socialism, but this did not amount to a clash between the writer's prejudices and reality.

The contrast in the sphere of art is all the sharper. Zola's method, which hampered not only Zola himself but his whole generation, because it was the result of the writer's position as solitary observer, prevents any profoundly realistic representation of life. Zola's 'scientific' method always seeks the average, and this grey statistical mean, the point at which all internal contradictions are blunted, where the great and the petty, the noble and the base, the beautiful and the ugly are all mediocre 'products' together, spells the doom of great literature.

Zola was a far too naive liberal all his life, far too ardent a believer in *bourgeois* progress, ever to harbour any doubts regarding his own very questionable, positivist ' scientific ' method.

Nevertheless the artistic implementation of his method was not achieved without a struggle. Zola the writer was far too conscious of the greatness of modern life (even though the greatness was inhuman) for him to resign himself without a struggle to the grey tedium which would have been the result of a method such as his, if consistently carried through. Zola hated and despised far too much the evil, base, reactionary forces which permeate capitalist society, for him to remain a cold, unsympathetic ' experimenter ' such as the positivist-naturalist doctrine required him to be.

As we have seen, the struggle resulting from this was fought out within the framework of Zola's own creative method. In Balzac it was reality and political bias that were at war with each other, in Zola it was the creative method and the ' material ' presented. Hence in Zola there is no such universal break-through as the ' triumph of realism ' in Balzac, there are only isolated moments, details, in which the author breaks the chains of his own positivist, ' scientific ', naturalist dogmas in order to give free scope to his temperament in truly realist fashion.

We can find such a break-through in almost every one of Zola's novels and hence there are admirably life-like *single episodes* in every one of his major books. But they can not permeate the entire work, for the doctrine still triumphs in the general lay-out of each of them. Thus the strange situation is created that Zola, although his life-work is very extensive, has never created a single character who grew to be a type, a by-word, almost a living being, such as for instance the Bovary couple or Homais the apothecary in Flaubert, not to mention the immortal figures given us by such creators of men as Balzac or Dickens.

But there was an urge in Zola, to go beyond the grey average of naturalism in his composition. Thus it is that he created many extraordinarily effective pictures. No reader can fail to be deeply impressed by his admirable descriptions of pits and markets, the stock exchange, a racecourse, a battlefield or a theatre. Perhaps no one has painted more colourfully and suggestively the outer trappings of modern life.

But only the *outer* trappings.

They form a gigantic backdrop in front of which tiny, haphazard people move to and fro and live their haphazard lives. Zola could never achieve what the truly great realists Balzac, Tolstoy or Dickens accomplished : to present social institutions as

human relationships and social objects as the vehicles of such relationships. Man and his surroundings are always sharply divided
in all Zola's works.

Hence, as soon as he departs from the monotony of naturalism,
he is immediately transmuted into a decorative picturesque romanticist, who treads in the footsteps of Victor Hugo with his bombas-
tic monumentalism.

There is a strange element of tragedy here.

Zola, who as we have seen, criticized Balzac and Stendhal so
vehemently for their alleged romanticism, was compelled to have
recourse to a romanticism of the Victor Hugo stamp in order to
escape, in part at least, from the counter-artistic consequences of
his own naturalism.

Sometimes Zola himself seemed to realise this discrepancy. The
romantic, rhetoric and picturesque artificiality of style produced by
the triumph of French naturalism, was at variance with Zola's
sincere love of truth. As a decent man and honest writer he felt
that he himself was much to blame for this. " I am too much a
son of my time, I am too deeply immersed in romanticism for me
to dream of emancipating myself from certain rhetorical prejudices . . . Less artificiality and more solidity—I should like us to be
less brilliant and to have more real content . . ."

But he could find no way out of this dilemma in the sphere of
art. On the contrary, the more vigorously he participated in the
struggle of opinions, the more rhetorical his style became.

For there are only two roads leading out of the monotonous
commonplace of naturalism, which results from the direct, mechanical mirroring of the humdrum reality of capitalism. Either the
writer succeeds in revealing the human and social significance
of the struggle for life and lifting it to a higher plane by artistic
means (as Balzac did)—or else he has to overstress the mere out-
ward scenery of life, rhetorically and picturesquely, and quite independently of the human import of the events depicted (like
Victor Hugo).

Such was the romantic dilemma which faced French naturalism.
Zola (as before him Flaubert) took the second road because he
was in sincere opposition to the ideology of the post-revolutionary
bourgeoisie; because he hated and despised that glorification of
false ideals and false ' great men ' which was the fashion of his
time and because he was quite determined to expose all this without mercy. But the most honest and sincere determination to fight
for such things could not make up for the artistic falsity of the

method and the inorganic nature of the presentation resulting from it.

Goethe in his old age had already seen this parting of the ways, the ' romantic ' dilemma of the nascent new literature. In the last years of his life he read almost simultaneously Balzac's *The Asses' Skin* and Victor Hugo's *Notre Dame Of Paris*. About Balzac's novel he wrote in his diary : " I have continued reading ' The Asses' Skin '...it is an excellent work of the latest literary method and excels among other things by moving to and fro between the impossible and the intolerable with vigour and good taste and succeeds in most consistently making use as a medium of the miraculous and of the strangest states of mind and events, to the details of which one could give much more praise."

In other words, Goethe saw quite clearly that Balzac used the romantic element, the grotesque, the fantastic, the bizarre, the ugly, the ironically or sententiously exaggerated only in order to show up essential human and social relationships. All this was for Balzac merely a means, if a roundabout one, to the creation of a realism which, while absorbing the new aspects of life, would yet preserve the qualities of the older great literature.

Goethe's opinion of Victor Hugo was the exact opposite of his attitude to Balzac. He wrote to Zelter : " Victor Hugo's 'Notre Dame' captivates the reader by its diligent study of the old scenes, customs and events, but the characters show no trace of natural animation. They are lifeless lay figures pulled about by wires; they are cleverly put together, but the wood and steel skeletons support mere stuffed puppets with whom the author deals most cruelly, jerking them into the strangest poses, contorting them, tormenting and whipping them, cutting up their bodies and souls, —but because they have no flesh and blood, all he can do is tear up the rags out of which they are made; all this is done with considerable historical and rhetorical talent and a vivid imagination; without these qualities he could not have produced these abominations . . . "

Of course Zola cannot simply be identified with Victor Hugo, although Hugo, too, had gone a little way in the direction of realism. *Les Miserables* and " 1793 " doubtless show a higher level of characterization than *Notre Dame Of Paris* although of *Les Miserables* Flaubert angrily remarked that such a characterization of social conditions and human beings was impermissible in an age in which Balzac had already written his works.

But Hugo was never able to get away from his basic mistake,

which was that he portrayed human beings independently of their social environment—and from the resulting puppet-like nature of his characters. The aged Goethe's judgment of Hugo is valid, with some mitigation, in respect of all Hugo's novels. Zola, who followed this tradition, is equally incapable of penetrating and convincing characterization.

Zola depicts with naturalist fidelity the biological and 'psychological' entity of the average human being and this preserves him from treating his characters as arbitrarily as Victor Hugo. But on the one hand this method sets his characterization very narrow limits and on the other hand the combination of two contradictory principles, i.e. of naturalism and romantically rhetorical monumentality again produce a Hugoan discrepancy between characters and environment which he cannot overcome.

Hence Zola's fate is one of the literary tragedies of the nineteenth century. Zola is one of those outstanding personalities whose talents and human qualities destined them for the greatest things, but who have been prevented by capitalism from accomplishing their destiny and finding themselves in a truly realistic art.

This tragic conflict is obvious in Zola's life-work, all the more as capitalism was unable to conquer Zola the man. He trod his path to the end, honourably, indomitably, uncompromisingly. In his youth he fought with courage for the new literature and art (he was a supporter of Manet and the impressionists) and in his riper years he again played the man in the battle against the conspiracy of the French clericals and the French general staff in the Dreyfus affair.

Zola's resolute struggle for the cause of progress will survive many of his one-time fashionable novels, and will place his name in history side by side with that of Voltaire who defended Calas as Zola defended Dreyfus. Surrounded by the fake democracy and corruption of the Third Republic, by the false so-called democrats who let no day pass without betraying the traditions of the great French revolution, Zola stands head and shoulders above them as the model of the courageous and high-principled *bourgeois* who—even if he failed to understand the essence of socialism --did not abandon democracy even when behind it the Socialist demands of the working class were already being voiced.

We should remember this to-day when the Republic has become a mere cover for a conquest-hungry colonial imperialism and a brutal oppression of the metropolitan working class.

The mere memory of Zola's courageous and upright figure is

an indictment of the so-called "democracy" represented by the men who rule France to-day.

1940.

CHAPTER FIVE

The International Significance of Russian Democratic Literary Criticism

BIELINSKI, CHERNYSHEVSKI and Dobrolyubov, the classics of Russian literary theory and criticism are still almost unknown to the non-Russian public. Although many translations of Russian literary works were published in mass editions in all civilized countries, the more resolutely democratic section of Russian literature and literary criticism was almost entirely excluded from this spate of publication. While even second and third-rate authors were translated and praised, the great satyrist of the Russian democratic movement, Saltykov-Schedrin, a contemporary of equal rank to Tolstoy and Dostoyevski is still accessible only to a very small circle of readers.

This is no accident. Although Russian literature was progressive, the policy of the *bourgeois* publishers who made use of it for their own ends, was at bottom decidedly anti-democratic and often even reactionary. The world-wide success of Tolstoy or Dostoyevski, of Chekhov or Gorki was so great that business interests prevailed over anti-democratic convictions. But wherever such massive material considerations were lacking, the publishers freely indulged their reactionary opinions. They pushed the sales of the few reactionary Russian writers such as Merezhkovski and neglected the representatives of the democratic trends in Russian literature.

Reactionary literary theorists have thoroughly exploited the situation thus created. The histories of Russian literature, written by non-Russians, are full of errors and misrepresentations regarding the literary critics of Russian revolutionary democracy. It is alleged that they mechanically subordinated the interests of literature to those of the political propaganda of the day, that they despised all aesthetic considerations, that they knew nothing about art, etc., etc. These allegations are based on nothing more than that these great critics were sharply opposed to many prejudices still current in modern literary criticism, such as for instance the idea of " art for art's sake " and also certain vulgar-propagandistic tendencies.

The reactionary legends woven around Russian democratic

97

literary criticism have this much truth in them : the great critics were in fact convinced and staunch democratic revolutionaries, who skilfully outwitted all the chicanery of the censorship of their time and succeeded in spreading and popularising the principles of revolutionary democracy among the greatest possible number of people. Thus their successful struggle has gained them the mortal enmity of all reactionaries, and the calumnies spread about them are mostly borrowed from the arsenal of reaction.

1.

The specific position occupied by Russian democratic criticism in the development of æsthetic thought in Europe can be understood only if we are clear on the changes produced everywhere outside Russia by the defeat of the 1848 revolutions. The forties were a period in which democratic ideas were still spreading and developing. It might be sufficient in this connection to mention the critical essays of Heinrich Heine. The defeat of the 1848 revolution brought the collapse of all these trends. Much of the literature and literary criticism of the time follows the reactionary lead given by the leading European *bourgeoisie,* which in its fear of a revolution, betrayed its own formerly revolutionary convictions and in all countries made a compromise with reaction : in Germany with the Hohenzollerns, in France with Napoleon III, in England with the Victorians. The literature and literary criticism of the leading European countries shows the distinct influence of this sudden change. Some writers devoted themselves fanatically to the new gospel; one need only compare Carlyle's writings dating from before and after 1848. Others, the really great writers of the period sank into a profound depression and hopelessness—like Flaubert and in his later years, Dickens. Others again—and these are the majority—chose to enter into an ideological compromise with triumphant reaction.

Bielinski, the founder of revolutionary democratic criticism in Russia was a contemporary and equal of the greatest European thinkers of the pre-1848 period. In Germany this was the period of the disintegration of Hegelianism, in England the period of the crisis of classical political economy, in both France and England the period when Utopian Socialism was spreading widely and at the same time already becoming problematical. In Germany this greatest and most fruitful crisis of European thought led to the emergence of historical materialism. The *Communist Manifesto* was written in the year in which Bielinski died.

As the economic and political struggles in the Russia of that day could not as yet have reached the sharpness of those in Central and Western Europe, Russian thinkers could not as yet arrive at the ideas of scientific Socialism. Even in Central and Western Europe it was only a tiny section of the revolutionary intelligentzia which understood the great transformation produced in the thinking of mankind by the work of Marx and Engels. Even the most versatile and progressive German writer of the period, Heinrich Heine, had contented himself with ' cleansing ' of its openly conservative components, the dialectical philosophy of evolution put forward by Hegel, reconstructing it in a radical direction and bringing the thus transformed Hegelian teaching into harmony with Saint-Simon's Utopian Socialism.

Bielinski's development runs in many respects parallel to that of Heine. But the coincidences by no means rested on any psychological kinship—one could scarcely imagine a greater contrast than that which existed between the human and literary characters of Heine and Bielinski—but rather on a relative similarity of the historic conditions and tasks confronting them. Both great thinkers advanced as far as their social milieu permitted, but Bielinski is more resolute and radical than Heine. Originally he was more strongly influenced by orthodox Hegelianism than Heine, but overcame it on the other hand more thoroughly and more profoundly. Hence, the materialist influence on him of Feuerbach was stronger and his acceptance of the ideas of Utopian Socialism, especially of its social criticism, clearer and more decided. He resembles Heine, however, in that neither of them, although they accepted much of the doctrines of philosophical materialism, ever repudiated the Hegelian dialectic, like Feuerbach himself and especially his philo-sophical followers and successors. Bielinski retained the great historical perspectives of the Hegelian dialectic and thereby stands in the foremost rank of the most advanced European vanguard in the great world-view crisis that convulsed Europe in the period preceding 1848.

We repeat : the defeat of the revolutions of 1848 did not bring about the same swerve towards reaction in the ideological development of Russia as in the rest of Europe. A certain, though quite short, period of depression was of course inevitable. But comparatively soon, in the middle of the fifties, a new upsurge of democratic ideas began in Russia. The economic, social and political evolution of the country squarely posed the issue of the inevitable abolition of serfdom and the general unrest bound up with this had forced the government of the time to grant temporarily a somewhat greater freedom of opinion. The classical leaders and representatives of this new upsurge of democratic thought were the two great heirs to Bielinski's life-work : Chernyshevski and Dobrolyubov.

The central problem around which the thinking of Russian society revolved at the time of their activities was the issue of the abolition of serfdom. Everyone knew that the last hour of serfdom had come. Differences of opinion in the progressive camp—and very sharp ones at that—concerned only the method of liberation. It was on this issue that liberalism and democracy first parted company in Russia. The democrats wanted a radical change in the feudal agrarian structure of Russia, both on the economic and in the social sphere. These aspirations divided them sharply from the timid liberals who were constantly making compromises with autocracy and although they, too, desired a progressive change in the agrarian structure of the country, were ever seeking to avoid any conflict with the feudal landowners, the bureaucracy and the autocracy. Throughout the fifties this political division was reflected in every ideological sphere, from philosophy to literature. Chernyshevski and Dobrolyubov were the ideological leaders of the radical democrats in their struggle against the flabby and submissive philosophy of the liberals.

This new upsurge of revolutionary democracy in Russia thus took place in politically and socially more advanced conditions than those in which Bielinski fought his ideological battle a decade earlier. This higher level of the political struggle is apparent in all the writings of Chernyshevski and Dobrolyubov. The most striking new feature of their literary activities was that they now directed their criticism not only against the traditional enemies of freedom but also against their own unreliable allies, the liberal *bourgeoisie* and its ideological representatives. In Bielinski's eyes the chief enemy was still the despotism of autocracy and feudal reaction. Chernyshevski and Dobrolyubov attacked these forces no less resolutely than their master, but in their time another problem had already arisen : the differentiation in the camp of the opponents of absolutism and feudalism, the incipient split between liberalism and democracy.

This new situation naturally affected the philosophical foundations of the new critical school. Chernyshevski and Dobrolyubov no longer, like Bielinski, based themselves on Hegel's philosophy, but on the materialism of Ludwig Feuerbach. Their social criticism was to a large extent determined by the analysis of *bourgeois* society given by the classics of Utopian Socialism. Bielinski lived in a period when Hegelian idealism was the accepted philosophy and when the historical process was supposed to demonstrate with increasing clarity the gradual triumph of reason. Chernyshevski and Dobrolyubov took up a more realistic, and less ideological attitude to history and historical thought. They were also witnesses of the decadence of Hegelian philosophy, its degradation into a philosophy of liberal compromises. Chernyshevski wrote a brilliant criticism of F. Th. Vischer's *Aesthetic* from this viewpoint, a criticism which is not outdated to this day.

This position of Chernyshevski and Dobrolyubov is unique in the history of nineteenth-century thought. Ludwig Feuerbach, the last great materialist thinker of the *bourgeoisie,* was unable to influence permanently the ideological evolution even of his own country (not to mention the other western countries) and left no deep impression behind. This fact holds no mysteries for the theorists who base themselves on historical materialism. Old-style materialist philosophy, that mechanistic materialism whose last great representative was Ludwig Feuerbach, always appeared as the ideology of the democratic revolution. Hence in England it was in the seventeenth, and in France in the eighteenth centuries that materialist doctrines flourished. In the second half of the nineteenth century materialism in the social sciences had no original representatives or any deep roots in either England or France. At a time when a democratic revolution was hatching in Germany, Feuerbach's materialist teaching had an inspiring, electrifying effect. Before 1848 the most advanced group of the literary vanguard in Germany (Richard Wagner, Gottfried Keller, Georg Herwegh, etc.) were all under the influence of Feuerbach, and his activities gave the young Marx and the young Engels the urge to put Hegelian dialectic on its feet, to turn it materialistically upside down.

This extensive and intensive effect of materialistic philosophy among the *bourgeois* intelligentsia of Germany in the forties of the nineteenth century was, however, of very brief duration. The defeat of the 1848 revolution, the betrayal by the German *bourgeoisie* of their own revolution, the compromise already being negotiated with Bismarck and the Hohenzollerns, put an end to the further fruitful influence of materialist philosophy. Only among those engaged in the natural sciences did materialism live on— but even here it lost its revolutionary élan, the universality it had possessed in the pre-revolutionary period and its application to philosophical and social problems grew increasingly pedestrian and vulgar. (Vogt, Ludwig Büchner, etc). In Germany those who were disciples of Feuerbach in the years preceding 1848 all without exception turned their backs on their former teacher. Schopenhauer, the pessimist and irrationalist remained for several decades the leading philosopher of reactionary Germany and the evolution of Richard Wagner is a good illustration of this process. Even those German ideologues who never openly repudiated Feuerbach's philosophy transformed his militant materialism to an increasing extent into a toothless positivism (an instance of this is the evolution of Hermann Hettner, the famous historian of literature of this period). The great Swiss novelist Gottfried Keller alone remained true to the materialist philosophy of his youth; but of course he lived and wrote in democratic Switzerland and not in reactionary Germany.

If one is to understand the significance and historical place of Chernyshevski's and Dobrolyubov's militant materialism, one must take this general historical situation of philosophy into consideration. Chernyshevski and Dobrolyubov are to this day the last great thinkers of revolutionary-democratic enlightenment in Europe. Their work is to this day the last great, inwardly unbroken offensive thrust of the democratic philosophy of enlightenment. Both were enthusiastic adherents of Feuerbach's materialism, but in their social philosophy, their social criticism and their conception of history they far outrun their teacher who was himself much more interested in natural science and the materialist solution of purely philosophical problems and who in the ideological sphere had subjected only religion to a concrete analysis. This one-sidedness of Feuerbach, as compared with the great materialists of the seventeenth and eighteenth centuries, mirrors the general weakness of the *bourgeois*-democratic movement in Germany.

Thus Chernyshevski and Dobrolyubov have done much more than merely to apply the philosophy of Feuerbach to new spheres. They, too, were naturally unable to carry their last principles, their methodology, forward into a dialectical-materialist philosophy. And because they went beyond Feuerbach in their practical philosophy without completely transcending his philosophical principles, their methodology had of necessity to contain many contradictions. But even these contradictions were of a fruitful nature because they pointed towards the future. Chernyshevski's and Dobrolyubov's revolutionary genius manifests itself precisely in the fact that whenever they examined social facts and historical correlations and drew revolutionary conclusions from them, they never allowed themselves to be hampered by their own conscious philosophy, by the limits of mechanistic materialism.

In this respect their philosophical position is often reminiscent of Diderot in the second half of the eighteenth century. Diderot, too, was an old-style materialist, an adherent of mechanistic materialism, but when faced with problems incapable of being solved on this basis, this revolutionary of genius relied on his instincts, on his realistic faculty of observation sharpened by his materialist views and on his ability to interpret facts, and blithely overstepped the limits of his own conscious philosophy. We need recall only his *The Nephew of Rameau* that work of genius, in which Diderot the mechanistic materialist turned himself into a precursor of dialectical materialism.

Making allowance for the difference in the historical situation, the same applies on a higher level to Chernyshevski and Dobrolyubov.

2.

Chernyshevski and Dobrolyubov were democrats. But there are many varieties of democrats. For Chernyshevski and Dobrolyubov any democratic change meant in the first place the political and social liberation of the lower, plebeian section of the people, i.e. first of all the complete emancipation of the poor peasantry, materially and morally crushed by serfdom. Here they part company with the liberalism of their time. The Liberals also wanted to abolish serfdom, but their ideal was a solution which would have brought about liberation without any real damage to the interests of the landowners. Hence they wanted the method of liberation to be quite free of any revolutionary measures. The Liberals were afraid of anything that might bring them into conflict with the autocracy or with the feudal landowners and on the other hand they were no less afraid of the spontaneous movement of the peasantry, of any attempt on their part to take their fate into their own hands. Caught between these two dangers, they manoeuvred and prepared a compromise with absolutism.

The democrats Chernyshevski and Dobrolyubov were genuine, fearless and uncompromising revolutionaries, in the sense in which Marat or St. Just were revolutionaries in the days of the French revolution. Of course there are many contradictions and much lack of clarity in the views of all these great revolutionaries:

none of them could foresee what the putting into practice of a revolutionary democracy would lead to and they all harboured all sorts of nebulous illusions as to its prospects. But Dobrolyubov and Chernyshevski lived sixty years later than the French revolutionary democrats and they already knew Socialism, if only in its Utopian, not its scientific, form. And they were true democrats for they put the total liberation of the suffering people above all other considerations and for the sake of this liberation they did not flinch from any unforeseen course the form of social evolution might take. They thus deflected Utopian Socialism in the direction of revolutionary activity at a time when its classic representative still rejected on principle all participation in revolutionary politics, even in any politics at all.   It is this faith in the people, this devotion to the oppressed and exploited masses that constitutes the revolutionary-democratic greatness of Chernyshevski and Dobrolyubov.   Here they parted company with even the best of their Liberal contemporaries and here lies the basis of the ideological conflict between them and the Liberals.

The depth of this democratic-revolutionary feeling in Chernyshevski and Dobrolyubov is the foundation on which the greatness of their literary criticism rests. These criticisms always served the end of the liberation of the plebs, always pointed towards the revolutionary way of emancipating the peasantry. Latter-day academic literary historians went so far as to say that Chernyshevski's and Dobrolyubov's literary criticism was merely a means of eluding the vigilance of Tsarist censorship and smuggling revolutionary ideas into the masses in this disguise.

Such a conception is of course quite incorrect, mainly because it contains a narrow and one-sided conception of what revolution is and of the tasks revolutionary ideologies have to fulfil. Chernyshevski and Dobrolyubov, like all truly great democratic revolutionaries before them, always conceived a social cataclysm, a revolution in the universalist sense, as a radical change in all human relations and in all human manifestations of life, from the most massive economic foundations to the highest forms of ideology. Seen from this angle, literature can of course no more be an end in itself than philosophy or even politics. Throughout their life Chernyshevski and Dobrolyubov sought for ways of revolutionary change and in all manifestations of human activity they looked for the tendencies which would advance or hinder the great changeover. What they longed for was ever the universal freedom of men to develop their faculties in every direction. In this respect they remained true disciples of Feuerbach and of the great thinkers of the Enlightenment. Feuerbach's saying : "Our ideal should be not a castrated, disembodied, denuded creature, our ideal should be a whole, real, many-sided, complete, fully developed man," could serve as a motto for their own ideological battles.

The difference between them and the old thinkers of the Enlightenment lies in the fact that Chernyshevski and Dobrolyubov could historically and philosophically gain insight into and digest the period following upon the great French revolution. Hence they were not confronted with a problemless "empire of reason" like the thinkers of the Enlightenment in the eighteenth-century. They saw that the great French revolution had not swept away the contradictions of *bourgeois* society but had raised them to a higher level and reproduced them in enhanced form. Thus they could look at the obstacles to the liberation of the popular masses with fewer illusions and much more concretely than their great precursors, but for this reason their final outlook is also more full of contradictions than that of the earlier thinkers of the Enlightenment. But these contradictions are the fruitful contradictions of life itself, the fearless recognition and philosophical assimilation of which makes Chernyshevski's and Dobrolyubov's writings so exciting and interesting.

At the same time such a conception extends—of course without clear consciousness of the fact—the application of Feuerbachian materialism to the phenomena of social life. The basic principle of materialist thinking is that being takes priority over consciousness, that being determines consciousness and not the other way round. The epistemological limits of the old mechanistic materialism lay precisely in the fact that within this quite correctly recognized priority of being the notion " being " was rigidly and unilaterally conceived; on the one hand the old materialists were unable to achieve a correct understanding of the objectivity of social being and on the other hand their concept of "being" was undialectical, containing neither evolution nor movement nor inner forward-driving contradictions. These limitations of mechanistic materialism can be very clearly discerned in Feuerbach.

Chernyshevski's and Dobrolyubov's conception of society strives to go beyond these limits of mechanistic materialism. That is why we find in the concrete analysis of certain phenomena by them a striking and lively dialectic, although the epistemological principles of their philosophy derive from Feuerbach's mechanistic materialism. This contradiction which can often be observed in the history of philosophy, is very conspicuous in them, but is by no means the first instance of such a contradiction. Friedrich Engels mentions that eighteenth-century French materialism thinks mechanically and metaphysically, at least in its theory of knowledge. But outside the sphere of philosophy in the narrower sense, we find—for instance in Diderot—masterpieces of dialectic. The social struggles of Chernyshevski's and Dobrolyubov's day were more open and acute than those of the middle of the eighteenth-century. It is therefore easy to understand that this fruitful contradiction, this forward-driving element of human thought, was stronger and more manifest in their work than in Diderot's.

Such a widening and deepening of the notion of "being" which accordingly comprises—if not in the conscious theory of knowledge, but certainly in literary practice—the observation and recognition of the contradictory movement of society, its evolution by contradiction, determines the nature of Chernyshevski's and Dobrolyubov's critical writings. This is of course much too general a statement. It indicates merely why and how Chernyshevski and Dobrolyubov concerned themselves with social problems, but not why literary criticism occupied a central position in their literary activities.

3.

Franz Mehring, in his analysis of Lessing, makes some very interesting remarks about the reason why literary criticism had played a dominant part in the struggle for freedom of the German *bourgeoisie* in the eighteenth century. He is quite right in pointing out this fact, which applies with certain qualifications to eighteenth-century France as well. But Mehring attaches too much importance to the circumstance that Lessing and the other champions of German enlightenment were compelled by external political considerations to concentrate above all on literary problems. There is of course some truth in this, but formulated too rigidly it results in a half-truth. Mehring's observations require to be qualified in the sense that the emancipatory strivings of the classes develop only very slowly and are full of contradictions. In various spheres of life the deep-seated contradictions of the new level of social being become visible long before a class—for instance the German *bourgeoisie* of the eighteenth century—has economically and ideologically reached a point at which it can enter into a direct political struggle for emancipation.

In the preparation of social groups for the struggle for emancipation, the ideological clarification, the internal discussion of moral and philosophical problems, plays a very important part. The contradictions and antagonisms thrown up by social being itself, the ideological consequences of new forms of social being, do not all appear simultaneously in the sphere of human manifestations and cannot be clarified all at once, quickly, in a direct line. The more intricate and many-sided such problems are, the greater the part literature can play in social evolution, in the ideological preparations for some great crisis in social relations. It follows from this that the great revolutionary ideologues of such preparatory periods give the greatest attention to literary phenomena and that the critical analysis and appreciation of literature occupies a considerable proportion if not the central position of their philosophical and publicistic work. Thus it was with Diderot and Lessing and thus with Bielinski, Chernyshevski and Dobrolyubov.

Histories of literature usually class the work of the great democratic critics as "publicistic criticism." This description is not incorrect but requires closer definition if misunderstandings are to be avoided. Bielinski, Chernyshevski and Dobrolyubov were all engaged in a bitter struggle against the "aestheticist" critics of their time, against those who consciously or unconsciously advocated "art for art's sake," who attempted to separate the conception of artistic perfection from the realistic reproduction of social phenomena, and who regarded art and literature as phenomena independent of social strife and untouched by it. In contrast to such ideas, Bielinski, Chernyshevski and Dobrolyubov laid the greatest emphasis on the connection between literature and society. For them life itself was the criterion for artistic beauty; art grew out of life and creatively reproduced it; the fidelity and depth of this reproduction was the true measure of artistic perfection.

Closely related to this conception is their basic idea that life itself, deeply conceived and faithfully reproduced in literature, is the most effective means of throwing light on the problems of social life and an excellent weapon in the ideological preparation of the democratic revolution they expected and desired. Inasmuch as the great Russian critics concerned themselves with the origins, the nature, the value and the effect of literature, inasmuch as they strived to deepen, widen and accelerate by their positive and negative criticism the practical, revolutionary influence of literature, their work can rightly be described as publicistic criticism.

But such a description is immediately distorted into a falsification if it is interpreted to mean that the publicistic viewpoint takes precedence over artistic considerations or even excludes them. The exact opposite is the case. Wherever modern literature and especially modern literary criticism is poor and infertile, it is certain that there has been some weakening of its most important artistic basis, some loosening of the close ties that unite it with life; that thus it no longer springs straight from life itself and in return influences life. When this tie with life is broken, literature and literary criticism lose sight of the organic, essential unity of artistic form and life-content and of their living, dialectic mutual influence on each other. As a result, not only is content subordinate to form, but the concept of form itself—now regarded as paramount both theoretically and practically—is given a narrow, one-sided and superficial definition.

In contrast, Diderot and Lessing, Bielinski, Chernyshevski and Dobrolyubov concerned themselves with genuine great artistic values. The reactionary detractors of the great Russian critics involved themselves in strange contradictions on this point. On the one hand they denied that these critics understood and loved art and accused them of one-sided political partisanship and of having subordinated the interests of art to political considerations. On the other hand they are compelled to admit that it was these critics who established the scientific foundations of Russian literary history, demarcated its periods and gave valid appreciations of its great figures.

Above all, we owe to Bielinski the really adequate appreciation of Pushkin and of his central, leading position in modern Russian literature; the recognition of the fact that new Russian literature began with Pushkin and found in him its first classic, unsurpassed to this day in artistic perfection. And it was again Bielinski who won for Lermontov the place in Russian literary appreciation which was his due.

But Bielinski also knew that even while Pushkin was still alive, a new period had begun in Russian literature, the period of modern realism, the period of Gogol. His appreciation of Pushkin as artist and poet was closely linked with this division of Russian literature into well-defined periods. Bielinski's conception of Russian literature closely resembles Heine's conception of the evolution of German literature. Both insist that the great central figures of the classic period, Goethe in Germany, Pushkin in Russia, stand higher in artistic merit than the representatives of the realistic period. When Heine speaks of "the end of the period of art" he sharply differs from those critics (e.g. Börne) who thought to advance

the new, realistic democratic literature by minimizing the importance of Goethe. In this Bielinski followed Heine : he opposed with
the greatest vigour Menzel's attack on Goethe. His conception of
Pushkin's artistic perfection is dialectic in the best sense of the
word. He regards it by no means as a mere formal impeccability,
but as a harmonic unity of the artistic principles with the faithful
reproduction of all the phenomena of life. It was not by chance
that in his analysis of Pushkin's *Onegin* Bielinski described this
work as "an encyclopaedia of Russian life"; he derived Pushkin's
artistic perfection from this all-embracing universality of his reproduction of life.

In Bielinski's view, the emergence of the Gogolian period, the
struggle for the triumph of Gogolian realism, coincided with the
growing intensity of the democratic-revolutionary struggle against
absolutism and feudalism. In similar fashion, Lessing's devastating criticism of the dramas of Corneille and Voltaire were
linked in indivisible ideological unity with the preparations of the
morally arming democratic movements directed towards the establishment of German unity and the destruction of that small-state
tyranny which perpetuated the division and slavery of the German
people. According to Bielinski the great social and political importance of Gogol's realism lay in its merciless exposure of the social
realities of its time and in its faithful mirroring of the harsh dis-
cordances of life. In Gogol's art this is not some alien tendency
grafted on literature from outside. Absolutism, tyranny, feudalism
made everyone's life so terrible and inhuman that the faithful
reproduction of daily life was in itself the most effective
propaganda.

Needless to say Gogol's realism is not a naturalist, photographic
reproduction of petty details of everyday life; it is a concentrated
artistic presentation of the outstanding features of social reality.
If the reader or spectator who reads or watches the realistic pictures painted by Gogol notes with horror the revelation of the
hidden truths of his own life, its hidden meaning or hidden senselessness, then it is not the writer who uncovers these things by
means of external devices, such as tendencious additions or com-
mentaries—no, it is the dreadful truth which unmasks itself through
the artistic instrumentality of a great realist. "What are you laughing at?" asks the police chief at the end of Gogol's *The Government Inspector*. "You are laughing at yourselves." In the sphere
of aesthetics, the support given to such a literature of exposure by
a critic is a struggle for realism, against both petty naturalism and

the ivory tower of an academic theory of art and an aestheticist literature.

But it is not only in respect of Gogol's art that Bielinski was the critical and historical interpreter of the new period in Russian literature. Many of his contemporaries, critics as well as poets, complained—as did later the contemporaries of Chernyshevski and Dobrolyubov—that the critic Bielinski tore everything to pieces but created nothing "positive." It is quite true that Bielinski, with his critical analyses, destroyed the literary career of many of his contemporaries. But in these controversies posterity has invariably endorsed Bielinski's judgment; there is not a single instance on record in which an author whom the great critic had subjected to one of his violent attacks had been later proved undeserving of such treatment. The alleged cruelty of Bielinski's criticism was just as much a thunderstorm that cleared the air in Russian literature as that of Lessing's had been in German literature. And Bielinski lived to see the first works of the new realist generation appearing before the Russian public. Here the inexorable critic is transformed into a sensitive, understanding and enthusiastic discoverer of new talent, who acclaimed the appearance of Turgenyev, Goncharov, Dostoyevski with great warmth. It was Bielinski who helped these great realist writers to occupy the places due to them in Russian literature.

But it is Chernyshevski and Dobrolyubov who are the theorists, critics and historians of the Gogolian period of literature, the period of the great Russian realists of the nineteenth century. In a great historical monograph Chernyshevski summarized the main social, ideological and artistic trends of this period. He and Dobrolyubov have given us a profound and comprehensive analysis of the greatest representatives of Russian realism, who were their contemporaries. It is to their work as critics that the correct appreciation of the personalities of Turgenyev, Goncharov, Saltykov-Shchedrin, Ostrovski, Dostoyevski and of the works they produced in the 'fifties of the nineteenth century is chiefly due. They welcomed with the same understanding and enthusiasm the first appearance of the younger generation of realists, as Bielinski in his time welcomed the writers who in Chernyshevski's and Dobrolyuboy's day were in their maturity. Chernyshevski wrote the finest and most adequate analysis of the first works of Leo Tolstoy, recognizing even at that early stage the specific new traits in Tolstoy's realism, traits which sharply divide him from all his predecessors. For a really correct appreciation of Tolstoy Chernyshevski's comments are still a valuable guide today.

Briefly, from Pushkin to Tolstoy the most outstanding figures of Russian literature live in the memory of posterity essentially in the form in which they were characterized by the three great critics at the time of the former's appearance on the literary scene. They thus laid down once and for all the historical and aesthetical foundations of Russian literary history. From all this it is clear that the concept "publicistic criticism" can be applied to these great writers only if carefully defined and qualified. In order to define the concept more concretely, more should be said about their critical method.

4

As already stated in the preceding, Bielinski, Chernyshevski and Dobrolyubov always insisted that literature must never be detached from the evolutionary process of life itself; that every work of art must be regarded as a product of the social struggle and playing a more or less important part in it. The methodological consequence of this premise is that every work of art is considered as a reflection of social life. The essence of Bielinski's, Chernyshevski's and Dobrolyubov's critical method is therefore to juxtapose life and literature, the original and the reflection. This conception of art as a mirror of reality is a common trait of all aesthetic theory based on a materialist philosophy.

But the old mechanistic materialism is unable to resolve theoretically the dialectic intricacies of this process of reflection. It was these limits of the old materialism which Goethe criticized in discussing Diderot's aesthetical writings. We have already seen that as a result of their revolutionary democratic convictions, the three great Russian critics' conception of society transcended the boundaries of their own epistemological and aesthetical theories. The life with which they compare the works of art produced by it and for which it serves as a measure, is never static, never merely the immediate surface of existence. Bielinski, Chernyshevski and Dobrolyubov brought to light the deepest, most hidden problems of Russian social evolution and made them the subject of their analyses. In comparing the "originals" thus found with their artistic counterparts, they obviously could not be satisfied with a mere naturalist reproduction of the surface of life; on the contrary they flayed any such attempt with the most biting irony. They demanded of the writers that in faithfully depicting the everyday destinies of men they should demonstrate the great problems agitating Russian society, and those decisive, fateful social forces which determine its evolution.

This way of posing the problem naturally determined the method of Bielinski's, Chernyshevski's and Dobrolyubov's negative criticisms. Such comparisons of "original" and reflection as we have just described, are in themselves a devastating criticism of all literature devoid of content. It would be a superficial criticism of a bad writer to discuss only his formal deficiencies. But if a trivial and superficial reproduction of life is confronted with the genuine human and social reality of which bad writers spontaneously give only an involuntary caricature, then the formal deficiencies appear merely as a negative form of the basic insubstantiality of the writing in question; the confrontation with life itself automatically exposes the emptiness of a feeble artistic reproduction of it.

The question grows more complicated if we consider how the great critics interpret artistic value in the works of the outstanding realists. Here again the basic method is the comparison of the original with the reflection. This comparison is founded on the assumption that a work of art is a specific objective form of mirroring reality. The stress is laid on the term "objective." The great Russian critics sharply reject all psychological quibbles, that false and misleading expedient of the literary theory of decadent periods in which explanations for works of art are sought in the mental peculiarities or biographical circumstances of their authors.

Such tendencies necessarily arise whenever the link—a link of which authors and critics are mostly unaware—is broken between artistic forms and the motive forces and structural principles of social reality. This loss of the true basis of realist art and genuine aesthetics is always due to the social causes in which the intricately intertwined complex of the objective and subjective factors making up modern bourgeois society finds its expression. It is above all the anti-artistic nature of capitalist society (already pointed out by Marx) that manifests itself with increasing effect, and although it does not, of course, form an unsurmountable obstacle in the path of true art and aesthetics, it does demand an exceptionally deep penetration into the essence of the motive forces, an indefatigable and resolute swimming against the current of the superficial phenomena of everyday life in a capitalist society.

The social evolution of Central and Western Europe after the defeat of the 1848 revolution certainly opposed a formidable obstacle to the emergence and development of such qualities in artists and their critics. The more the writers become subject to the influence of the ideological depression, the more they are prone to segregate themselves and withdraw from public life in order to preserve the integrity of their aesthetic ideals—not to mention those who are influenced by the apologetics of the reactionaries or even actively assist them—the less capable they grow of penetrating to the very fountainheads of art, of sensing the connection between aesthetic form and social structure, at least instinctively if not consciously. For those who are subject to such influences but nevertheless retain their artistic feeling are left with only a single stable foothold : the soul of the artist himself, the world of his own experiences. But instead of regarding this as the necessary bridge between objective reality and the objectivity of reproduction, they endow this intermediate link with an absolute quality and see in it the sole, the sovereign source of artistic production. Here the road leads in a straight line from Sainte-Beuve to Nietzsche and the present-day epigones—a road leading into the morass of arbitrary subjectivism.

The great Russian critics never lost sight of this connection. On the contrary, the freshening and sharpening of the class struggles in Russia in the 'fifties of the nineteenth century, the important task of enlightening the popular masses imposed by the revolutionary unrest—a task which they undertook with passionate devotion—all this not only preserved them from the dangers of the ideological decline which had seized the West in the same period, but helped them to continue the line of social objectivity in their attitude to the problems of art appreciation and to apply the methodology of the classics of aesthetics in a consistently democratic sense. In other words the Russian revolutionary-democratic critics emphatically refused to dive into the poets' soul and to regard works of art from that viewpoint, as the product of a mysterious creative subjectivity. For them the starting-point is the finished work of art and its relation to the reality which it mirrors, is for them the proper subject of criticism. Dobrolyubov says : "What the author intended to express is much less important for us than what he really did express, possibly unintentionally, simply as a result of the correct reproduction of facts as he saw them." In another passage we read : "A work of art may be the expression of a certain idea, not because the author had this idea in mind while he was producing it, but because he was impressed by certain features of reality from which this idea automatically arises."

It is precisely this objectivism that many critics and historians of literature in the period of the decline of the arts regard as an anti-aestheticist trend. This entirely false opinion is a result of the pseudo-aesthetic prejudices of a period of decline. For it is precisely by means of this method that Bielinski, Chernyshevski and Dobrolyubov were able to throw light on what the writer had really created, and why in happy moments of creative inspiration he had been able to raise what he had seen and formed high above the barriers of his own subjective opinions or prejudices. The true nature of artistic creation was thus explained here for the first time, in contrast to the psychologising mystifications of the subjectivist school of aesthetics.

This method reaches its culminating point in Friedrich Engels' analysis of Balzac's life-work. He shows that Balzac has created something different, something much greater and deeper than he consciously intended and even than was compatible with his conscious world-view. Engels calls the extremely important, fundamental aesthetic result of this analysis "the victory of realism." This Engelsian "victory of realism" shows not only a relative independence of the work of art from the opinions (and above all from the social prejudices) of even an author of genius but sometimes finds them to be diametrical opposites. The great Russian critics were no less distinctly aware of this dialectic, although they lacked the methodological clarity of Engels. Dobrolyubov, for instance, illustrated this position with the following simile : "It is like the case of Balaam who wanted to curse Israel, but in the solemn moment of elation, a blessing instead of a curse involuntarily rose to his lips."

We said that we can discern this method in the works of the great Russian critics even though sometimes only in rudimentary form. The principle of the "victory of realism" emphasizes precisely the important part played by art in the evolution of mankind. It shows that in the forming of human consciousness, in the uncovering of social tasks and objectives and in the struggle for them, the great artist is no mere secondrate camp-follower of philosophical thought and political activity, but a comrade-in-arms of equal value.

Great artists have ever been pioneers in the advance of the human race. By their creative work they uncover previously unknown interconnections between things — interconnections which science and philosophy are able to put into exact form only much later. Dobrolyubov says : "Such writers were blessed with so rich a nature that they could instinctively assimilate the genuine ideas and aspirations which most of the contemporary philosophers with their strictly scientific approach could at best merely surmise. Yes, writers of genius could bring to life and express in actions the truths for which the philosophers only dimly groped."

Dobrolyubov is quite aware of the fact that the process is a most intricate one and not merely a simple matter of the 'influencing' of a writer by the ideas current in science or philosophy. He continues : 'Usually this does not happen in the simple form that a writer borrows the ideas of the philosophers and expresses them in his works. No, both writer and philosopher work independently, both take the same thing for their starting-point and this thing is real life. The difference lies only in their approach to life.' The appeal to reality, the materialist theory of mirroring the objective world through the medium of human consciousness, through art, science and philosophy thus does not by any means lead the great Russian critics towards an intellectualisation of art and even less towards its mechanical politization—but on the contrary towards establishing the independence of art, not of course in the sense of the subjectivistic-idealistically inflated spurious isolation found in the theories of the post-1848 period of decline, but in such a manner that in demonstrating the interdependence of art and life and in showing the real function of art in the process of social evolution, they facilitate the philosophical understanding of the true independence of art.

Thus did the great Russian critics, in contrast to the modern, narrow, subjectivist, distortingly aestheticist overestimation of art, establish the true and epoch-making part played by art in the history of mankind.

If we go more closely into the application of this critical method we see that these critics—here again treading the same paths as Engels—centre their investigations around the power of a writer to create types. Here again the road of revolutionary-democratic criticism leads away from the modern perverse overestimation of art towards the recognition of its true greatness and its true function. Just as the past lives in the memory of mankind in the shape in which it was formed by the great classics, so the self-knowledge of the present is based on the work of great artists. *Hamlet, Don Quixote* and *Faust* convey to us the innermost essence of past epochs. It is because of the creation of such comprehensive types that the greatest values of the past have remained immortal. Dobrolyubov says : 'The value of a writer or of a book is determined by the degree to which they express the true aspirations of an age or of a people.' Genuine, lasting types are born out of the sensitivity of the writer for the things about which the community feels deeply, and out of his ability to incarnate them in concrete characters and human destinies.

It is the creation of such characters, such types, that the Russian critics demand of their contemporaries. It is by no means accidental that in this the revolutionary demands of militant democracy coincide with the defence of the true interests of art. Their demand for a comprehensive, type-creating realism organically follows from their political-propagandistic objectives. This programme culminates in the aesthetic imperative : 'Create a realistic literature equal to the classics of the past in the deep understanding and plastic reproduction of the outside world; create out of the life of the present typical characters as deep and true as Don Quixote, Hamlet or Faust !' The essential aesthetic values of literature could not be more effectively defended than by 'publicistic criticism' of this kind.

Chernyshevski and Dobrolyubov thus reject all probing into the so-called 'depths of the poet's soul.' In its place they put the basic question : how does the evolution of the community itself create typical problems and typical characters, how are certain types which mutually supplement each other and develop each other to a higher plane, spontaneously produced by the process of social evolution itself. In his analysis of Goncharov's novel *Oblomov,* Dobrolyubov gives a classical example of this new critical method. He shows the growing discontent and opposition of the Russian nobility and gentry in its evolution from Pushkin's *Onegin* to Goncharov's *Oblomov.* He shows how the unity of the social process necessarily and spontaneously produces cognate problems for all men actively participating in it and demonstrates how several great writers (in accordance with their own social position, time, and personality) depicted different stages in the development of this type and the typical conflicts in which it was involved, until at last the type found its historical and aesthetical completion in Goncharov's *Oblomov.*

This Russian democratic-revolutionary criticism advanced to a point where the social genesis and the aesthetic value of a literary work linked up with each other. While the aesthetes and critics of the West either overstressed the formal elements in art in subjectivist-mystificatory fashion or adopted a rigidly exaggerated objectivism concerned solely and directly with the superficial phenomena of social life, Russian revolutionary criticism probed for and found the live trends in which social evolution finds its true, aesthetic reflection, its artistic fulfilment. The creation of genuine and lasting types depends on the correct understanding of permanent and dominant social processes, and is at the same time the fulfilment of the fundamental requirements of art itself. It is the great achievement of Russian realism that it has created many such truly typical characters. The discovery and revelation of the social and historical significance of such typical characters and typical destinies are the main task Bielinski, Chernyshevski and Dobrolyubov set themselves in their work as critics.

This method does not, of course, confine itself to assessing the typicality of the characters in works of literature, although the principle of comparing the literary work with the social reality it mirrors applies to this as well. The social concretization of the method at the same time involves its aesthetic concretization. The psychological and moral analysis of the human types created, at the same time reveals the merits and validity of the method used in their creation; the investigation of their destinies develops into a penetrating examination of the genuinely poetic—not formally conceived—composition of the work. Questions such as why in the Russian novels of this period, the female characters are humanly and morally superior to the men; why Turgenyev, when he wished to depict an active hero, had to pick on a Bulgarian revolutionary; why the suicide of the heroine in Ostrovsky's *Thunderstorm* has not a depressing but a tragically inspiring effect; why Stoltz, the positive counterpart to Goncharov's *Oblomov,* had to be painted in artistically less vivid colours than the slothful hero who is for-ever sprawling on a sofa—all these things show how intimately social, political and aesthetical problems are intertwined and how the latter, precisely as a result of such intertwinement, find a deeper, true and more artistic solution than those produced by the Western contemporaries of Chernyshevski and Dobrolyubov.

It is obvious that in all this the two great Russians deal with the basic problems of literature. They do on occasion refer to " the laws of aesthetics," but it is with contemptuous irony and one should always concretely examine in what connection and with what object they were made and to what aesthetic conclusions the analysis in which they occur finally leads. (Bielinski's terminology is somewhat different on this point; he wanted a radical reconstruc-tion of Hegel's aesthetic but with the preservation of its funda-mental principles). Dobrolyubov, for instance, violently attacked the so-called "laws of dramaturgy" in an analysis of one of Ostrov-

ski's plays. But if we read the whole article, what do we find ?
What Dobrolyubov attacked so sharply was the niggling, formalistic, academic dramaturgy, which attempted to slaughter Ostrovski's
new, revolutionary, realistic plays on the grounds that they broke
these laws. When Dobrolyubov analysed Ostrovski in detail, he
deduced concretely and critically, without any abstract theoretical
discussion—the new principles of dramaturgy by means of which
Ostrovski succeeded in putting on the stage with great power and
profound effect important trends of his time.

Essentially Dobrolyubov's method is thus to re-establish and defend the laws of aesthetics—laws periodically changing their forms
of manifestation—against the danger of academic-abstract modifi-
cation. Lessing followed the same method in his time and openly
admitted as much, when in his polemic against the dramaturgy of
the French classics, he demonstrated on the one hand the essential
unity of Sophocles and Shakespeare, and their essential acceptance
of the dramaturgy of Aristotle. A similar argument is contained
in Dobrolyubov's concrete analyses, but here it is tacitly immanent
and not openly expressed.

This slight divergence between Dobrolyubov and Lessing makes
no real difference to the essential coincidence of their methods, but
it is still somewhat more than a mere superficial, terminological
divergence. The basic unity of Sophocles and Shakespeare is not
regarded by Lessing either as a purely aesthetic and much less a
formalist principle; he goes back to Aristotle because he finds in
Aristotle's dramaturgy an, until then, unsurpassed expression of the
natural laws of tragedy, of the poetic form of the tragical in life
and in history. The Russian critics for their part appeal directly
to life itself, without accepting as canonically obligatory any previous concrete performance either in poetic practice or in aesthetic
theory. By so doing they made the materialist view that art should
mirror objective reality far more vigorously and consistently the
foundation of aesthetic theory than Lessing, whose materialism was
much more spontaneous and much less conscious than theirs. On
the other hand, Lessing's acceptance of the Aristotelian aesthetic
as a canon and above all his stressing of the ideal consummation of
the Aristotelian doctrine in the works of Sophocles and Shakespeare
contains a stronger emphasis on the dialectic character of the thesis
of reflection, even though again spontaneously, not as a conscious
expression of method. For with these trains of thought Lessing
stresses more strongly the relative independence of poetic form and
with it the active part played by creative subjectivity, than his great

successors. Further, the demonstration of the ultimate identity of the creative principle in Shakespeare and the ancient classics also expresses the historical dialectic of aesthetics, the dialectic connection between changing forms of manifestation and enduring essential laws.

The divergence is thus not one of principle, but merely a difference in emphasis arising out of the difference in historical conditions, and partly out of the nature of their philosophical backgrounds : Lessing is a link in the chain of idealist philosophy leading from Leibnitz to Hegel, while the Russian crtics are the greatest representatives of pre-Marxian philosophical materialism; independent, even though not methodologically conscious, pioneers of dialectical materialism. The divergence further arises from the different nature of the opponents against whom Lessing on the one hand, and the Russians on the other, had to fight for their aesthetic and critical theses. Lessing's chief objective was to destroy the courtly aesthetic based on a misunderstanding of Aristotle and a distorted conception of ancient classic art, while the Russians were mainly concerned with the theories of decline put forward by the academic-formalistic art-for-art-sake school, and with the various trends of subjective idealism in the theory and practice of literature.

This conflict of such divergent accentuations was resolved into harmony in the aesthetic of Karl Marx who carried the theory of reflection on to its dialectical fulfilment. Consistent materialism in the epistemological foundations and a correct dialectic conception of the relationship between being and consciousness allot to creative subjectivity, and with it to artistic form, their proper place in the faithful reproduction of the objective world, without in the least undermining the priority of being; on the contrary, they are the only possible means of expressing this priority in a formally and objectively adequate manner. At the same time the canonic validity of the classics—both of antiquity and of later times (Shakespeare)—is lifted out of Lessing's occasionally somewhat dogmatic spontaneity and given a historical objectivity by determining the social and human factors which raise the works of the classics to the level of norms, of unattainable models.

The concentration on the objective characteristics of works of art is the essence of critical method and is closely linked with the revolutionary-democratic aims of these great critics. But in seeking and finding in the realistic literature of their time a powerful ally against reaction and feudal survivals, they always evoked the creative effect of the works and never the subjective political or philosophical opinions of the writers. What these critics were concerned with was what the great authors of their time were uncovering with the realistic pictures they brought up from the depths of Russian life. For this reason they were glad to accept as a comrade-in-arms in the great work of liberation every serious writer who depicted reality faithfully and with talent. In this they more than once went beyond not only the limits of Russian literature but the narrow conception of realism as well. Chernyshevski, for instance, hailed with enthusiasm the good Russian translations of Schiller's poems and declared that Schiller was a precious and imperishable part of Russian literature, a poet whom all progressive Russia regarded as their own.

Such an objective viewpoint acquired a decisive importance in the specific conditions in which the two Russian critics had to pursue their political activities. We have already noted that the incipient struggle between liberalism and democracy was one of the central battlegrounds of this activity. Most of the great writers of the time inclined towards the Liberal philosophy; but inasmuch as they depicted Russian reality faithfully, they involuntarily aided revolutionary democracy in many ways, among them in the exposure of the policy and philosophy of Liberalism itself. The sharp criticisms which expressed this circumstance in polemic form, were not—as is often alleged—directed against the writers themselves but on the contrary were the fruit of a genuine respect for what they had objectively created.

This attitude is expressed very clearly in Chernyshevski's famous criticism of Turgenyev: *The Russian at the Rendez-vous.* In this essay Chernyshevski showed that Turgenyev, as a sincere and gifted realist writer who portrayed life as it is, has in his story *Asya* quite unintentionally but quite inevitably produced a shattering exposure of the type of the Liberal intellectual, a type psychologically and in outlook very close to Turgenyev and very dear to his heart. Thus an analysis of the objective content and objective presentation of this story written by the Liberal Turgenyev served Chernyshevski as a starting-point for a devastating criticism of the Liberal outlook and of the Liberal intellectual as a human type. It was precisely because Turgenyev was a genuine, serious realist, that his work could supply weapons against his own political philosophy.

The same critical essay touches upon another very important methodological problem. Turgenyev's novelette is a simple and beautiful love-story and there is no mention in it of politics or the social struggle. A Russian intellectual living abroad falls in love with a young girl. But when the girl returns his feeling with a genuine passion which breaks through the barriers of convention, he takes fright and runs away. Chernyshevski's criticism of this story is a political and social criticism. What then is the connection between the criticism and its subject? Does not Chernyshevski's political criticism break up the organic, artistic structure of the story, does he not approach it from a viewpoint irrelevant to it?

Here we can deal only very briefly with the basic methodological problem. Gottfried Keller, the great Swiss democratic writer, said once "Everything is politics." He did not mean that everything was politics in the direct sense, but only that the same social forces which at their most acute, at the culminating point of action, determine political decisions, are also exercising their influence in all phenomena of daily life, in work, in love, in friendship, etc. In every period of history these social forces produce certain types of men whose characteristic traits manifest themselves in the same way in every sphere of life and human activity, even though in different directions, with different contents and with different intensity. The greatness of the great realist writers consists precisely in their ability to discern and render visible these typical human traits in every sphere of life.

In his story *Asya,* the subject of Chernyshevski's critical essay, Turgenyev did this very successfully. The human and philosophical weakness of nineteenth-century Russian Liberalism is shown in an artistically concentrated form in the behaviour of the hero of the story towards the object of his love. Whether this is what Turgenyev himself wanted to express does not matter at all, nor does it matter whether he had so much as thought of such a connection while he was writing the story. What does matter is that this connection is clearly before us in the story; that Chernyshevski recognized and analysed this connection; and that the connection did in reality exist in the form in which Turgenyev depicted and Chernyshevski analysed it, i.e. that the Liberals shirked the democratic tasks arising from the liberation of the serfs in the same cowardly fashion and with the same 'high-minded' excuses as Turgenyev's hero, who shamefully ran away from his tryst.

5.

What Chernyshevski uncovered here was the connection between political action and all other phenomena of social life. What is new and epoch-making in this analysis is the acumen with which

Chernyshevski penetrates to the human-typical core of the love-story and brings to light its political content and meaning. The recognition of this unity of all manifestations of the human soul and spirit is the common property of all writers and critics who understand the great, eternal and therefore always topical functions of art. In this basic problem of art Goethe and Pushkin are on the side of Chernyshevski and not of modern aesthetics. When for instance Balzac, a political conservative, but a great realist, analysed the historical novels of Walter Scott, he summed up their artistic merit in this fashion : Walter Scott does not depict the great historical events themselves; what he is interested in is the wherefore of those events; hence he gives no complete description of a decisive battle, no analysis of the strategy and tactics employed —what he gives us is a picture of the human, social and moral atmosphere in both camps, presented in little everyday incidents which merge into more general action to demonstrate to the reader why it was inevitable that the victor should win the battle. This aesthetic approach of Balzac is quite in line with Chernyshevski's critical principles.

Such conceptions are by no means as self-evident as they may appear once they have been correctly put. Important trends in contemporary bourgeois literature take up a diametrically opposite position. Zola, for instance, categorically rejected as unscientific and inartistic, the introduction of casual motivation and demanded that the writer should confine himself to the description of how, not why, things happen. Zola backed up this polemic contrast by allegedly 'scientific' arguments and by a reference to the methods of modern natural science—as he understood them. On closer examination it becomes obvious, of course, that his arguments were based not on the real practice and method of natural science, but on the epistemological agnosticism which in connection with the general crisis of the bourgeois ideology had spread also to the conception of scientific method.

The rejection of casual motivation, which was as yet in its incipient stage in Zola's works, had fatal consequences both for the author and the critic; on the one hand it tended to discourage the search for deeper motives which could reveal the essence of social and human relationships, directed the attention of writers and critics towards the superficial occurrences of everyday life (Taine's milieu theory) and thereby made them dependent on the theories in fashion for the moment, which they then exaggerated in a mechanistic, anti-artistic manner. (Biologism and genetics in

Zola.) It produced on the other hand—as a necessary polar complement to this unreal, psychologizing subjectivism—a no less mistaken mechanical, pseudo-objective sociologism. Instead of organically and artistically developing through the manipulation of living human characters the real intrinsic totality of the decisive driving forces which determine the social process, they resorted to purely external, pseudo-universal descriptions of a superficially conceived social totality, in the merely decorative or naturalistic setting of which human beings appeared as mere puppets.

Naturally the great Russian critics could not deal with these tendencies which did not develop fully until considerably later; but in their methodology, in their way of judging an author or a book, the foundations for the refutal of such false theory and such art-distorting practice are already laid down quite clearly. (Thus in Saltykov-Shchedrin's appreciation of Zola one can distinctly perceive the application of Chernyshevski's and Dobrolyubov's critical principles.) Zolaism and in general the aesthetic ideology of sham objectivism and sociological vulgarisation has often been attacked in bourgeois literary theory. But these attacks came almost exclusively from the right, from reactionary trends in literature, from the point of view of subjectivist psychologism, which could not of course bring any real clarity into the discussion. Sham objectivism is still effective today; it occupies a very important position in literature and literary criticism even though it sails under quite different colours; it diverts writers from their specific and most important tasks and—in exactly the same way as its opposite pole, i.e. subjectivism—it destroys in the sphere of criticism all valid judgment of a work by the proper standard of the coincidence in it of social significance and aesthetic values.

It follows from this that the methodology of Russian revolutionary-democratic criticism as conceived here, is of the greatest importance even today. It would be a grievous error to consider Bielinski, Chernyshevski and Dobrolyubov merely historically, as prominent representatives of a past epoch, who have now ceased to be a live and effective force. The exact opposite is the case. If in the present profound crisis in the evolution of mankind we are to advance towards a genuine literary culture, if we want literature and literary criticism to rise to the level of the great problems of the epoch, then we can and must, today more than ever before, learn a great deal from Bielinski, Chernyshevski and Dobrolyubov.

Here we can make only a few brief remarks regarding this great and complex problem. There is first of all the artistic presentation of politics itself. It is one of the main weaknesses of present-day bourgeois literature that in this respect, as in so many others, it mostly moves between two false extremes. On the one hand is pictured political action in a stark and abstract immediacy and disjunction, without any serious and penetratingly realist portrayal of the human essence of the politically active characters. On the other hand bourgeois literature often escapes into an abstract, fabricated, in reality non-existent private ' psychology ' which in its artificial isolation from social life comes into being on paper only and ever remains without substance. In contrast to these two false extremes, every true lover of literature cannot repeat too often and too insistently Keller's saying that 'everything is politics.' Naturally this applies only to real, serious, realist writers who in showing life as it is, are able to dig down to those roots which in the last instance determine that this human type is viable and that other fated to perish, that this one is valuable and that one useless, etc. Today it is more important than ever to understand that only in truly deep realism can literary greatness be organically and inseparably united with a pervading political influence.

But not only the basic outlook, even the methodology of the Russian revolutionary critics is topical, even indispensable for the solution of the literary problems of our own time. While Cherny-shevski and Dobrolyubov were still alive, another false dilemma had already arisen in modern bourgeois literature and literary interpretation among their Western contemporaries. On the one hand there was the limitation of literature to the portrayal of a naturalist 'average,' and on the other the escape into the hair-splitting of a subjectivist psychologism. We find these false extremes in the entire Western literature after the defeat of the revolutions of 1848. True, some of the greatest writers of the age struggled incessantly—and so far as their own works were concerned, successfully—creatively to overcome these false extremes. But the leading lights of Western criticism—Taine for one, a still very influential critic—contributed by their analyses more to the perpetuation of these false extremes than to their elimination, as did the great Russian critics. In Taine, for instance, we find unorganically jumbled together a mechanistic theory, which makes man a mere product of the so-called milieu (from which all naturalism derives its theoretical arguments) and a purely subjective, psychologising analysis of abstract passions quite detached from social reality (in which abstract psychologism found its theoretical arsenal). We recall Taine's description of Balzac's heroes as 'monomaniacs.'

But these false extremes crop up on every issue of principle in modern bourgeois criticism. On the one hand we find a so-called "purely aesthetical" criticism, a criticism approaching its subject from the viewpoint of 'art for art's sake,' and apportioning praise or blame according to superficial formal characteristics without so much as admitting even the existence of the really important problems of literature, and of the laws which govern artistic form and which arise from the development of society and of its culture. On the other hand there is what is called 'publicistic criticism,' a 'purely' social or political attitude to literature, which judges past and present according to the superficial slogans of the day, without considering the real artistic content of the work in question, or caring whether it is a great work of art or a piece of worthless trash; it is concerned solely with the slogan of the day, which may be completely forgotten tomorrow. If we are to fight and overcome these two wrong trends in contemporary criticism—which can sometimes be observed simultaneously in one and the same author, so that we are faced with an eclectic mixture of vulgar-sociology and an irrational admiration of some sort of 'mastery'; if we are to create a genuine critical style which is simultaneously and inseparably both political and aesthetical, then we can and should learn a great deal, more than ever before, from Bielinski, Chernyshevski and Dobrolyubov.

The history of criticism in the past centuries shows that its great periods, its immortal figures were linked—and not by accident—with the passionate advocacy of genuine democratic principles. Thus did Diderot and Lessing act in the eighteenth century achieving an influence extending far beyond the confines of their own country; Bielinski, Chernyshevski and Dobrolyubov occupied a similar position in the history of aesthetical thinking in the nineteenth century, although they have not as yet made any impression outside Russia. But the social scene and the demand for its reproduction in literature are such that a universal recognition of their international significance can only be a question of time and that not long.

CHAPTER SIX

Tolstoy and the Development of Realism

THE OBJECT of the present study is to define Tolstoy's place in world literature and outline his part in the development of realism. It is based on Lenin's evaluation of Tolstoy's work. On this point as on many others relating to problems of method and of the historical application of Marxism, the whole depth of Lenin's conception was not fully understood for a long time. Because of Tolstoy's world-wide fame, and the important part he played in the working-class movement during the period preceding and following the revolution of 1905, nearly every literary critic within the orbit of the Second International felt bound to discuss him at length. Needless to say everything they wrote radically diverged from Lenin's views. At that time the intricate social processes reflected in Tolstoy's works were understood little or not at all and faulty interpretations of the social background of Tolstoy's writings resulted in a superficial, and often quite incorrect appreciation of the writings themselves.

Lenin called Tolstoy "the mirror of the Russian revolution," and adds that many have at first found this description strange. "How can something be called a mirror which gives so obviously incorrect a reflection of events?" But here as everywhere else, Lenin does not stop at the contradictions presented at first sight by the phenomena of life; he probes deeper, down to the roots. He shows that contradiction, precisely because of its contradictory nature, is the necessary and adequate form of expression for the richness and intricacy of the revolutionary process. In Lenin's view the contradictions in Tolstoy's views and images, the inseparable mixture of historical greatness with childish simple-mindedness forms an organic unity which is the philosophical and artistic reflection of both the greatness and weakness of the peasant movement between the liberation of the serfs in 1861 and the revolution of 1905. Lenin fully appreciated the supreme mastery with which Tolstoy painted some of the most important characteristics of this period and the consummate art with which he portrayed landowner and peasant alike. Lenin also demonstrated most convincingly that when Tolstoy so aptly and so venomously criticized the Russian society of his time, he did so almost entirely from the viewpoint of a naive 'patriarchal' peasant. What Tolstoy expressed was in Lenin's view the feeling of those millions of Russians who had already reached the point of hating their masters, but had not yet reached the stage of entering on a conscious, consistent and merciless struggle against them.

This is why Lenin always regarded Tolstoy as a writer and artist of universal, world-wide significance. Maxim Gorki in his memoirs quotes Lenin as saying about Tolstoy :

' " What a colossus, eh? What a gigantic figure ! Ah, there's an artist for you, my boy ! . . . And do you know what is even more amazing? It's his peasant voice, his peasant way of thinking ! A very peasant in the flesh ! Until this nobleman came along, there was no real peasant in our literature . . ." Then he looked at me with his little Asiatic slant-eye, and asked : "Who in Europe could be put in the same class with him?" and immediately answered himself : "No one !" '

The leading social-democratic critics misinterpreted Tolstoy because they did not understand the revolutionary significance of the revolt of the peasantry. Because they failed to grasp the core, the basic meaning of Tolstoy's artistic work, they naturally clung to the immediately visible and superficial phenomena, Tolstoy's obvious choice of subjects. And because at the same time they did not accept the sham universality which the Russian and European bourgeoisie had ascribed to Tolstoy's *entire activities,* they were driven to deny the universality, even of Tolstoy's literary production. When for instance Plekhanov asked "from what point and up to what point" progressives could accept Tolstoy, he of course put the emphasis on Tolstoy's social criticism. But his assessment of this social criticism is diametrically opposed to Lenin's, and this is entirely in keeping with their basic difference of viewpoint. Plekhanov says : "The progressive representatives of the working class, respect Tolstoy above all as a writer who, even though he failed to understand the struggle for the transformation of social conditions and remained entirely indifferent to it, yet felt that the present social order was undesirable. They admire in him chiefly the writer who used his mighty literary gifts to show up this undesirability, even though only episodically."

We find a similar false estimate of Tolstoy's art in the writings of Franz Mehring and Rosa Luxemburg.

It was Plekhanov's opinion which provided the centre and the left-wing of pre-1914 social democracy with the theoretical and historical basis for their appreciation of Tolstoy. He greatly influenced especially Rosa Luxemburg; but even Mehring, who had a fine sensibility and was often quite original in his aesthetical judgments, failed to emancipate himself from these misconceptions and achieve a depth of understanding in his appreciation of Tolstoy such as we owe to Lenin. But Mehring showed at least some glimmering of comprehension. He realized that the reason why *The Power of Darkness* made such a strange impression was that it depicted Russian life as it really was. Mehring also saw what was truly of the people in *War and Peace*. He wrote: ". . . the age in which the Russian people constituted itself as a nation. For the Russian nation was not created by the Tsar, nor by his generals, nor by his ministers, nor by the ruling classes in general. All these are merely insignificant, indifferent, subordinate figures, who either do nothing at all or only cause trouble when they act on their initiative and who can achieve great things only when they are the instruments of a mysteriously and irresistibly operating popular force." But such passages are rare even in Mehring and he, too, judges Tolstoy on the whole along the lines laid down by Plekhanov.

One cannot simply disregard the misjudgment of Tolstoy by the social democrats, because the same misjudgment crops up again later in vulgar-sociology. Thus V. M. Fritsche, for a long time an influential historian of Russian literature, in a preface written to Lenin's papers on Tolstoy, called Tolstoy a 'subjective artist' and (in agreement with bourgeois critics) put forward the view that Tolstoy could depict really convincingly only his own class, the aristocracy, and that not only was he restricted to the aristocracy in respect of subject, he also 'patently idealized the phenomena which he depicted, nor did he describe them objectively from every angle, but with a bias.' If this had been Tolstoy's method, as Fritsche attempts to prove, only vulgar-sociology could explain how he was nevertheless one of the greatest realists of all time and not merely a commonplace, if gifted, panegyrist of the Russian nobility. No such explanation has, however, ever been given.

If then we wish to analyze the part played by Tolstoy in world literature, we must not only set aside the spurious myths spread about his art, but also the views of vulgar-sociology and must base our analysis on the only correct view, that of Lenin. In addition to this, only the view put forward by Russian revolutionary-democratic criticism can help us to reach a better understanding of Tolstoy and we shall therefore repeatedly make use of Chernyshevski's appreciation of Tolstoy in the following pages.

In developing realism a stage further, Tolstoy's oeuvre marks a step forward not only in Russian literature but in the literature of the world. This step forward was made, however, in rather peculiar circumstances. Although Tolstoy continued the great realistic traditions of the eighteenth and nineteenth centuries, the traditions of Fielding and Defoe, Balzac and Stendhal, he did so at a time when realism had already fallen into decay and the literary trends which were to sweep away realism had triumphed throughout Europe. Hence Tolstoy, in his literary work, had to swim against the current in world literature, and this current was the decline of realism.

But Tolstoy's position in world literature was unique for more reasons than this. It would be quite misleading to stress this divergence unduly and define Tolstoy's place in the literature of his age as though he had rejected all the literary trends and all the writers of his own time and had obstinately clung to the traditions of the great realists.

In the first place : what Tolstoy carried on was not the artistic and stylistic tradition bequeathed by the great realists. We do not wish to quote here Tolstoy's own judgments on the older and newer realists; these judgments are often contradictory and—like the judgments of most great writers — they vary a great deal according to the concrete requirements of each period of their work. What never varied, however, was Tolstoy's healthy—and angry—contempt of the petty naturalism of his own contemporaries. In a conversation with Gorki he spoke of Balzac, Stendhal, and Flaubert as the greatest writers in French literature (not qualifying this judgment in the case of Flaubert as he did in the case of Maupassant) but described the Goncourts as clowns. In an earlier preface to Maupassant's works we find no criticism of certain decadent tendencies in Maupassant's realism.

The older great realists had no demonstrable immediate influence on Tolstoy's style. The principles he followed in his realism objectively represent a continuation of the great realist school, but subjectively they grew out of the problems of his own time and out of his attitude to the great problem of his time, the relationship between exploiter and exploited in rural Russia. Of course the study of the old realists had a considerable influence on the development of Tolstoy's style, but it would be wrong to attempt to derive the Tolstoian style of realism in art and literature in a straight line from the old great realists.

Although Tolstoy continued and developed the traditions of the older realism, he always did so in his own original way and in accordance with the needs of the age, never as an epigone. He was always in step with his time, not only in content, in the characters and social problems he presented, but also in the artistic sense. Hence there are many common traits in his literary method and that of his European contemporaries. But it is interesting and important to note in connection with this community of method that artistic traits which in Europe were the symptoms of the decline of realism and contributed to the dissolution of such literary forms as the drama, the novel and the short story, regained their vitality and originality in Tolstoy's hands and served as the elements of a nascent new form which, continuing the traditions of the old great realism in a novel manner and in relation to new problems, rose to heights unsurpassed by the realist literature of any nation.

If we analyze Tolstoy's works from the angle of world literature, we must take for our starting-point the peculiarities of Tolstoy's style and his specific place in literature.

Without these peculiarities the world-wide success of Tolstoy's works cannot be understood. For one must always keep in mind that Tolstoy achieved this success as an essentially modern writer, modern in form as well as in content. From the seventies of the nineteenth century onwards his success was world-wide success in a literary world and with a reading public from whose memory the traditions of the pre-48 European literature were rapidly fading and the greater part of which even went so far as to oppose quite sharply and definitely those very traditions. (Stendhal's vogue in this period is based partly on misunderstanding, partly on falsification; it was an attempt to turn Stendhal into a precursor of subjective psychologism.) Zola, for instance, in rejecting Balzac's and Stendhal's alleged romanticism, criticized in them that they went beyond the workaday 'average' of life, i.e. precisely the trait which made them great realists. And in Flaubert and especially in *Madame Bovary* he saw fulfilled all that he thought valuable in Balzac. The lesser representatives of naturalism, both writers and critics (and the adherents of trends subsequent to naturalism) show this deviation from the great traditions of realism even more unmistakably than Zola.

It is in this atmosphere that Tolstoy achieved his world-wide success. One should not underrate the enthusiasm with which his works were received by the adherents of the naturalist school and of other later literary trends. This world-wide success was not of course, based exclusively or even in the first place on such enthusiasms. But on the other hand such enduring international success (still unabated to this day) could not have been possible had not the adherents of the various literary trends found or thought they had found important points of affinity with themselves in Tolstoy's works. The various naturalist "free stages" in Germany, France and England first performed the *Power of Darkness* imagining it to be a model naturalist play. Not long afterwards Maeterlinck, in his theoretical motivation of his "new" dramatic style, cited as his witnesses Ibsen's experiments and the same *The Power of Darkness*.

This same thing has been going on to this day. A study of this incongruous effect of Tolstoy's works will be found at the end of the present book.

2.

However specific Tolstoy's influence on European literature may have been, it was not an isolated phenomenon. Tolstoy's irruption into world literature occurred simultaneously with the unprecedentedly rapid rise of Russian and Scandinavian literature to a leading position in Europe, where until then the great literary trends of the nineteenth century had had their origins in the leading western countries—Germany, England and France.

Writers of other nations very rarely achieved world-wide significance, until the seventies and eighties of the nineteenth century brought a sudden change. True, Turgenyev had become known in Germany and France before other Russian authors, but his influence cannot be compared with that of Tolstoy and Dostoyevski; besides, Turgenyev had achieved his fame precisely by those of his traits which really had some affinity with the French realism of the time. But in the case of Tolstoy and the Scandinavian writers who rose to fame at the same time (Ibsen in the first place) it was unfamiliarity of their subject and method which also played an important part. In a letter written by Engels to Paul Ernst about Ibsen, the former emphasises: "In the last twenty years Norway has experienced a literary upsurge like no other country except Russia . . . The performance of these fellows is far superior to that of others and they leave their mark on other literatures, not least on the German."

Although we have mentioned the factor of unfamiliarity, the effect of this must not be mistaken for the decadent chase after exotic subjects which appeared in the later imperialist age. The cult of medieval mystery-plays, of negro sculpture, of the Chinese theatre, are symptoms of the complete dissolution of realism; the bourgeois writers—with the exception of a few outstanding humanists— are no longer able even to get near the real problems of life.

On the other hand the influence of Russian and Scandinavian literature begins when bourgeois realism has reached a crisis. Although naturalism had destroyed the artistic foundations of the greater realism, the greatest of the destroyers, such as Flaubert, Zola and Maupassant, still knew what great art was and in some of their works or parts of them they themselves did reach up to its level.

The same applies to their adherents and readers.

The impression made by Russian and Scandinavian literature is undoubtedly connected with the fact that the readers felt the decline of European realism and longed for a great realist contemporary art. Even Russian and Scandinavian writers of much less merit than Tolstoy still showed in their works the traces of the "great art" which was already lost in Europe; their composition and characters were forceful, the intellectual level of their problems and solutions high, their general conception bold and their attitude radical.

Even so critical a spirit as Flaubert hailed Tolstoy's *War and Peace* with loud enthusiasm, criticising only the passages in which Tolstoy's own philosophy of history is openly expressed.

"Thank you," he wrote to Turgenyev, "for sending me Tolstoy's novel. It is first-rate. What a painter and what a psychologist! . . . I feel that there are things of Shakespearean greatness in it! While I was reading it I cried out aloud in my delight . . . although the novel is long."

The same enthusiasm was evoked among the western European intelligentsia, and, at the same time, by Ibsen's plays.

Faithful to his world-view, Flaubert expressed his enthusiasm exclusively from an artistic point of view. But the effect of Russian and Scandinavian literature in Europe was, as we have already mentioned, not limited to the artistic sphere. The effect was due in the first place to the fact that these writers dealt with problems similar to those occupying the minds of the western reading public, but the problems were much more widely posed and their solutions, even though unfamiliar, much more radical. In the hands of the greater Russian and Scandinavian authors this topicality of subject stood in strange contrast with the almost classical form, which did not, however, appear academic and antiquated; on the contrary, it expressed contemporary problems in an entirely contemporary form. The purely epic character of Tolstoy's great novels—which appeared so improbable to the European reader of the time—we shall discuss later. Here we are for the time being discussing the effect on Europe of these works and not the works themselves, and it will suffice here to point out the severe structure and composition of Ibsen's plays.

At a time when the drama was increasingly disintegrating into mere milieu-painting, Ibsen built strictly concentrated dramatic plots, the qualities of which reminded the readers and audiences of the Greek and Roman dramatists (see the things written about *Ghosts* at the time). In those days, when dialogue had lost most of its dramatic tension and had degenerated into a gramophone record of everyday speech, Ibsen wrote a dialogue every sentence of which revealed new traits of the speaker's character and carried the plot a step further, a dialogue which was in a much deeper sense true to life than any mere copy of everyday conversation could ever be. Thus wide circles of the western European radical intelligentsia gained the impression that Russian and Scandinavian literature were the 'classical' literature of their own time, or at least the artistic precursors of a coming classical literature.

To what extent the Ibsenian drama was problematic in the deeper sense, how imperfectly its formal perfection concealed the inner instability of Ibsen's conception of society and hence of his real dramatic form—to elucidate all this would require a special and longer analysis. Here it will be enough to say that the Ibsenian drama, however intrinsically problematic it may be, was vastly superior to the western European dramatic attempts of the time, both in dramatic concentration and in form. This superiority is so great that even other Scandinavian writers who were far more subject than Ibsen to the general European decay, were yet superior to the westerners in tension, concentration, and the avoidance of the banalities of naturalism and of the empty artifices of formal 'experimentation.' In Strindberg, for instance, there are definite naturalist tendencies, and he went much further than Ibsen in the dissolution of dramatic form. His conflicts and characters grow increasingly subjective and even pathological. But his first plays show a simplicity of structure, an economy of means of expression and a concentration of the dialogue which one would seek in vain among the playwrights of the German and French naturalist school.

The hope of the European literary vanguard that this Russian and Scandinavian literature marked a new dawn of European literary development was of course based on an illusion; those who harboured such hopes had no clear notion of the social causes either of the decline of their own literatures or of the strange flowering of literature in Russia and the Scandinavian countries.

Engels saw quite clearly the specific quality of this literary development and pithily characterized the main traits of its social basis. He wrote to Paul Ernst about Ibsen : "Whatever the faults of e.g. the Ibsen plays may be, they mirror for us a world small and petty-bourgeois, it is true, but nevertheless a world as far removed from the German as heaven from earth; a world in which people still have character and initiative and act on their own, even though often rather strangely from the outsider's point of view. I prefer to take a closer look at such things before I pass judgment."

Engels thus pointed out the essential reason for the success of Russian and Scandinavian literature in Europe : in an age in which force of character, initiative and independence were increasingly disappearing from the everyday life of the bourgeois world and in which honest writers could depict only the difference between the empty careerist and the stupid dupe (like Maupassant) the Russians and Scandinavians showed a world in which men struggled with fierce passion—even though with tragic or tragi-comic futility—against their degradation by capitalism. Thus the heroes of the Russian and Scandinavian writers fought the same battles as the characters in western literature and were defeated by essentially the same forces. But their struggle and their defeat were incomparably greater and more heroic than that of similar characters in western literature. If we compare Nora or Mrs. Alwing with the heroines of the domestic tragedies depicted in western European novels and plays, we can see the difference, and this difference was the basis of the great Russian and Scandinavian success and influence.

It is not difficult to uncover the social roots of this success and influence.

After the revolutions of 1848, the June rising and especially the Paris Commune, the ideology of the European bourgeoisie entered upon a period of apologetics. With the unification of Germany and of Italy, the decisive tasks of the bourgeois revolution had been accomplished for a time, so far as the great powers of western Europe were concerned. It is of course characteristic that both in Germany and in Italy these tasks were accomplished not by revolutionary, but decidedly reactionary methods. The class struggle between the bourgeoisie and the working class had visibly become the central issue in every social problem. The ideology of the bourgeoisie evolved increasingly towards the protection of capitalism against the claims of the workers as the economic conditions of the imperialist age matured at an accelerating pace, exercising a rapidly growing influence on the ideological evolution of the bourgeoisie.

This of course does not mean that all western European writers of the time were conscious or unconscious defenders or panegyrists of capitalism. On the contrary, there is no prominent writer of the time who did not oppose it, some with indignation, some with irony. But the general scope of this opposition and the opportunities of its literary expression were determined, limited and narrowed by the development of bourgeois society and the change in bourgeois ideology. All initiative, independence and heroism disappeared for a long time from the western European bourgeois world. The writers who attempted to depict the world in a spirit of opposition, could depict only the contemptible baseness of their own social surroundings and thus the reality which they mirrored drove them into the narrow triviality of naturalism. If, spurred on by their thirst for better things, they wanted to go beyond this reality, they could not find the life-material which they could have stepped up to greatness by true-to-life poetic concentration. If they attempted to depict greatness, the result was an increasingly empty, abstractly Utopian, in the worst sense romantic, picture.

In Scandinavia and Russia, capitalist development began much later than in western Europe and in them, in the seventies and eighties of the nineteenth century, bourgeois ideology had not as yet been driven to apologetics. The social conditions which favoured realism and which determined the development of European literature from Swift to Stendhal were still in existence in these countries, even though in a different form and in greatly changed circumstances.

In his analysis of Ibsen's plays Engels sharply contrasted this trait of Norwegian social evolution with the German situation in the same period.

The social basis of realism in Russia must not, however, be regarded as identical with that existing in Scandinavia. If we were concerned with the effect on western Europe of Russian and Scandinavian literature (and not with Tolstoy) we might confine ourselves to saying that both in Russia and in Scandinavia conditions were more favourable to realistic literature than in western Europe. The development of capitalism had been delayed in both, the part played by the class struggle between bourgeoisie and proletariat in the total social process was smaller and in accordance with this the general ideology of the ruling class was not yet, or less, apologetic.

But the backwardness of capitalist development had a totally different character in Norway and in Russia. Engels carefully pointed out the 'normal' traits of Norwegian development. He wrote : "The country is backward because of its isolation and its natural conditions, but its general condition was always appropriate to its conditions of production and hence normal." Another point is that even the advance of capitalism was comparatively slow and gradual in the specific circumstances existing in Norway. "The Norwegian peasant was *never* a serf . . . the Norwegian petty-bourgeois is the son of a free peasant and in these circumstances he is a man in comparison with the German philistine."

All these favourable traits of Norwegian capitalist backwardness brought about the strange flowering of Norwegian literature. The favourable advance of capitalism rendered temporarily possible the development of a vigorously realist, extensive and promising literature. But with time Norway had to be aligned with the general capitalist evolution of Europe, in a way, of course, which preserved as far as possible the specific conditions governing the country's development. Norwegian literature distinctly mirrors this assimilation to the rest of Europe. The aged Ibsen himself manifested a growing uncertainty in his opposition and as a result he absorbed more and more of the decadent traits of western European literature and modes of expression (symbolism). The careers of the younger oppositional and realist writers show them increasingly succumbing to the general reactionary, anti-realist ideological and literary influences of western Europe. Even before the war the career of Arne Garborg, a highly gifted realist writer ended in religious obscuration and after the war Knut Hamsun capitulated to reactionary ideologies in literary trends and even fascism.

The capitalist backwardness of Russia was of a totally different character. The irruption of capitalism into the semi-Asiatic serfdom of Tsarism brought about widespread social unrest which lasted from the abolition of serfdom to the revolution of 1905. Lenin says that Tolstoy was the mirror of this epoch. Its specific development determined the specific traits of Tolstoy's art and with it the difference between the influence on Europe of Tolstoy on the one hand and of the Scandinavians on the other. Any realistic and concrete analysis of Tolstoy's influence on world literature must therefore be based on an analysis of that epoch. Lenin gave us such an analysis while the views on Tolstoy expressed by the Russian vulgar-sociologists reveal only that the influence exercised by the great writer was as much a mystery to them as it was to their contemporaries in Europe.

Lenin defined very clearly the specific quality of this revolutionary epoch, comparing it with previous revolutions directed against feudal or semi-feudal social orders. He says: "Thus we see that the conception 'bourgeois revolution' is insufficient to define the forces which may win the victory in such a revolution. There may be and there have been bourgeois revolutions in which the commercial or commercial-and-industrial bourgeoisie played the part of the principal motive force. A victory of such revolutions was possible as the victory of the corresponding section of the bourgeoisie over its opponents (for instance over the privileged nobility or the absolute monarchy). But in Russia matters are different. A victory of the bourgeoisie in our country is impossible as a bourgeois victory. This seems a paradox, but it is a fact. The preponderance of our peasant population, its frightful oppression by the feudal landowners, half of whom own immense estates, the strength and class-consciousness of the working class, already organized in a Socialist party—all these circumstances lend our bourgeois revolution a specific character."

Tolstoy had of course no conception of the true nature of the Russian revolution. But being a writer of genius, he faithfully recorded certain essential traits of reality and thus, without his knowledge, and contrary to his conscious intentions, he became the poetic mirror of certain aspects of the revolutionary development in Russia. The boldness and sweep of Tolstoy's realism rests on the fact that it is carried by a movement of world-wide significance, a movement revolutionary in its basic social tendency. The writers of western Europe had at that time no such foundations to build on. Before 1848 the great writers of the west also had their feet firmly planted on such soil. Tolstoy's affinity to them rests on the community of the primeval social foundations of art. He differs from them because his own social basis—the specific character of the Russian revolutionary development—differs from theirs.

It is a condition *sine qua non* of great realism that the author must honestly record, without fear or favour, everything he sees around him. This subjective condition of great realism may require a more exact definition. For the merely-subjective candour of the realist writers survived the decline of realism itself, but could not avert the consequences brought about by this decline in the sphere of art and philosophy. The subjective honesty of the writer can engender true realism only if it is the literary expression of so extensive a social movement that its problems drive the writer to observe and describe its most important aspects and on the other hand stiffen his backbone and give him enough strength and courage to fertilize his sincerity. Such great historical movements are by no means simply covered by the trite conception of 'progress.' Vulgar-sociology distorts the social conditions of poetic subjectivity by banalizing the relationship between society and the writer in a liberalistic-mechanistic direction. For instance, a writer may be alleged to be absolutely 'progressive' (Balzac, for instance, is represented as a champion of industrial capitalism) and then the greatest opposite, precisely because they cannot be made to fit in with the Liberal conception of 'progress.'

An author may be able to uncover and depict the essential factors of some phase of social development even though he holds views containing reactionary elements; this will not lessen the objective value of his sincerity. In such cases the writer's sincerity will yet enable him to depict truly the realities of a social movement, provided that social movement poses real problems and finds solutions for them. The sincerity of great writers must not, of course, be judged by the statements of some 'average' representative of such a social movement, nor by the statements of such great writers themselves. The scope of their sincerity depends on the scope of the problems posed by such movements and their importance in the evolution of mankind.

In his analysis of the evolution of the revolutionary movement in Russia up to 1905, Lenin clearly showed that the specific position of the Russian peasantry and the part it played in the collapse of the semi-feudal despotism of the Tsar was of essential importance in determining the character of the Russian revolution and its place in the history of the world. Lenin quite rightly regarded Tolstoy as the poetic mirror of this peasant revolution and found in this the explanation why Tolstoy could develop into a realist writer as great as the greatest realist classics, although in his time realism in Europe was already in its decline. Lenin also showed that this specific character of the Russian peasant revolution was

an essential factor in the highest form of bourgeois revolution—
a bourgeois revolution in which the bourgeoisie could no longer
be victorious—and in explaining this he explained at the same
time why Tolstoy was able to develop realism one step further
than any of his predecessors.

We have said that reactionary traits in the world-view of great
realist writers do not prevent them from depicting social reality
in a comprehensive, correct and objective way. But here again
we must be more specific. For this does not apply to any and
every world-view. Only illusions motivated by the social movement
depicted, i.e. illusions—often tragic illusions—which are historically
necessary, do not prevent the writer from depicting social reality
with objective truth.

Such were the illusions of Balzac, of Shakespeare, and such too,
in the final count, were Tolstoy's illusions. Lenin said : "The contradictions in Tolstoy's views . . . are a true mirror of those contradictory circumstances in which the historical activity of the
peasantry in our revolution took place."

All Tolstoy's illusions and reactionary Utopias — from Henry
George's world-liberating theory to the theory of non-resistance to
evil, were all without exception rooted in the specific position of
the Russian peasantry. Recognition of their historical necessity
does not of course make them less Utopian or less reactionary. But
the effect of the historical necessity of these illusions is that, far
from hampering Tolstoy's realism, they actually contribute to its
greatness, depth and feeling, although naturally in a very contradictory fashion.

Obviously these illusions and reactionary traits often play an
important part in determining Tolstoy's influence on western Europe. Even though by this means a bridge was made between the
western reader and the poet of the Russian peasantry, Tolstoy
nevertheless translated the reader into a quite different poetic world
than the one his philosophy led the former to expect. The reader
was suddenly faced with the 'cruelty' and 'coldness' of a great
realist, with an art which, although in its form and subject quite
appropriate to the time, yet in its innermost essence seemed to
come from an entirely different world.

Only the greatest bourgeois humanists of the post-war period
began to understand that this entirely different world was nothing
but their own past, which had seemed lost to them—the world
of the great bourgeois revolution. It is characteristic that they
understood this all the better, the nearer their bourgeois-revolution-

ary humanism approached the new democracy, the humanism of the victorious proletarian revolution.

3.

The evolution of bourgeois society after 1848 destroyed the subjective conditions which made a great realism possible. If we regard the problem of this decline from the subjective viewpoint of the writer, we see in the first place that in this period the writers of Europe were increasingly turning into mere spectators and observers of the social process, in contrast to the old realists who had themselves experienced this process and participated in it. Their conclusions were the results of their own life-struggle and constituted only one part of the resources they had at their disposal in depicting reality.

The question whether the writer must experience or need merely observe what he describes is by no means an isolated question limited to the sphere of art—it embraces the writer's entire relationship to social reality. The old writers were participants in the social struggle and their activities as writers were either part of this struggle or a reflection, an ideological and literary solution, of the great problems of the time. In reading the biographies of the great realists of old, from Swift and Defoe to Goethe, Balzac and Stendhal, we see that none of them were writers throughout their life and writers only, and their multiple and combative ties with society are richly reflected in their works.

But this mode of life was not a consequence of their personal preferences. Zola was by instinct certainly a more active and combative type than Goethe. But it is the social surroundings which determine the degree to which intricate and combative relationships can arise between the writer and society, such as those which resulted in a life so rich in experience as that of Goethe. It depends on whether the society in which the writer lives contains historically significant social and ideological trends to which the writer can dedicate himself with all the fervour of his personality.

On capitalist society reaching its apologetic stage, such possibilities grew increasingly rare for the great bourgeois writers. Of course there were plenty of writers who experienced the evolution of the bourgeoisie in the period following upon 1848 with a complete engagement of their personality. But what was this evolution like and what literary results could a dedication to it bring a writer? Gustav Freytag and Georges Ohnet experienced the development of the German and French petit bourgeoisie respectively and owe their ephemeral popularity to the 'warmth' of their experience. But they depicted a debased, narrow, trivial life full of concealments and hypocrisy, and they did so by correspondingly narrow, trivial, untruthful means. Only in very few cases did an experience related to reactionary tendencies result in literarily valuable (even though historically insignificant) products, as for instance the experience of the problems of British imperialism in the works of Rudyard Kipling.

The really honest and gifted bourgeois writers who lived and wrote in the period following upon the upheavals of 1848 naturally could not experience and share the development of their class with the same true devotion and intensity of feeling as their predecessors. They were far more likely to repudiate with hatred and loathing the way of life now thrust on the world by that development. And because in the society of their time they found nothing they could support whole-heartedly (for the proletarian class struggle and its implications were beyond their understanding) they remained mere spectators of the social process, until the new humanist movement which began at the end of the nineteenth century and to which the best of the now living writers belonged, posed the problem of a new democracy and thereby put the whole matter in a different light; but there is no room here to deal with this : the point will be discussed in the last essay of this volume.

The change in the writer's position in relation to reality led to the putting forward of various theories, such as Flaubert's theory of impartiality ('impassibilité') and the pseudo-scientific theory of Zola and his school. But much more important than the theories are the realities on which they are based. If the writer merely occupies an observation post in relation to reality, that means that he regards bourgeois society critically, ironically and often turns away from it in hatred and disgust.

The new type of realist turns into a specialist of literary expression, a virtuoso, an 'armchair scientist' who makes a 'speciality' of describing the social life of the present.

This alienation has for its inevitable consequence that the writer disposes of a much narrower and more restricted life-material than the old school of realism. If the new realist wants to describe some phenomenon of life, he has to go out of his way specially to observe it. It is clear that he will first take into account the superficial traits which meet the eye. And if the writer is really gifted and original, he will seek for originality in the observation of detail and will attempt to carry the literary expression of such originally observed detail to ever higher levels.

Flaubert advised the young Maupassant, who was his personal disciple, that he should observe a tree until he discovered the traits which distinguished it from all other trees and then seek for the words which would adequately express this unique quality of that particular tree.

Both master and disciple often achieved this aim with great artistry. But the task itself was a narrowing of the purpose of art itself, and a blind alley so far as realism was concerned. For—to consider only this particular example—the task set by Flaubert isolated the tree from nature as a whole and from its relationship with man. One may thus discover in what the unique character of the tree consists, but this uniqueness amounts to nothing more than the originality of a still-life.

But when Tolstoy in *War and Peace* describes the leafless gnarled oak which the despondent Andrey Bolkonski contemplates and which later, on his return from the Rostovs, he at first cannot find at all and afterwards discovers transformed and covered with fresh leaves, then, although Tolstoy has given the tree no 'originality' in the Flaubert-Maupassant still-life sense, he has thrown light in a flash and with great poetic vigour on a very intricate psychological process.

We cannot give here a detailed theory and critique of the realist literary development in Europe after 1848 and must confine ourselves to merely touching in principle on its basic features. We then see that the social evolution which forced the most sincere, upright and gifted *bourgeois* writers into the position of observers, at the same time inevitably drove them to fill the place of the missing essentials with literary substitutes.

Flaubert recognized this new position of the realist writer very early and with tragic clarity. In 1850 he wrote to Bouilhet, a friend of his youth :

"We have a many-voiced orchestra, a rich palette, varied sources of power. As for tricks and devices, we have more of those than ever. But we lack inner life, the soul of things, the idea of the writer's subject."

This bitter confession should not be regarded as the expression of a mood, of a transient fit of despair. Flaubert saw only too clearly the true position of the new realism.

Let us consider so important a modern novel as Maupassant's *Une Vie*, which Tolstoy regarded as one of the best works, not only of Maupassant, but of newer literature as a whole. In this book Maupassant took his subject from the past. The novel begins in the time of the restoration of the Bourbons and ends shortly before the revolution of 1848. Thus it depicts mainly the same period of which Balzac was the great historian. But—to point out only one important feature—the reader, although the scene of the novel is set among the nobility, is never made aware of the fact that the July revolution has come and gone and that the position of the nobility in French society is totally different at the end of the novel from what it was at the beginning.

Let no one say that what Maupassant *wanted* to depict was, after all, not this change but the disappointment of his heroine in her marriage and in the child born of it. But the fact that Maupassant posed the problem in this way shows that he considered love, marriage and mother-love separately from the historical and social foundations on which alone they could be realistically depicted. He isolated the psychological problems from the social problems. For Maupassant society was no longer a complex of vital and contradictory relationships between human beings, but only a lifeless setting.

The social being of the nobility, which in Balzac's works is a great, varied process rich in tragedies and comedies, is narrowed to a 'still-life' in Maupassant. He describes the castles, parks, furniture, etc., of the aristocracy with the most consummate skill, but all this has no real, live connection with his subject proper. And this subject proper, too, is relatively meagre, shallow and unilinear.

If then we wish to summarize the principal negative traits of western European realism after 1848 we come to the following conclusions :

First, that the real, dramatic and epic movement of social happening disappears and isolated characters of purely private interest, characters sketched in with only a few lines, stand still, surrounded by a dead scenery described with admirable skill.

Secondly, the real relationships of human beings to each other, the social motives which, unknown even to themselves, .govern their actions, thoughts and emotions, grow increasingly shallow; and the author either stresses this shallowness of life with angry or sentimental irony, or else substitutes dead, rigid, lyrically inflated symbols for the missing human and social relationships.

Thirdly (and in close connection with the points already mentioned) : details meticulously observed and depicted with consummate skill are substituted for the portrayal of the essential features of social reality and the description of the changes effected in the human personality by social influences.

This transformation of the writer from a champion of social progress and a participant in the social life of his time into a mere spectator and observer, was of course the result of a long development. The connection between the last great realists of the nineteenth century and the social life of their time was already paradoxical and full of contradictions. We need only think of Balzac and Stendhal and compare them with the English and French realists of the preceding century in order to see how contradictory the former's experience of the social life of their time necessarily was. Their relation to society was not only critical—we find a critical attitude in the older realists as well, although their connection with the *bourgeois* class was far less problematic—but profoundly pessimistic and replete with hatred and loathing.

Sometimes only very loose threads, very transparent illusions, very fragile Utopias connect these writers with the *bourgeois* class of their day. With advancing age Balzac's foreboding of the collapse of both aristocratic and *bourgeois* culture throws an ever darker shadow on his outlook. But for all that Balzac and Stendhal still gave an extensive and profoundly conceived picture of the *bourgeois* society of their time, and the reason for this is that they both had a deep and extensive experience of every important problem and stage in the development of *bourgeois* society between the first revolution and 1848.

In Tolstoy this relationship is even more paradoxical and contradictory. His development shows a growing aversion to the Russian ruling classes, an increasing loathing and hatred of all oppressors and exploiters of the Russian people. At the end of his life he sees them as a mere gang of scoundrels and parasites. Thus, at the terminal point of his career, Tolstoy comes very close to the western realists of the second half of the nineteenth century.

How is it then that in spite of this Tolstoy the writer never turned into a Flaubert or a Maupassant? Or, if we want to extend the question to the earlier stage of Tolstoy's development, to the time when he still believed or wished to believe that the conflict between landowner and peasant could be solved by patriarchal methods : how is it that not even in this earlier Tolstoy is there any trace of the provincialism so evident in the later realists, even the most gifted ones? How is this to be explained, since Tolstoy understood the socialist movement of the working classes as little or even less than most of his western contemporaries?

It is on this point that Lenin's admirable analysis provides a key to the understanding of Tolstoy.

The vulgar-sociologists compiled statistics of the characters depicted by Tolstoy and on the basis of these figures they proclaimed that Tolstoy had depicted mainly the life of the Russian landowner. Such an analysis can at best facilitate the understanding of quite uninspired naturalists, who, when they depict something, describe only what lies immediately in front of them, without any relation to the sum of social reality. When great realists depict social evolution and the great social problems, they never do so in so simple and immediate a fashion.

In the works of a great realist everything is linked up with everything else. Each phenomenon shows the polyphony of many components, the intertwinement of the individual and social, of the physical and the psychical, of private interest and public affairs. And because the polyphony of their composition goes beyond immediacy, their *dramatis personae* are too numerous to find room on the playbill.

The great realists always regard society from the viewpoint of a living and moving centre and this centre is present, visibly or invisibly, in every phenomenon. An instance is Balzac. Balzac shows how capital, which he—correctly at that time—saw incarnated in financial capital, takes over power in France. From Gobseck to Nucingen, Balzac creates a long procession of the immediate representatives of this demoniacal force. But does this exhaust the power of financial capital in Balzac's world? Does Gobseck cease to rule when he leaves the stage? No, Balzac's world is permanently saturated with Gobseck and his like. Whether the immediate theme is love or marriage, friendship or politics, passion or self-sacrifice, Gobseck is ever present as an invisible protagonist and his invisible presence visibly colours every movement, every action of all Balzac's characters.

Tolstoy is the poet of the peasant revolt that lasted from 1861 to 1905. In his life-work the exploited peasant is this visible-invisible ever-present protagonist. Let us look at the description of Prince Nekhlyudov's regimental life in *Resurrection*, one of Tolstoy's late works :

"He had nothing else to do than to don a beautifully pressed and brushed uniform, which not he but others had made and brushed, put on a helmet and gird on weapons which were also made, cleaned and put into his hands by others, to mount a fine charger which had again been bred, trained and groomed by others, and ride to a parade or an inspection . . ."

Such descriptions, which we find in great numbers in Tolstoy's writings, of course also contain many details. But these details are not meant to throw light on the specific qualities of the objects described but to stress the social implications which determine the use of such objects. And the social implications point to exploitation, the exploitation of the peasants by the landowners.

But in Tolstoy's life-work the exploited peasant is visibly or invisibly present not only in every greater or lesser phenomenon of life—he is never absent from the consciousness of the characters themselves. Whatever their occupation, every implication of this occupation and everything human beings think of it, hinges consciously or unconsciously on problems which are more or less immediately linked with this central problem.

It is true that Tolstoy's characters and Tolstoy himself raise these issues on an almost purely individual ethical basis : how can life be arranged in a way that men should not ruin themselves morally by exploiting the labour of others? In his own life and out of the mouth of many of his characters, Tolstoy has given plenty of incorrect and reactionary answers to this question.

But what is important in Tolstoy is the putting of the question and not the answer given to it. Chekhov said quite rightly, in connection with Tolstoy, that putting a question correctly is one thing and finding the answer to it something quite different; the artist absolutely needs to do only the first. Of course the term 'putting the question correctly' should not be taken too literally in the case of Tolstoy. What is important are not the muddled and romantic ideas put forward by, say, the hero of one of his early novels; what is essential are not his fantastic and Utopian plans for the salvation of the world, or at least not only these are important and essential. They are organically linked with the reaction of the peasants to these plans of salvation, their hostile distrust, their instinctive fear that the squire's new plan cannot possibly be anything but some new way of cheating them and the better it sounds the more cunning the deception must be—only in connection with these things can we speak, with Chekhov, of Tolstoy's 'correct putting of the question.'

Tolstoy's correct putting of the question consists among other things in this : no one before him ever depicted the 'two nations' as vividly and palpably as he. There is a paradoxical greatness in the fact that while his conscious striving was constantly directed towards the moral and religious overcoming of this rigid division of society into two hostile camps, in his literary production the reality which he depicted with relentless fidelity constantly exposed the impracticability of this the author's favourite dream. Tolstoy's development followed very tortuous paths; he lost many illusions and found new ones. But whatever Tolstoy wrote, as the truly great poet that he is, he always depicted the inexorable division between the 'two nations' in Russia, the peasants and the landowners.

In the works of his youth, for instance in *The Cossacks,* this implacability manifested itself in as yet idyllic, elegiac form. In *Resurrection* Maslova gives this answer to Nekhlyudov's words of remorse : "So you want to save your soul through me, eh? In this world you used me for your pleasure and now you want to use me in the other world to save your soul!"

In the course of the years Tolstoy changed all his internal and external means of expression, he made use of and discarded all sorts of philosophies, but the portrayal of the 'two nations' remained the backbone of his life-work from start to finish.

Only if we have discovered this central problem in Tolstoy's art does the contrast in presentation between Tolstoy and the contemporary western realists become evident, in spite of the common affinity of subject. Like all honest and gifted writers of the period, Tolstoy grew more and more estranged from the ruling class and found their life to an increasing degree sinful, meaningless, empty and inhuman.

But the writers of the capitalist West, if they took this attitude towards the ruling class and took it seriously, were forced into the position of isolated observers, with all the artistic drawbacks attendant on such a position—for only an earnest understanding of the struggle of the working classes for their freedom could have shown them the way out of this isolation. Tolstoy, the Russian, lived in a country in which the *bourgeois* revolution was still the order of the day and in depicting the revolt of the peasants against their exploitation by both landowner and capitalist, in depicting the 'two nations' of the Russian scene he could become the last great *bourgeois* realist of the age.

4

The true artistic totality of a literary work depends on the completeness of the picture it presents of the essential social factors that determine the world depicted. Hence it can be based only on the author's own intensive experience of the social process. Only such experience can uncover the essential social factors and make the artistic presentation centre round them freely and naturally. The hallmark of the great realist masterpiece is precisely that its intensive totality of *essential* social factors does not require, does not even tolerate, a meticulously accurate or pedantically encyclopaedic inclusion of all the threads making up the social tangle; in such a masterpiece the most essential social factors can find total expression in the apparently accidental conjunction of a few human destinies.

In contrast to this, the exact copying of reality by a mere onlooker offers no principle of grouping inherent in the subject matter itself. If artistic presentation goes on further than the reproduction of such superficial visible traits of everyday life as meet the eye, the result is a 'bad infinity' (to use the Hegelian phrase) i.e. a chaotic mass of observations the beginning, sequence and end of which are left entirely to the arbitrary choice of the author. Should the author, on the other hand, introduce into the world of observed fact a system originating in his own mind and in nothing else, he may bring some order into the chaos, but the order would be an order determined by abstract considerations, an order external to the material it marshals, an order foreign to real life. The resulting literary work would inevitably be dry and unpoetic and this will be the more obvious the greater the efforts the author makes to counterfeit, by means of descriptions, lyrical passages, symbolism, and the like, a mysticized link between the human destinies depicted in the work and the social forces that rule them. The more superficial the author's observation, the more abstract must be the connections which aim to conjure *aposteriori* some sort of order and composition into such a work.

The inner truth of the works of the great realists rests on the fact that they arise from life itself, that their artistic characteristics are reflections of the social structure of the life lived by the artist himself. The history of the structure of the great realistic novel —from Le Sage's loose sequence of adventures, through Walter Scott's attempts at dramatic concentration to Balzac's partly novelistic-dramatic, partly cyclically intricate compositions—is the literary reflection of a process in which the categories of capitalism as forms of human living gradually penetrate *bourgeois society*. In the dramatic concentration which Balzac built into his all-embracing cycle we can already discern the beginnings of the crisis into which triumphant capitalism plunges the arts. The great writers of our age were all engaged in a heroic struggle against the banality, aridity and emptiness of the prosaic nature of *bourgeois* life. The formal side of the struggle against this banality and insipidity of life is the dramatic pointing of plot and incident. In Balzac, who depicts passions at their highest intensity, this is achieved by conceiving the typical as the extreme expression of certain strands in the skein of life. Only by means of such mighty dramatic explosions can a dynamic world of profound, rich and many-hued poetry emerge from the sordid prose of *bourgeois* life. The naturalists overcame this 'romanticism' and by so doing, lowered literary creation to the level of the 'average,' of the banality of everyday life. In naturalism capitalist prose triumphed over the poetry of life.

Tolstoy's life-work embraces several phases of this literary process, which runs parallel to the stages of social evolution in Russia. He began his career as an author in a pre-Balzacian stage, in terms of western literary development, and the work of his old age extended into the period of the decline of great realism.

Tolstoy himself was well aware that his great novels were genuine epics. But it was not only he himself who compared *War and Peace* with Homer—many known and unknown readers of the book had the same feeling. Of course the comparison with Homer, while it shows the profound impression made by the truly epic quality of this novel, is more an indication of the general trend of its style than an actual characteristic of the style itself. For in spite of its epic sweep, *War and Peace* is still from first to last a true novel, although of course, not a novel with the dramatic concentration found in Balzac. Its loose, spacious composition, the cheerful, comfortable, leisurely relationships between the characters, the calm and yet animated abundance of the epic episodes indispensable to the true story-teller—all these are related more to the great provincial idylls of the eighteenth-century English novel than to Balzac.

But this affinity expresses an opposition to the general line of development of the nineteenth-century European novel more than anything else. The old society, only just beginning to submit to capitalist domination, still possessed in its daily life the variety and interest of the pre-capitalist era. Tolstoy's great novels differ from those of his English predecessors in the specific nature of the social reality which they mirror and are superior to their English parallels in artistic richness and depth precisely because of this specific character of the reality presented. The world depicted by Tolstoy is a world much less *bourgeois* than the world of the eighteenth-century English novelists, but — especially in *Anna*

Karenina—it is a world in which the process of capitalist development is more strongly apparent than in the English novels which nearly always depict only one particular phase of it. In addition, the great English novelists of the eighteenth century lived in a *post-revolutionary* period, and this gave their works (especially those of Goldsmith and Fielding) an atmosphere of stability and security and also a certain complacent shortsightedness.

In contrast to this, Tolstoy's literary career began and ended in a period of approaching revolutionary storms. Tolstoy is a *pre-revolutionary* writer. And precisely because the central problem in his works was the Russian peasant problem, the decisive turning-point in the history of western literature, i.e. the defeat of the 1848 revolutions, left no traces on them. In this connection it matters little how far Tolstoy himself, in the various phases of his development, was aware or unaware of this cardinal issue. What is important is that this issue is at the core of all his works, that everything he wrote revolves around this issue; it is only for this reason that he still remained a pre-revolutionary writer even after the disaster of the European revolutions of 1848.

But the village idylls of Tolstoy's great novels are always threatened idylls. In *War and Peace* the financial disaster of the Rostov family is enacted before our eyes as the typical disaster of the old-fashioned provincial nobility; the spiritual crises of Bezukhov and Bolkonski are reflections of the great current which broadened politically into the Decembrist rising. In *Anna Karenina* even darker clouds menace the village idyll and the enemy has already openly shown its capitalist countenance. Now it is no longer a question of financial disaster alone — here one can already feel the undertow of capitalism, against which Tolstoy makes so passionate a protest.

Constantine Levin, who really takes up the problems where Nikolai Rostov left them in *War and Peace,* can no longer solve them as simply and light-heartedly. He fights not only to recover his material prosperity as a landowner (without falling a victim to the capitalisation of the land) but has to carry on an incessant inner struggle, a struggle moving from crisis to crisis in trying to convince himself that his existence as landowner is justified and that he has the right to exploit his peasants. The incomparable epic greatness of Tolstoy's novels is based on the illusions which caused him to believe that this was not a tragic conflict out of which there was no way out for the honest representatives of the class, but a problem capable of solution.

In *Anna Karenina* these illusions were already shaken to a much greater extent than in *War and Peace*. This manifests itself among other things in the fact that the structure of *Anna Karenina* is much more 'European,' much more closely-knit and the unfolding of the story far less leisurely. The closer assimilation of the theme to those of the European novels of the nineteenth century is a further, even though external, indication of the approaching crisis; although the style of *Anna Karenina* still has the characteristics of Tolstoy's early period, certain traits of his later critical period are already showing themselves. *Anna Karenina* is far more novel-like than *War and Peace*.

In *The Kreutzer Sonata* Tolstoy takes another long step in the direction of the European novel. He creates for himself a great form of *novella* which resembles the perfected form produced by European realism and which is both broad and dramatically concentrated. He inclines more and more towards presenting the great catastrophes, the tragically-ending turning-points in human destinies by a detailed portrayal of all their manifold inner motives, i.e., in the most profound sense of the word, epically.

Thus Tolstoy approaches to some extent the form of composition used by Balzac. Not that Balzac had influenced his literary style; but the reality which they both experienced and the manner in which they experienced it drove both of them by an inner necessity to create such forms. *The Death of Ivan Ilyich* marks the culminating point of this later style of Tolstoy, but its effects can also be traced in his last great novel *Resurrection*. It is no accident that Tolstoy's dramatic works were also written in this period.

But the thematic assimilation to European literature does not mean artistic assimilation to the prevalent literary trends there, the very trends which broke up the artistic forms of the epic and the drama. On the contrary, to the end of his life Tolstoy remained, in all questions relating to art, a great realist of the old school, and a great creator of epic form.

The epic presentation of the totality of life—unlike the dramatic —must inevitably include the presentation of the externals of life, the epic-poetic transformation of the most important objects making up some sphere of human life and most typical events necessarily occurring in such a sphere. Hegel calls this first postulate of epic presentation 'the totality of objects.' This postulate is not a theoretical invention. Every novelist instinctively feels that his work cannot claim to be complete if it lacks this 'totality of objects,' that is, if it does not include every important object, event and sphere of life belonging to the theme. The crucial difference between the genuine epics of the old realists and the disintegration of form in the declining newer literature is manifested in the way in which this 'totality of objects' is linked with the individual destinies of the characters.

The modern writer, the looker-on, can very well achieve such an awareness of this totality of objects. And if he is a great writer, he may conjure it up before us by the force, the suggestive power of his descriptions. Every reader will remember, for instance, Zola's markets, stock exchanges, underworld haunts, theatres, racetracks, etc. So far as the encyclopaedic character of his contents and the artistic quality of his descriptions is concerned, Zola, too, possessed this 'totality of objects.' But these objects have a being entirely independent of the fate of the characters. They form a mighty but indifferent background to human destinies with which they have no real connection; at best they are the more or less accidental scenery among which these human destinies are enacted.

How different are the classics!

Homer tells us about the weapons of Achilles, weapons made by the gods. But he does not do so as soon as Achilles takes the stage. Only when Achilles has angrily retired to his tent, when the Trojans have triumphed, when Patrocles has been killed in the borrowed armour of Achilles, when Achilles himself is preparing for the mortal combat with Hector—a combat mortal in every sense of the word, for Achilles knows that he himself must die soon after Hector's death—it is just before this dramatic moment of the combat with Hector, when the weapons of the two champions decide the fate of two nations and the better weapons of Achilles, apart from his god-like strength, become a factor deciding the outcome of the duel—only then does Homer describe how Hephaistos forged these weapons for Achilles.

Thus the description of the weapons of Achilles is truly epic, not only because the poet describes their *making* and not their *appearance* (Lessing points this out in the famous chapter in his *Laokoon*), but also from the point of view of the composition as a whole, for it occurs exactly where these weapons of Achilles play a decisive part in the story, in the characterization and fate of the heroes. Thus these arms of Achilles are not objects independent of the characters in the story but an integrating factor of the story itself.

The really great novelists are in this respect always true-born sons of Homer. True, the world of objects and the relationship between them and men has changed, has become more intricate, less spontaneously poetic. But the art of the great novelists manifests itself precisely in the ability to overcome the unpoetic nature of their world, through sharing and experiencing the life and evolution of the society they lived in. It is by sending out their spontaneously typical heroes to fulfil their inherently necessary destinies that the great writers have mastered with such sovereign power the changeful texture of the external and internal, great and little moments that make up life. Their heroes set out on their career and encounter quite naturally the specific objects and events of their sphere of life. Precisely because the characters are typical in the most profound sense of the word, they must of necessity meet the most important objects of their sphere of life more than once in the course of their typical career. The writer is free to introduce these objects when and where they have become typical and necessary requisites in the drama of life he is describing.

There is perhaps no other modern author in whose works the 'totality of objects' is so rich, so complete as in Tolstoy. We need not think only of *War and Peace* in which every detail of the war is shown, from the court and the general staff down to the guerilla fighters and prisoners of war and every phase of peaceful private life from birth to death. We can recall the dances, clubs, parties, social calls, conferences, work in the fields, horse-races and card games described in *Anna Karenina* and the court and prison scenes in *Resurrection*. But if we subject to a closer analysis any of these pictures—which Tolstoy paints with such pleasure, so broadly and in such detail that each of them becomes a separate picture within the framework of the whole—we cannot fail to see how different they are from the pictures painted by modern realists and how similar to those we find in the old epics.

These pictures of Tolstoy are never mere scenery, never merely pictures and descriptions, never merely contributions to the 'totality of objects.' The Christmas fancy-dress procession in *War and Peace* marks a crisis in the love of Nikolai Rostov and Sonia; the victorious cavalry charge signals a crisis in the life of Nikolai Rostov; the horse-race is a turning-point in the relations between Anna Karenina and Vronski; the trial of Katyusha leads to the fateful meeting between her and Nekhlyudov and so on. Each such separately presented section of the 'totality of objects' contains some decisive point which makes it a necessary factor in the evolution of one or more of the characters in the novel.

In reality the interconnections and relationships in Tolstoy's novels are much more intricate and varied than merely such points of contact between objective happenings and the subjective experiences of the characters, as have been referred to in the preceding; such points of intersection also mark more or less important turning-points of the whole story. Every phase of such crises, every thought and emotion of the characters is inseparably intertwined with the turning-point, with the event which provides the opportunity for the crisis in the story. For instance : when it is already inevitable that a crisis in the relationship of Anna and Vronski to Karenin should arise, the race and Vronski's accident is nevertheless not merely an opportunity for the crisis to become manifest, it also determines the nature of the crisis. It reveals traits in each of the three characters which in other circumstances would not have manifested themselves in the same way and with the same typicality. Because of the internal threads which link the horse-race with the characters and the plot, the race entirely ceases to be a mere picture—it grows into the fateful culminating scene of a great drama, and the fact that riding in races is a typical pastime of Vronski, that attending horse-races at which royalty is present is a typical habit of the bureaucrat Karenin, renders the manifold relationships between individual destinies and the 'totality of objects' even more manifold and typical by the intervention of social factors.

Such a presentation of the 'totality of objects' dispenses Tolstoy --like every truly great epic poet—from giving dry and tedious descriptions of a setting, the connection between which and individual destinies is always general and abstract and hence always remains coincidental. The 'totality of objects' in Tolstoy always expresses, in immediate, spontaneous and palpable form, the close bond between individual destinies and the surrounding world.

5.

Such a manner of presenting the 'totality of objects' is a condition *sine qua non* of depicting truly typical characters. Engels stressed the importance of typical circumstances in close connection with the typicality of characters, as a prerequisite of true realism. But typical circumstances may be depicted abstractly or concretely, even if they are correctly described, so far as their social nature is concerned. In the works of the newer realists such descriptions increasingly tend to be abstract. If the characters in a work of art, their mutual relationships, the stories of their lives, etc., cannot be shown in such a manner that the relationships between them and their environment appear as the natural results of the characterization; if the settings and instruments of the story are from the viewpoint of the individual merely accidental (i.e. if artistically they make the impression of mere scenery), then it is impossible for the artist to depict typical circumstances in a really convincing manner. For it is one thing for the intelligence to admit that a certain *milieu,* complete with all the phenomena pertaining to it, has been perfectly described, and quite another to become a participant in the profoundly moving experience of seeing how the destinies of individual men and women grow out of an infinite wealth of circumstances they have encountered and how the turning-points in their lives are indissolubly linked with the typical conditions prevailing in their sphere of life.

It is obvious that changes in the style of presentation are reflections of the changes in social reality itself, that they mirror the fact that capitalism is increasingly becoming the dominant factor in every form of human existence.

Hegel very clearly recognized the harmful effect of this change, on art in general and on epic literature in particular. He says about this : "What man requires for his external life, house and home, tent, chair, bed, sword and spear, the ship with which he crosses the ocean, the chariot which carries him into battle, boiling and roasting, slaughtering, eating and drinking—nothing of all this must have become merely a dead means to an end for him; he must feel alive in all these with his whole sense and self in order that what is in itself merely external be given a humanly inspired individual character by such close connection with the human individual. Our present-day machinery and factories together with the products they turn out and in general our means of satisfying our external needs would in this respect—exactly like modern state organisation—be out of tune with the background of life which the original epic requires."

With this Hegel has accurately stated the central problem of style confronting the modern *bourgeois* novel. The great novelists have ever fought a heroic battle to overcome, in the sphere or art, that coldness and harshness in *bourgeois* existence and in the relationships of men with each other and with nature, which opposes such a rigid resistance to poetic presentation. But the poet can overcome this resistance only by seeking out the surviving live elements of these relationships in reality itself, by culling from his own rich and real experience and expressing in concentrated form the moments in which such still living tendencies manifest themselves as relationships between individuals. For the mechanical and 'finished' character of the capitalist world, described by Hegel and so often repeated after him, is, it is true, an existing and growing evolutionary tendency in capitalism, but it must never be forgotten that it is still only a tendency, that society is objectively never 'finished,' fulfilled, dead, petrified reality.

Thus the decisive artistic problem of *bourgeois* realism was this : is the writer to swim against the current or should he allow himself to be carried by the stream of capitalism?

In the first case he may create live images, which it is of course extremely difficult to hew out of the refractory material but which are nevertheless true and real, for they depict the still existing spark of life, the struggle against the 'finished' world. Their truth rests on the fact that what they depict, in an extremely exaggerated form, is substantially correct in its social content.

In the second case—and this is the method followed by newer realism since Flaubert—there is less and less swimming against the current. But it would be quite wrong and superficial to say that this brought literature into closer contact with daily life; that it was the way of life that had changed and literature had merely adapted itself to the change. For writers who, in their own literary activity, yield to the undeniably existing social evolutionary tendency referred to in the preceding, must in their works inevitably turn what is merely a tendency into a generalized, all-embracing reality. Their writings, which cannot strike a spark of life from capitalist reality, thus become even more petrified, even more 'finished' than reality itself and are even more dull, hopeless and commonplace than the world they purport to depict.

It is naturally impossible to preserve among the realities of capitalist society the Homeric intensity of the relations between men and the outer world. It was a piece of good fortune quite exceptional in the history of the modern novel that Defoe, in his *Robinson Crusoe,* succeeded in turning all the tools required for the satisfaction of elementary human needs into components of a thrilling story and by means of this vital connection with human destinies, endow them with a significance poetic in the highest sense of the word. And although *Robinson Crusoe* is an isolated, unrepeatable instance, it is yet most instructive because it indicates the *direction* in which the imagination of the writer should move if it is to find an artistic solution to the problem of overcoming the prose of capitalist reality. It is futile for a writer to adorn his descriptions with the choicest, most brilliant, most adequate words, futile to make his characters feel the deepest sorrow and the greatest indignation at the emptiness, hopelessness, inhumanity and ' petrification ' of reality. It is all in vain, even if this sorrow is expressed with the greatest sincerity and in the most beautiful lyrical form. The example of *Robinson Crusoe* shows that the struggle against the prose of capitalist reality can be successful only if the author invents situations which are not in themselves impossible within the framework of this reality (although they may never really occur) and then, given this invented situation, allows his characters to develop freely all the essential factors of their social existence.

Tolstoy's unique epic greatness rests on such a power of invention. His stories roll on with apparent slowness, without vehement turnings, seemingly following in a straight line along the track of the ordinary lives of his figures. But always and everywhere along this track Tolstoy invents situations arising with internal poetic necessity from the concrete stage of development reached by the characters, situations in which they are brought into a living relationship with nature. *War and Peace* in particular is full of such significant and magnificently living pictures. Think for instance of the splendid hunting party organized by the Rostov family and the idyllic evening with the old uncle with the sequel to it. In *Anna Karenina* the relationship to nature has already become much more problematic. All the more admirable is the genius with which Tolstoy creates such pictures as Levin's mowing of a field, letting them grow out of the problematic nature of Levin's relationship with his peasants and his sentimental attitude to physical labour.

It would be a mistake, however, to limit this problem of the poetic animation of the world depicted by Tolstoy to the relationship between man and nature. The increasing division of labour between town and countryside, the growing social weight of the towns necessarily shifts the action more and more to the urban scene, and to the modern great city and even in such cities no poetic invention can restore a Homeric relationship between man and nature, between man and the objects now turned into commodities. That does not imply, of course, that the realist writer must surrender without a battle to the 'finished' prose of this urban world. The great realists have never capitulated, on this point least of all. But here again the writer is compelled to invent situations in which the world of the great city is endowed with life and poetry. Such poetry can here be born only if the human figures themselves are

deeply imbued with life and their relationships with each other
are rendered profoundly dramatic. If the writer succeeds in invent-
ing such situations, situations in which the struggles and mutual
relationships between the characters widen into a great dramatic
spectacle, then the objects in which these mutual human relationships find expression and which are the vehicle for them, will—
precisely as a result of this their function—be endowed with a
poetic magic. How conscious the great realists were of this, is
shown by a passage in Balzac's *Splendeur et Misère des Courtisanes,*
when the duel between Vautrin 'the Cromwell of the hulks' and
Corentin, the greatest police spy of his time, has reached its culminating point. Corentin's assistant, Peyrade, feels that he is in
constant danger. "Thus the terror, which is spread in the depths
of the American forests by the ruses of hostile tribes and from
which Cooper has derived so much advantage, enveloped with
its glamour the tiniest details of Parisian life. Passers-by, shops,
carriages, some man at a window—all this aroused in the human
numbers entrusted with protecting old Peyrade (for whom this
was a matter of life and death) the same engrossing interest which
the trunk of a tree, a beaver lodge, a pelt, a buffalo robe, a motionless boat or an overhanging tree at the water's edge possesses in
Cooper's novels."

Naturally this glamour is no longer the clear, bright, simple
magic of the infancy of the human race, such as we find in Homer.
The striving of the great realists to remain true to the realities
of life has for its inevitable result that when they portray life under
capitalism and particularly life in the great cities, they must turn
into poetry all the dark uncanniness, all the horrible inhumanity
of it. But this poetry is real poetry : it comes poetically to life
precisely because of its unrelieved horror. This discovery and
revelation of poetic beauty in the dreadful ugliness of capitalist
life is worlds apart from those photographic copies of the surface
which use the hopelessness and desolation of the subject as the
medium of presentation. An instance of this is the masterpiece
of Tolstoy's late period *The Death of Ivan Ilyich.* Superficially,
what is painted here is the everyday story of an average human
being, such as any modern realist might have painted. But Tolstoy's
gift of invention turns the inevitable isolation of the dying Ivan
Ilyich into an almost Robinson Crusoe-like desert island—an island
of horror, of a horrible death after a meaningless life—and inspires
with a terrible dark poetry all the figures and all the objects
through which the human relationships are conveyed. The fading

world of court sittings, card-parties, visits to the theatre, ugly furniture, down to the nauseating filth of the dying man's bodily
functions, is here integrated to a most vivid and animated world
in which each object eloquently and poetically expresses the soul-
destroying emptiness and futility of human life in a capitalist
society.

In this their poetic quality the late works of Tolstoy have strong
affinities with the creative methods of the great realists of the
nineteenth century, although the artistic and historical differences
are very considerable. Balzac and Stendhal got over the 'finished'
unpoetic nature of *bourgeois* society by resolving social life into a
struggle, an interplay of mutual passionate relationships between
individuals; thus society does not confront the human beings living
in it as a 'finished' force, as a dead machine, as something fateful
and inalterable. Not only is society—objectively as well as in the
picture given of it in these writings—undergoing constant change
(the period in question is that between 1789 and 1848) but the
characters depicted by Balzac and Stendhal do actually 'make
their own history.' In a Balzac novel a court of law is not simply
an institution with certain social functions, as in the books written
after 1848. It is a battlefield of various social struggles, and
every interrogation of a suspect, every drawing-up of a document,
every court sentence is the result of intricate social tugs-of-war
whose every phase we are invited to witness.

One of the principal themes of Tolstoy's *oeuvre* is the transformation of the social scene. In writing about Tolstoy Lenin
quotes these words of Levin : "How everything has been turned
upside down with us now, and is only just getting settled again."
One could scarcely describe the period between 1861 and 1905
more strikingly. Everyone—or at least every Russian—knows what
was 'turned upside down' then. It was serfdom and the whole old
régime tied up with it. But what is 'only just getting settled again'
is quite unknown, strange, and incomprehensible to the masses of
the people! The extraordinary poetic sensitivity to all the human
implications connected with this 'turning upside down' of old Russia was one of the essential elements of Tolstoy's greatness as a
writer. However wrong or reactionary his political and other
opinions about this development may have been, he had certainly
seen with extraordinary clarity the changes wrought in the various
strata of society by this transformation of old Russia and seen
them in motion, in all their mobility, never as an established condition, as a static, rigid state.

Let us consider the figure of Oblonski in *Anna Karenina.* Tolstoy shows him, not as a naturalistically conceived landowner-bureaucrat who has reached a certain level of capitalist development; what he shows is the increasing degree of capitalist transformation as it affects Oblonski's own personal life. As a human type, Oblonski is much more of an old-world country squire, who much prefers a comfortable, leisurely, broad foundation for a life of ease and pleasure to a however brilliant career at court, in the administration, or in the army. That is why his metamorphosis into a half-capitalist, capitalistically-corrupted type is so interesting. Oblonski's officialdom has purely material motives : on the income of his estates alone he can no longer live the life he wants to live.   The transition to closer ties with capitalism (a seat on a board of directors, etc.) is the natural consequence of his evolution, the natural widening of the new parasitic foundations of his life. On this basis the old pleasure-loving outlook of the landowner evolves in Oblonski into a superficially good-natured, superficially epicurean Liberalism.   He takes over from a modern *bourgeois* world-view all that can ideologically justify and support his undisturbed enjoyment of life. But he still remains the old country gentleman when he instinctively despises the ruthless place-seeking of his colleagues-in-office and interprets and practises the Liberal 'laissez-faire' in his own good-humouredly egoistic way as 'live and let live,' 'après-moi le déluge,' and the like.

But what is decisive for the difference between Tolstoy's last principles of composition and the great realists of the early nineteenth century is that the social formations, institutions and the like are much more 'finished,' lifeless, inhuman and machinelike in Tolstoy than they ever were in either Balzac or Stendhal. The essential reason for this conception springs from the very fountain-head of Tolstoy's genius : that he regards society from the viewpoint of the exploited peasantry. In Balzac's world, too, the social and political institutions are transformed into militant mutual relationships solely for the representatives of the classes immediately participating in the struggle for power; for the plebeian social groups these institutions, too, are a 'finished' world, complete in itself and confronting them with machinelike apathy. Only the gigantic figure of Vautrin rises up to fight, with changing fortunes, a battle against the powers of the state; the other criminals lead a miserable existence in the pores of society and the police confronts them as an impersonal and irresistible force. Naturally this applies even more to the peasants and the lower middle class.

Hence, needless to say it is obvious that Tolstoy, who regarded the world from the angle of the Russian peasant, could not but have a similar conception of society and the state.

But this does not completely explain the attitude of Tolstoy to all these problems.   For even the members of the ruling class take up a different attitude to state and social institutions in Tolstoy and in Balzac. Tolstoy's characters, even if they belong to the upper classes, regard these institutions as a 'finished' objectivized world in itself. The reasons for this are obvious enough. The first of them was the character of Tsarist autocracy, which permitted intervention by individuals in social and political events only in the form of intrigue, corruption, backstairs influence—or revolt. No one of any high intellectual and moral quality could regard the Tsarist state as something in which he had a part, not even to the extent to which the characters of Balzac and Stendhal could do so in respect of the several states of their time. This 'finished,' this dead quality of the Tsarist state and its social institutions assumed ever greater rigidity in Tolstoy's writings, running parallel in this with the increasing estrangement between the forces of the state and the life of Russian society. From the remote distance of the historic past single figures still protrude into Tolstoy's world, figures of whom he thinks that they might possibly still have some influence over the state. Such is old Prince Bolkonski in *War and Peace*. But even he has retired, angry and disappointed, to his estates and the career of his son already consists of nothing but a chain of disappointments, a progressive destruction of the illusion that a decent and gifted man might actively participate in the military or political life of Tsarist Russia. This chain of disillusionment is shown by Tolstoy not merely as the individual destiny of Andrey Bolkonski or Pierre Bezukhov. On the contrary it very clearly reflects the ideological repercussions in Tsarist Russia of the French revolution and of the Napoleonic period, i.e. those human and psychological motives, those human and psychological conflicts, which drove the flower of the Russian nobility of the time to the Decembrist insurrection. Whether Pierre Bezukhov's road would have led to such a consummation is a point left open by Tolstoy. But the fact that for some length of time Tolstoy considered the plan of writing a novel about the Decembrists shows that the perspective was at least not foreign to his conception of such aristocratic rebels.

True, the political and social world, as Tolstoy saw it in his youth and early manhood, was a fairly loose structure. The semi-patriarchal form of bondage existing in the world of *War and Peace* gave elbow-room enough for free movement, for independence and autonomy in the local and personal sphere. One need only think of the life led by the independent country squires, the activities of the partisans and the like. There can be no doubt that Tolstoy observed and reproduced these traits with complete historical fidelity. But the eyes with which he regarded them were themselves conditioned by the level of his own development, and by the stage reached in the evolution of Russian society at the time when he wrote these books. With the transformations brought about by historical development and hence with the change in Tolstoy's views on the state and on society, his manner of presentation changes too. His *The Cossacks* and other early Caucasian stories show, in their central conception of society, traits very similar to those found in *War and Peace,* while the late and unfinished *Hadji Murat,* although related to the previous in subject, has a much firmer structure, with less opportunities for private human activities.

The driving force in this transformation of reality was the growth of capitalism. But in order to understand Tolstoy's world it is very important to see clearly that capitalism in the form in which it emerged in Russia, was—in Lenin's words—an Asiatic, and 'Octobrist' capitalism.

This form of capitalist development aggravated even further the social conditions unpropitious to art and literature and increased the deadness and rigidity of the resulting social formations. What Marx had in his time said of German developments applied no less to the Russia of Tolstoy's later years : "In all other spheres we are tormented . . . not only by the development of capitalist production but also by the lack of its development; side by side with modern troubles we are oppressed by many inherited troubles arising from the survival of ancient and antiquated methods of production with their accompaniment of out-of-date social and political conditions. We suffer not only from the living but also from the dead."

Precisely because Tolstoy's immediate attention was directed mainly towards describing the upper classes, he expressed in the most vivid and plastic fashion this 'Asiatic' character of nascent Russian capitalism and its tendency not to destroy or eliminate the worst aspects of an autocracy already superseded by historical development but merely to adapt them to the requirements of capitalist interests. In *Anna Karenina* Tolstoy already created

superb types showing this 'capitalization' and corresponding bureau-
cratization of the Russian nobility. Here is Oblonski, in whom
Tolstoy has painted a wonderfully rich and subtly modelled picture of the Liberal tendencies at work within this social group;
here, also, we find the type of the modern aristocrat in the person
of Vronski. Vronski changes his mode of life as a result of his
passion for Anna; he gives up his military career and develops
into a capitalist landowner, who transforms the traditional husbandry of his estates into a capitalist enterprise, champions Liberalism and progress in the political counsels of the nobility and
attempts to revive the 'independence' of the nobles' way of life
on a capitalist basis. Thus the effect, from the social point of view,
of an accidental passion is to induce in Vronski a typical evolution
proper to his class. To round off the picture, there is a third
character, the type of the already completely bureaucratized, reactionary, obscurantist, hypocritical and empty administrative official
in the person of Karenin. Capitalist division of labour increasingly
permeates all human relationships, it becomes the way of life, the
decisive determinant of thoughts and emotions; Tolstoy depicts
with an increasingly bitter irony how in this world of divided
labour human beings are transformed into parts of an inhuman
machine. This division of labour is a most suitable instrument
for the oppression and exploitation of the working masses and
Tolstoy hates it precisely because it is an instrument of oppression
and exploitation. But as the great and universal genius that he is,
Tolstoy presents this *whole* process as it affects *all* classes of the
population; he reveals its inner dialectic, the way in which this
capitalist-bureaucratic division of labour not only dehumanizes and
transforms into mere malignant robots the human beings (even
those of the ruling class) which it has enmeshed, but also how this
whole process turns against these same human beings at every
point in their lives, whenever they attempt to defend their own
elementary vital interests or manifest a remnant of humanity still
surviving within themselves.

An instance of this is the wonderful scene between Ivan Ilyich
and his doctor. Ivan Ilyich has become the complete bureaucrat,
a paragon of a judge, who strips his cases of all humanity with
consummate bureaucratic skill and who has turned himself into
a perfectly functioning cog in the great Tsarist machinery of opres-
sion. In vain do the accused, caught in the wheels of this machine,
plead the special, the human implications of their case—the expert
judge calmly and politely shepherds them back to the path of the

paragraphs on which they are crushed by the juggernaut of the law in accordance with the requirements of the Tsarist system. But now Ivan Ilyich himself is dangerously ill and wants to find out from his doctor what his condition and expectations are. The doctor, however, is just such another superior bureaucrat, just such another perfect piece of machinery as Ivan Ilyich himself; he treats Ivan Ilyich exactly as Ivan Ilyich treats the accused who come before him. "All this was exactly the same as what Ivan Ilyich had himself so brilliantly performed in front of the accused a thousand times. The summing-up of the doctor was just as brilliant and he looked as triumphantly, even cheerfully, at the accused over his spectacles . . . The doctor looked at him severely with one eye, over his spectacles, as if to say : 'Prisoner, if you will not restrict yourself to answering the questions put to you, I shall be constrained to order your removal from this courtroom.' " What is so horrible in the death of Ivan Ilyich is precisely that he is confronted with this sort of rigidity in every human contact, when in the face of approaching death he first becomes aware of an urge to establish human relationships with human beings and overcome the futile senselessness of his life.

The development of Russian society deepens the double hideousness, an autocracy combined with ' Asiatic ' capitalism. As this objective development drives inexorably on towards the revolution of 1905, Tolstoy's hatred and contempt of the dehumanized nature of such a society grows rapidly. In Karenin's figure this dehumanization is already put before us in completed form. Karenin and his wife are at a party when Karenin becomes aware of the nascent love between Anna and Vronski. He prepares to have it out with her. ". . . And everything that he would now say to his wife took clear shape in Alexey Andreyevich's head. Thinking over what he would say, he somewhat regretted that he should have to use his time and mental faculties for domestic consumption, with so little to show for it; but nevertheless the form and train of thought of the speech he would make shaped itself clearly and distinctly, like an official report."

In Tolstoy's later works, particularly in *Resurrection,* his hatred of this inhumanity has deepened. The main reason for this is that in his later years Tolstoy saw much more clearly the connection between the dehumanization of the state machine and the oppression and exploitation of the common people. In Karenin's bureaucratic careerism this tendency was present only implicitly, in the complete indifference with which Karenin, concerned only with his own career, decides the fate of millions of human beings as if it were a mere piece of paper. (From the point of view of Tolstoy's own development it is interesting to note that in some passages of *War and Peace,* e.g. in the figure of Bilibin, he still treats this inhumanity which manifests itself in a formal-bureaucratic attitude to all problems, with a certain good-natured irony.) But in *Resurrection* he already brings the whole inhuman machinery into relation with the sufferings of its victims and gives a comprehensive, many-sided and accurate picture of the machinery of oppression in the Tsarist form of capitalist state—a picture nothing comparable with which can be found in the *bourgeois* literature of any country. Here the ruling class is already shown as a gang of vicious imbeciles who carry out their functions either with unsuspecting stupidity or malicious careerism and who are by now nothing but cogs in a horrible machine of oppression. Perhaps never since Swift's *Gulliver's Travels* has capitalist society been depicted with such powerful irony. As Tolstoy grew older, his presentation of characters belonging to the upper classes increasingly took this satirical, ironical form. The representatives of the ruling class show an increasing resemblance, for all their polite and polished exterior, to the stinking Yahoos of Jonathan Swift.

The fact that Tolstoy depicts the specific Tsarist form of capitalist machinery detracts nothing from the universal validity of the picture—on the contrary the resultant concrete, full-blooded, lifelike quality enhances this universal validity, for both the hideous tyranny of the oppressors and the utter helplessness of the victims is deeply and universally true. The specific form in which this tyranny manifests itself at the hands of the Tsarist bureaucracy is merely a concrete aggravation of its universal qualities. For instance, Tolstoy's Prince Nekhlyudov intervenes in the interest of an imprisoned woman revolutionary and for this purpose goes to see one of the Yahoos who wears the uniform of a general. Because the general's wife would like to have an *affaire* with Nekhlyudov, the revolutionary is released. "As they were starting, a footman met Nekhlyudov in the ante-room and handed him a note from Mariette : '*Pour vous faire plaisir, j'ai agi tout à fait contre mes principes et j'ai intercédé auprès de mon mari pour votre protégée. Il se trouve que cette personne peut être relâchée immédiatement. Mon mari a écrit au commandant. Venez donc* disinterestedly. *Je vous attends. M.*' 'Think of that,' said Nekhlyudov to the lawyer. 'Why, this is dreadful. A woman has been kept in solitary confinement for seven months and then turns out to

be quite innocent and a word suffices to get her released.' 'That
is what always happens.' " This is of course no isolated instance
in *Resurrection*. Tolstoy shows with an extraordinary fertility of
imagination, how the fate of a great many people immediately
depend entirely on such personal matters of chance, on such arbitrary personal interests of some member of the ruling class. But
the sum of all these arbitrary happenings and actions constitutes
a clear and coherent system; through all these chances and accidents the main purpose of the dehumanized machinery emerges—
it is the protection, by any and every means, even the most brutal,
of the private property owned by the ruling classes.

Thus Tolstoy in his later years created a hideous 'finished' world
of increasing horror. The pores of society in which human beings
could act with some measure of independence have been gradually
stopped up. Nekhlyudov can no longer harbour any illusions regarding life on the land, regarding a compromise between the
interests of the landowners and the interests of the peasants, such
as Konstantin Levin could still harbour, even though in a tormenting, problematic form. Nor does the private safety-valve of family
life, the possibility of an escape like that of Nikolai Rostov or Levin
exist any longer for Tolstoy in his later years. From the *Kreutzer
Sonata* onwards he sees love and marriage, too, in its modern
form; he sees in them all the specific forms of lies, hypocrisy and
dehumanization, which are brought about by capitalism. He once
said to Gorki : "Men must suffer earthquakes, epidemics, dreadful
diseases and all the torments of the soul, but the worst tragedy
in life was at all times, is now and ever will be the tragedy of the
bedroom." Here, as nearly everywhere else, Tolstoy expresses
his thoughts in a timeless form; but when he gives such thoughts
artistic expression he is incomparably more concrete and historical.
His later *descriptions* of the 'tragedy of the bedroom' may have
been conceived as documents of his ascetic philosophy, but his
earlier *artistic presentations* of the problem burst through this
abstract-dogmatic frame and depict the specifically capitalist
hideousness of modern *bourgeois* love, marriage, prostitution and
two-fold exploitation of women.

Where is there in such a world any room for action? The world
Tolstoy sees and depicts is to an increasing degree a world in which
decent people can no longer find any opportunity for action. As
capitalistically developing Russia, despite the 'Asiatic' character
of its capitalism, approaches ever closer to the normal forms of
fully developed capitalism, the material of life on which Tolstoy

draws must also approach ever closer to the material of life, the literary mirroring of which led to the naturalist disintegration of the great school of realism in western Europe. There was, of course, one objective possibility of action in the Russia depicted by Tolstoy : but only for democratic and socialist revolutionaries, and to depict such action was precluded for Tolstoy by his philosophy. When together with the strong and hopeful features of the approaching peasant revolt he also gives poetic expression to its half-heartedness, its backwardness, its hesitations and lack of courage, he leaves his characters no other possibility save the old dilemma of capitulation or flight. And we have seen that such a capitulation must of necessity take increasingly infamous and inhuman forms, and we have also seen that even the possibilities of flight are progressively narrowed for Tolstoy by the objective evolution of society and his own deepening poetical and philosophical insight into the structure of the society thus born.

It is true that Tolstoy also preached the need for good deeds, for individual non-participation in sin and the like and wrote many things in which reality, despite all the magnificent accuracy of detail, is manipulated in such a way as to provide evidence for the possibility and efficacity of such good deeds (*The Forged Coupon*, etc.). But the poetic greatness of the older Tolstoy manifests itself precisely in the fact that when he *writes,* he cannot help presenting the true circumstances of real life with inexorable fidelity, irrespective of whether they corroborate or refute his own favourite ideas. For instance, the impossibility of an active life in this world of which we have just spoken, is clearly expressed in *The Living Corpse* by Fedia into whose mouth Tolstoy, without mentioning his own favourite theory at all, even as a possibility, puts these words : "A man born in the sphere in which I was born has only three possibilities to choose from. Either he can be an official, earn money and increase the filth in which we live—that disgusted me, or perhaps I didn't know how to do it, but above all it disgusted me. Or else he can fight this filth, but for that he must be a hero and I have never been that. Or finally and thirdly he tries to forget, goes to the dogs, takes to drink and song—that is what I have done and this is to what it has brought me."

In Nekhlyudov's figure Tolstoy did of course attempt to present the individual good deed itself. But his inexorable truthfulness produces a quite different, bitterly ironical result. Only because Nekhlyudov himself belongs to the very ruling class he hates and despises, only because in his own social sphere he is regarded as a good-natured fool, as a harmless eccentric bitten by the bug of philanthropy, only because he can make use of old family and other connections, can he accomplish his 'good deeds' at all. And objectively all these good deeds are mere insignificant trifles; they are as nothing in comparison with the horrible inexorability of the machine, and they fit easily into the amorous or ambitious intrigues of those who are parts of the machine. Subjectively Nekhlyudov himself is forced—often unwillingly, often full of self-contempt, but sometimes also yielding to a temptation—to wear the mask of the courtier in order to be able to accomplish at least a few of his 'individual good deeds.' And where Nekhlyudov draws the Tolstoyan conclusions from the earlier critical vacillations of Konstantin Levin, he is faced with the hatred and distrust of the peasants who regard every 'generous' proposal of their landlord as a new cunning attempt to deceive them and take advantage of them.

Tolstoy thus pictures a world in which the relationships of human beings to each other and to society approach very closely the relationships depicted by western post-1848 realism. How is it then that Tolstoy, in spite of this necessary link with the newer realism, is yet a great realist of the old type and a heir to the tradition of the old great realists?

6.

The crucial difference of style between the old and the new realism lies in the characterization, i.e. in the conception of the typical. The older realism presented the typical by concentrating the essential determinants of a great social trend, embodying them in the passionate strivings of individuals, and placing these personages into extreme situations, situations devised in such a way as to demonstrate the social trend in its extreme consequences and implications. It is clear that such a method of presentation was possible only in conjunction with a plot full of movement and variety. Such a plot is not, however, an arbitrary formal principle, a mere technical vehicle which the writer can handle according to his pleasure or his ability. The plot is a poetic form of reflecting reality, i.e. that essential pattern which the relationships of human beings to each other, to society and to nature form in real life. The poetic reflection of reality cannot be mechanical or photographic. We have already pointed out that poetic concentration, the poetic form of reflecting reality can move in more

than one direction and follow more than one trend of development and that as a result it can either surpass or fall short of
reality in depicting the animated surface of social existence. We
have also pointed out that the static presentation of average characters in surroundings conceived as 'finished' must of necessity cause
literature to fall short of reality.

This has been the fate of the realist writers after 1848. The lack
of action, the mere description of *milieu,* the substitution of the
average for the typical, although essential symptoms of the decline
of realism, have their origins in real life and it is from there that
they crept into literature. As writers grew more and more unable
to participate in the life of capitalism as their own sort of life, they
grew less and less capable of producing real plots and action. It
is no accident that the great writers of this period, who reproduced
important features of social evolution more or less correctly, almost
without exception wrote novels without plots, while most of the
novels of this time which had intricate and colourful plots were
full enough of sound and fury, but signified nothing so far as social
content was concerned. It is no accident that the few significant
characters produced by this literature were almost still-life-like,
static portraits of average people, while the figures pretending to
above-the-average stature in the literature of this period could not
be anything but caricature-like pseudo-heroes, empty phrase-
mongers in a grandiloquent and hollow opposition to capitalism or
an even hollower hypocritical vindication of it.

Flaubert recognized early and clearly the difficulties besetting the
writer in this period. During the writing of *Madame Bovary,*
he complained that the book was not interesting enough : ' I have
filled fifty pages without recording a single event; it is a continuous
picture of a *bourgeois* life and of a non-active love, a love all the
more difficult to depict as it is both timid and deep, but alas !
without internal crises, for my *monsieur* has a placid temperament.
I have had something similar in the first part : my husband
loves his wife somewhat in the same manner as my lover—they
are two mediocrities in the same surroundings, who must nevertheless be distinguished from each other . . .'

Flaubert, as a true artist, consistently followed his road to the
end. He attempted to lend artistic colour and movement to his
dreary, dull scene by descriptive differentiation and an even more
subtle *milieu*-painting and psychological analysis of his average
people. This attempt was doomed to fail. For the average man
is mediocre precisely because the social contradictions which

objectively determine his existence are not given their supreme expression by him and in him, but on the contrary mutually blunt each other and seem to level each other out to a superficial equilibrium. This produces an immobility, a monotony in the essential problems of artistic presentation, which Flaubert admitted with severe self-criticism, but attempted to overcome by mere technical artifices. But the increased refinement of artistic technique only created a new problem, which Flaubert also admitted at times : a contradiction between the subtly artistic presentation of the subject itself and the dreary tedium of the subject. The newer western literature, Flaubert's much less gifted successors, trod the same path, hanging ever more magnificent purple mantles woven of words around the shoulders of ever more lifeless, ever more mass-produced lay-figures.

There can be no doubt that the development of Russian society and of Tolstoy's philosophy, which we have just described very briefly, drove Tolstoy in the same direction, i.e. towards making his characters somewhat more mediocre, more like the average. The rigid, "finished" world in which they lived, the impossibility of living full and purposeful lives in which their being could manifest itself in appropriate action, had to bring these characters to a certain extent within the range of the average and deprive them of some of the typicality which the characters of Balzac or Stendhal possessed through the colourful flurry of action in which they could develop their qualities.

This problem of style faced not only Tolstoy but every prominent Russian writer of the time. The Russian literature of the second half of the nineteenth century marks a new phase in realism as a whole, not only in Tolstoy's writings. The common problem of style facing all these writers was determined by a reality most unfavourable to the portrayal of passionate characters and even more completely permeated by the social trends which in western Europe had given rise to naturalism and the practice of portraying the average instead of the typical. They did their best to find artistic means enabling them to swim against the current; to find, even in a world such as the one in which they lived, that extreme expression of clearly revealed social determinants which makes possible a true typicality, far beyond the merely average.

The great achievement of the Russian realists of this period was that they succeeded in finding such possibilities and giving their characters a typicality mirroring all the social contradictions of their time. The primary, essential means of transcending the average is to create extreme situations in the midst of a humdrum reality, situations which yet do not burst through the narrow framework of this reality so far as social content is concerned, and which, by their extreme character, sharpen rather than dull the edge of social contradictions.

I have already mentioned Goncharov's *Oblomov* and contrasted its qualities with the mediocrity of the contemporary western realists. In this example it is obvious that it is precisely the extreme exaggeration of a trait in Oblomov (which if treated naturalistically would result in the dreariest, most humdrum average, i.e. his torpid inactivity) that provides the starting-point for this magnificently realistic presentation. By this ' exaggeration ' all the mental conflicts engendered by Oblomov's sloth are thrown into bold relief on the one hand and on the other hand it is thus made possible to show this trait in Oblomov against a background of wide social implications.

In all concrete details of poetic presentation Tolstoy has nothing in common with Goncharov's method, but he shares with him the great historical principle of overcoming the unpoetic nature of a society ever more strongly permeated by capitalism. Tolstoy very often tells stories which on the surface contain not a single trait going beyond the everyday average. But he builds these stories on the foundation of situations, makes his events centre around situations which expose with elemental force the lies and hypocrisy of everyday life. I again refer to the admirable *The Death of Ivan Ilyich*. It is precisely because Tolstoy here presents the life of a commonplace, average bureaucrat that he can, by sharply contrasting this drearily meaningless life with the stark fact of imminent and inevitable death, put before us all the features of middle-class life in a *bourgeois* society. In its content the story never oversteps the limits of the commonplace and average and yet gives a complete picture of life as a whole and is not commonplace or average in any of its moments.

It is in this connection that the difference in the function of detail in the works of Tolstoy and in those of the western realists should be dealt with. Tolstoy always gives a dazzling mass of brilliantly observed small detail; but his presentation never lapses into the empty triviality of his western contemporaries. Tolstoy devotes much attention to describing the physical appearance of his characters and the physical processes evoked in them by psychological influences, but yet never lapses into the psycho-physiological pedestrianism so prevalent in the writings of his contemporaries.

In Tolstoy details are always elements of the plot. The necessary result of this method of composition is that the plot is always dissected into small, apparently insignificant sections which follow each other minute by minute and in which these details play a decisive part; they provide, in fact, the vehicles for the plot. If the extreme situation is externally as well as intrinsically extreme, as in Balzac, then the plot can consist of a dramatic chain of great and decisive crises which the writer can present with a dramatic concentration sometimes bordering on the drama. But Tolstoy's extreme situations are extreme only intrinsically and intensively, not externally. And this intensity can be conveyed only step by step, minute by minute, in a ceaseless play of moods in which the dramatic fluctuation of the contradictions of life ripple under the motionless surface of the commonplace. The meticulous detail with which the death of Ivan Ilyich is described, is not the naturalist description of a process of physical decay—as in the suicide of Madame Bovary—but a great internal drama in which approaching death, precisely through all its horrible details, tears the veils one after the other from the meaningless life of Ivan Ilyich and exposes this life in all its appalling bleakness. But bleak and devoid of all inner movement as this life is, the process of its exposure is most exciting and vivid in its artistic presentation.

Naturally this is not the only method Tolstoy used in his writings. He created many characters and situations which are extreme even by the standards of the old realists, i.e. externally. Where his material permitted, Tolstoy was even inclined to favour such themes. His artistic temperament revolted against depicting the merely commonplace, as was so widely accepted in western literature. Wherever Tolstoy found it possible to create extreme situations of this kind, he did so quite in the manner of the old realists. The hero who acts extremely, is only consistently following to its end the same path which the others tread hesitatingly, half-heartedly or hypocritically. The character and fate of Anna Karenina is an instance of this type of Tolstoyan creation. Anna Karenina lives—with a husband whom she does not love and whom she has married for conventional reasons, and with a lover whom she loves passionately—a life just like the life of other women of her own sphere. The only difference is that she follows this road consistently to the end, ruthlessly drawing every conclusion and not permitting insoluble contradictions to blunt their edges in the banality of everyday life. Tolstoy stresses more than once that Anna is no exceptional case, that she is doing the same as other women do. But the average society lady, like Vronski's mother, is nevertheless scandalized by her conduct : ' No, you can say what you like, she was a bad woman. What sort of desperate passions are these ! Just to show that she was something special ! ' The average *bourgeois* simply cannot understand the tragedies which arise from the contradictions of *bourgeois* life itself and which cannot become tragic for him personally because he is too cowardly and base not to find a humiliating compromise as a way out of every situation.

Almost exactly as Anna Karenina is judged by the women of her sphere, is Balzac's Viscomtesse de Beauséant judged by the average aristocrats of her circle. But the similarity of the basic artistic conception of these two characters, the similarity of the deep social truth revealed in the portrayal of an extreme individual passion, provides an opportunity to show up clearly the great difference in the methods of Balzac and Tolstoy, those greatest representatives of two different periods of realism. Balzac depicts with the greatest dramatic-novelistic concentration the two catastrophes in the loves of Madame de Beauséant (in *Le Père Goriot* and *La Femme Abandonnée*). But he concentrates his interest on these great catastrophes. When Mme. de Beauséant's first romance collapses, Balzac describes nothing but the tragic turning-point of the story. Although in the second case he does describe in some detail the birth of a new love, the rupture and catastrophe again occur with dramatic ' suddenness,' although, as ever with Balzac, with great inner truth. Tolstoy, on the contrary, depicts in greatest detail every stage in the development of the love between Anna and Vronski, from their first meeting to the tragic catastrophe. He is much more epic than Balzac, in the classical sense of the word. The great turning-points, the catastrophic crises in the destiny of the lovers are always given a wide and broad epic background and only very rarely appear as dramatically concentrated catastrophes. Tolstoy stresses this epic character, in addition, by the even less dramatic and catastrophic parallel story of the destinies of Levin and Kitty.

In this novel, too, the inimitably realistic treatment of detail is an important medium of Tolstoy's creative method. He reproduces the attractions and estrangements in this love as a continuous, although clearly articulated process, and the junctions at which the changes occur are most distinctly underlined. But as these points of junction can rarely be dramatic in the external sense of the word, as they might often pass unnoticed if regarded externally, and yet must be shown as real turning-points, they are given prominence by picking some detail out of the flow of mental processes, some apparently small incident in the mental and physical life of the characters, and accenting it so that it acquires a pointed dramatic significance. Thus Anna Karenina, when after the ball in Moscow, she tries to escape from Vronski's love for her and her own budding love for him, looks out of the window of the railway carriage at the St. Petersburg station after her nightly conversation with Vronski, and suddenly becomes aware of the fact that Karenina has unusually prominent ears. In the same way, at a later time, in the period of the dramatic climax to the dying love between Anna and Vronski, after many bitter and angry quarrels which until then had always ended in a reconciliation, the hopeless rupture between the lovers is revealed by an apparently insignificant detail : ' She lifted her cup, with her little finger held apart, and put it to her lips. After drinking a few sips she glanced at him and by his expression she saw clearly that he was repelled by her hand and her gesture and the sound made by her lips.'

Such details are ' dramatic ' in the most profound sense of the word : they are sensually visible and vehemently experienced objectivations of decisive emotional turning-points in the lives of people. That is why they have none of the triviality found in the ever-so-faithfully observed details in the writings of the newer writers—details which are merely well-observed but play no real part in the story. But Tolstoy's specific manner of concentration enables him to insert such internally dramatic scenes in the broad, calm flow of his narration, enlivening and articulating the flow without hindering its broad, calm movement.

This renewal of the original epic character of the novel, after the dramatic-novelistic stage of its development in the early nineteenth century (as represented by Balzac), necessarily follows from the nature of the life-material which Tolstoy had to work on and out of the essential traits of which he crystallized his principles of form. We have already discussed the reasons which had compelled Tolstoy to keep, on the whole, within the outer framework of the commonplace, but within this framework there is one more new possibility open to Tolstoy in addition to those already described : his specific method of extreme intensification, which brings out the extreme possibilities latent in his characters. Balzac presents the extreme as the actual pursuit of some course to its end, as a tragic realisation of extreme possibilities which represent the contradictions of capitalist society in the purest form. He was still in the position to make this pursuit-to-the-end of extreme possibilities the typical fate of his heroes, precisely because, as we have already shown, his heroes were not as yet living in a 'finished' world—their world was one in which they could still play active parts in the great drama of society. For Tolstoy, as we have also shown, this possibility no longer existed. But because everything he wrote was set against a background representing an important phase in the history of mankind, and was part of a drama of world-wide historical importance and because this great social drama formed the backdrop to the private fortunes of all his characters, he, too, had to make the purest, most extreme, form of social contradictions the focal point of his presentations.

But only in the form of possibilities. This new and specific form of presenting the great social contradictions follows from that specific attitude of Tolstoy to revolutionary developments in Russia, which Lenin analysed so brilliantly. Like the works of the older great realists, so Tolstoy's works mirror a great social and historical change; but, regarded from the viewpoint of the characters depicted, they do so indirectly. The characters of the older realists were direct representatives of the motive forces and decisive trends and contradictions of the *bourgeois* revolution. They represented these trends in immediate form, and the connection between their individual passions and the problems of the *bourgeois* revolution was an immediate one; characters like Goethe's Werther or Stendhal's Julien Sorel show very clearly this direct connection between individual passion, social necessity, and the general representative significance of just such individual passions. The specific character, so well analyzed by Lenin, of the *bourgeois* revolution in Russia, and Tolstoy's own attitude to the peasant problem, that central question of that *bourgeois* revolution, make such direct presentation in the manner of the old *bourgeois* realists impossible for him. We know with what profound understanding and generosity Tolstoy has presented the Russian peasant. But his own specific attitude to the whole peasant movement had the necessary result that the central theme of his main works was always the reflection of the development of the peasant movement in the lives of that ruling class, who were the owners and beneficiaries of the ground-rents.

This choice of subject again forms a socially and historically necessary link between Tolstoy and the newer realism. After the end of *bourgeois*-revolutionary movements in central and western Europe, after the shifting of the core of social conflict to the clash between *bourgeoisie* and working class, the *bourgeois* realists could present only indirect echoes of this central problem of the *bourgeois* society of their time. If they were writers of talent, they observed and described the emotional reflexes, the human problems and realisations arising from social conditions. But as most of them were unable to understand the social problem which was the objective basis of the human conflicts they described, they unconsciously separated these human conflicts from the social basis with which they were objectively connected. Hence they were forced—again without knowing or wishing it—to leave the most decisive social determinants out of their plots and characters and place these, without any serious historical background, into a merely 'sociologically' or impressionistically-psychologically conceived *milieu*. This separation from the historical background created a dilemma for the newer realists : they could either make their characters commonplace; average men and women of *bourgeois* everyday life, in whom the great objective contradictions of social life appeared in blunted form and often paled into unrecognizability; or else, if they wanted to transcend this humdrum average, they could resort to a purely individual intensification of personal passions, thus making their characters hollow and eccentric or—if a psychological explanation was attempted—pathological figures.

In connection with the brief analysis of Anna Karenina's figure we have already pointed out how Tolstoy's method of presenting passions by their extreme poetic intensification overcame this dilemma. What is outside the average in Anna Karenina's figure and fate is not some individually pathological exaggeration of a personal passion, but the clear manifestation of the social contradictions inherent in *bourgeois* love and marriage. When Anna Karenina breaks through the limits of the commonplace, she merely brings to the surface in tragically clear intensification the contradictions latently present (although their edges may be blunted) in every *bourgeois* love and marriage.

It is not too difficult to understand why Tolstoy's presentation of passion and personal fate could not always take the form it has in *Anna Karenina*. The presentation of the men and women of the ruling classes and their destinies, was to an increasing extent and with increasing consciousness conceived by Tolstoy as a function of their connection with the exploitation of the peasantry. The poetic starting-point in the presentation of each character by Tolstoy was the question : in what way was their life based on the receipt of ground-rents and on the exploitation of the peasants and what problems did this social basis produce in their lives. As a truly great poet and worthy successor to the greatest realists of the past, Tolstoy saw these interconnections in all their intricacy and was never satisfied with the uncovering of the mere immediate link between exploiter and exploited. His genius as a realist expresses itself rather in the fact that he sees the whole intricate life of each character of the ruling class as an integral whole and reveals as the foundation of this unity the character's social position as an exploiter, as a parasite. In individual traits which on the surface seem to have nothing to do with exploitation—in what his characters think of the most abstract problems, in the fashions in which they make love and in many other such things, Tolstoy demonstrates with admirable realist artistry—which instead of merely analyzing and commenting, renders palpably obvious the true existential interconnections—the link between such traits in his characters and the parasitic nature of their existence.

This extraordinary concreteness of poetic vision enables Tolstoy to avoid all stereotyped presentation of either the social foundations of life or their reflections in men's souls. He carefully distinguishes between large and small landowners, between those who cultivate their land themselves and the absentee landlords living on their ground rents, between traditional and capitalist husbandry, between landowners and such bureaucrats or intellectuals who are landowners by origin and still live wholly or in part on ground rents but no longer live on the land. Tolstoy sees very clearly that the same social causes can produce very different human reactions and shape very different human destinies in different individuals, according to the differences in their natural inclinations, education, and the like.

The profound realism of Tolstoy's world thus rests on his ability to present an extremely intricate and differentiated world and yet to make it quite clear, by poetical means, that underlying all this intricate diversity of manifestations there is a coherent, unified foundation to all human destinies. This connection between all the human traits and destinies of his characters and the great social and historical background raises Tolstoy's realism far above the level of the commonplace. He has the same richness and the same natural, organic, non-artificial unity between man and fate which is found in the old realists and none of the meagreness smothered in a spate of superficial and unconnected detail that is characteristic of the new realists.

Tolstoy devised a concrete, creative method of overcoming the unpropitiousness of his essential life-material, the life lived by the parasitic landowners in capitalistically developing Russia; this method was to create types based on the mere possibility of an extreme attitude, an extreme passion, an extreme fate. The contradictions on which the life of these ground-rent-owning parasites rested, could not, given such human material, find expression in directly extreme action; and could do so the less, the closer their connection was with exploitation as the decisive human relationship. But it is precisely this relationship between exploiter and exploited and its echoes in the lives of the exploiting class which is one of Tolstoy's main themes. In his essay on art Tolstoy declares 'dissatisfaction with life' to be the characteristic trait of the newer art. This applies to his own work as much as to any other, but in his writings this 'dissatisfaction with life' is always based on the fact that the life of a parasite, of an exploiter can never permit him to be in harmony with himself and with others, unless he is a complete fool or a complete scoundrel.

It is this 'dissatisfaction with life' which Tolstoy translates into reality by the method of 'extreme possibilities.' In seeking to bring harmony into their lives, eliminate the conflict between their opinions and their actual way of life, and find a satisfactory occupation for themselves in the community, his Bezukhov and Bolkonski, Levin and Nekhlyudov and others strikingly expose the contradiction between the social basis of their lives and their desire for harmony and an adequate occupation.

This contradiction drives them from one extreme to the other. As Tolstoy, on the one hand, chooses subjectively honest representatives of this class as his heroes and, on the other hand, cannot and does not wish to bring them to the point of rupture with their own class, the vacillations due to the contradictions referred to remain within the sphere of the ruling class. 'Extreme possibilities' crop up and are earnestly considered; serious steps are taken towards their translation into reality; but before the decisive step is taken, contrary tendencies appear, which are in part nothing but the same contradictions on a higher level, in part leanings that drag the heroes down to a compromise with reality. This produces a ceaseless movement in which all the important determinants of this life find expression in all their richness, but which very rarely leads to a really dramatic crisis, to a clean break with the previous phase. The lifelike quality, the inner richness of the characters rests on the fact that such extreme possibilities arise again and again, that the thorn of the conflict between social existence and consciousness never ceases to prick.   But the movement is always almost a continuous circle or at best a spiral, never the rapid dramatic upheaval we see in the fortunes of Balzac's and Stendhal's heroes.

Every 'extreme possibility' always reveals some stark contradiction between social being and consciousness and is always closely bound up with the great problems of Russian social evolution, although not always in a directly visible form.   For this reason the vain searchings and gropings of these heroes, their inactivity or abrupt abandonment of intentions scarcely born, never degenerate into the triviality and banality which inescapably awaits the heroes of western naturalism in their purely private destinies.   It is because Tolstoy conceives his problems so broadly, because he follows the echoes of social conflicts deep into the innermost recesses of personal life, that his world is so rich and full of interest.   Tolstoy makes his favourite heroes share his own misconception that a man can withdraw from public life and individually escape from participation in its guilt and vileness.   But the way Tolstoy depicts such a withdrawal and its various stages, the vacillations on the road and the deviations from it, the way in which all problems of personal life become involved in this movement—all this tends to show precisely the inescapably social quality of all personal, private, individual life.

Thus 'extreme possibilities' in Tolstoy are not *real* and sudden turning-points, but a sort of power station, a centre of attraction around which the lives of individual characters revolve.   Nevertheless, the posing of social problems on so high a level of their contradictory quality suffices to raise Tolstoy's world to a great height of realistic presentation which, however, differs considerably in its artistic methods from the great realist literature of the past.   In brief it might be said that after the dramatically-novelistic phase of Balzac's time, Tolstoy restored to the novel its original epic quality. For if the characters move to and fro within a determined and socially strictly limited sphere of life, as they do in Tolstoy, a much greater epic calm and stability can be achieved, in spite of all the movement, than was possible for Balzac.

Goethe in *Wilhelm Meister* distinguishes thus between the novel and the drama. 'In a novel it is pre-eminently mental attitudes and events that are to be presented, in the drama characters and deeds. The novel should proceed slowly and the mental attitudes of the principal character in it should by whatever means available, hold

back the progress and development of the whole.   The drama
should hurry and the character of the protagonist should urge
matters to a climax and be hampered in this.   The hero of the
novel should be a sufferer, or at least not highly active; of the
dramatic hero one demands activity and deeds.'

This definition of the novel which applied perfectly to *Wilhelm
Meister,* was in many respects no longer valid for the later *Selective
Affinities* and even less for the novels of the great French realists.
But it is not a bad description of the Tolstoyan manner.   One
should not, of course, interpret Goethe's contrasting of mental attitude and character in the sense that what he had in mind were
blurred,   outlineless   creatures,   emotionally   swayed   by, and
merging with, their *milieu.* Wilhelm Meister himself shows clearly
that this was not Goethe's idea at all.   What Goethe meant by
'mental attitude' and 'character' were differing degrees of density
and concentration in the characterization.   'Mental attitude' contrasted with 'character' thus means an almost unlimited breadth of
characterization, a great wealth of seemingly incompatible traits,
which are nevertheless welded together—by some great social trend,
by human aspirations, by the moral and spiritual self-development
of the character—into an organic and mobile unity.   Dramatic
characterization, on the other hand, means the concentration of
the essential determinants of social conflicts and contradictions in
a compressed passion which explodes in one or more catastrophes
into which all the rich material of life must be condensed.   After
what has been said, it is scarcely necessary to explain at length
how closely Tolstoy's epic works approach this Goethean ideal.

This difference between Tolstoy and the great realists of the
early nineteenth century emerges most clearly perhaps in the presentation of the moral and spiritual life, the intellectual aspect of
their characters.   One of the reasons why Tolstoy is a worthy
successor to the earlier great realists is that the presentation of
this moral and spiritual side plays a decisive part in his portrayal
of human beings.   But the manner of presentation is again all his
own and differs radically from that of the earlier realists.

In Balzac, and in many cases in Stendhal, great dialogues which
throw light on the mental make-up of the characters, are at the
same time great duels of *Weltanschauung,* in which the quintessence
of the great social problems is uncovered and which result in
dramatic decisions that determine the fate of the characters. When
Vautrin and Rastignac discuss social and moral problems, a few
such conversations rapidly following each other—and   naturally

supported by the dramatic weight of the events which provoke them and which they raise to an abstract level—lead to a complete and irrevocable change in Rastignac's whole life.

The great and important dialogues and monologues in Tolstoy can have no such function. They always illustrate, with great acumen and ruthlessness, the ' extreme possibilities ' around which the development of the hero revolves. Such are for instance the conversations of Konstantin Levin with his brother and later with Oblonski about the justification of private property and the moral and spiritual justification of that compromise between the interests of the landowners and peasants, of which Levin dreams. These conversations cannot bring about any dramatic crisis, because neither a break with the system of private property nor a transformation into a ruthless exploiter with a good conscience are within the range of Levin's social and human possibilities. But they show up with merciless sharpness the central problem, the decisive sore spot in Levin's whole way of life and world-view. They show the focal point around which all his thoughts and emotions ceaselessly revolve, irrespective of whether he loves or is loved, whether he devotes himself to science or escapes into public activities. Thus they, too, are in a more general sense turning-points in a life, but on a very high level of abstraction, turning-points of a very special kind, in which the ' extreme possibilities ' of a human life emerge most clearly, which unmistakably outline the specific make-up of the man, but nevertheless remain mere possibilities and are not transformed into deeds, into realities. And yet they are not abstract artificial possibilities, but rather the very concrete central life-problems of a well-defined character.

In Tolstoy these intellectual utterances, these manifestations of the moral and spiritual life of the characters acquire a novel and fateful significance which again constitutes a radical difference between Tolstoy and the newer realists. That the characters of these newer realists lack spiritual life and that their intellectual physiognomy is blurred and colourless, is known well enough. The reason for this is, above all, that the extinction or blunting of the great objective social contradictions in the portrayal of individuals makes it impossible to portray them on a really high spiritual and intellectual level. Conversations or monologues raised to the level of abstraction can be concrete and alive only if they express the specific abstraction of a specific social contradiction as it manifests itself in one particular person. Detached from this foundation they remain abstract inventions. It is therefore no accident that the newer realists in the western countries increasingly avoid such spiritual or intellectual manifestations or depress them to the level of the average and commonplace.

This is of course at the same time a reflection, in the sphere of thought, of that "finished" capitalist world which these writers depict. In such a "finished" world all manifestations of the average human being are increasingly transformed into a tedious, endlessly repeated routine. It goes without saying that Tolstoy, having himself to devote considerable attention to depicting just such a world, could not himself dispense with depicting this tedious routine. In *War and Peace* we already find many conversations the sole object of which is to demonstrate the boring routine which governs social life in the highest spheres. But firstly, for Tolstoy this is only one side of the world he has to show and he uses it as a foil to provide a satirical contrast, and by ironically emphasizing the machine-like character of its functioning (Tolstoy repeatedly compares such conversations with the clacking of a loom), to stress the more vital quality of other manifestations. Secondly, Tolstoy often involves characters who are outside the routine (Bezukhov, Levin, etc.) in conversations of this sort again in order that they may serve as a foil and by their 'clumsiness' damage the artfully woven threads of the machine. Thus it can be seen even in the smallest details that Tolstoy, even where a similar subject-matter seems to bring him close to the newer realists, in fact represents a diametrically opposed artistic method.

There is, however, a considerable external resemblance between them which we must stress. The great dialogues in the works of the older realists, although they have a background of very concrete circumstances, yet rise so rapidly to great dramatic heights that the outer circumstances and environment have very little influence on the conversations themselves. The dramatically intensified concrete situation, the dramatic concretization of the characters in and through the conversation, make such an intervention of external circumstances almost completely unnecessary. In the modern realists the momentary, external, accidental and impermanent circumstances and factors nearly always blot out the content of the conversations. The more trivial the latter are and the closer they approach the commonplace, the more they need such interaction with the momentary setting in order to show some animation, at least on the surface.

Tolstoy's great dialogues are always closely bound up with the time and place in which they occur. Even the external features of the accidental place and the accidental time constantly crop up in the conversation itself. One need think only of the dialogue between Levin and Oblonski in the barn after the hunt. But the very concrete and ever-present quality of place and time in these conversations is with Tolstoy never a mere device to introduce more life into the scene. Precisely the stressing of such concrete and accidental circumstances shows that what is discussed is a permanent problem in the life of Levin; for instance, it is so actual in every instant of his life that he may burst into a discussion of it at any moment. In the instance quoted the subject happens to crop up in connection with the hunt. The emphasis placed on the concrete circumstances underlines precisely this quality at the same time necessary and accidental, this 'extreme possibility' of a permanent crisis which is always latently present but nevertheless never brings about a real change.

The same purpose is served by the mostly abrupt breaking-off of such conversations in Tolstoy, a device which again underlines their seemingly accidental, commonplace quality. Balzac's conversations must be carried on to the end, for only thus can the dramatic turn be brought about and motivated. The conversations of the modern realists mostly have neither beginning nor end. They are just chance fragments of an, in the poetic sense, incoherent, slice of life. But the breaking-off of Tolstoy's conversations is not really accidental, only apparently so. The conversations are carried on with the greatest skill to a point at which the contradictions and the impossibility of eliminating them are stated by the hero with merciless clarity and thoroughness. A conversation apparently evoked by some chance occasion leads to such a culminating point and then breaks off or runs out, again apparently by chance. But by then it has already fulfilled its specific object; for its object was merely to revolve around a specifically Tolstoyan, possible turning-point.

Thus the apparently accidental beginning and end of a conversation are intentional devices in Tolstoy's method of epic presentation. They lead out of the quiet flow of life and then lead back into it again after having thrown a bright light on what is constantly going on under the surface of this calm stream of life. Here as elsewhere, Tolstoy with extraordinary inventiveness creates new elements of form, elements still capable of raising his unfavourable subject-matter to the level of a great realist epic.

7.

Thus Tolstoy's continuation of the work of the great realists rested to a considerable extent on an increased flexibility of characterization and plot-unfolding; superficially seen, this method often recalls the devices used by modern realists (thereby greatly facilitating Tolstoy's great success in western Europe) but its formal purpose is the exact opposite of that of the superficially similar features of the newer realism, which here are symptoms of the disintegration of the great realistic forms, while in Tolstoy's writings they are elements of their further evolution.

Tolstoy did not develop such tendencies of form under the influence of the newer realists, although he knew their works well and studied them carefully. As early as in the sixties of the nineteenth century, immediately after the publication of Tolstoy's first writings, in which these tendencies were as yet only embryonic, the great Russian critic Chernyshevski had already clearly recognized this feature in Tolstoy's art. He spoke of Tolstoy's preoccupation with the way in which one thought or emotion develops out of another. He made a distinction between the psychological analysis of Tolstoy and of nearly every other writer. He says of the latter, as contrasted with Tolstoy : "Usually it (i.e. the psychological analysis) has a descriptive character, so to speak—it seizes on some static emotion and breaks it up into its component parts—it gives us what may be called an anatomical table. The works of great poets usually show the great dramatic changes from one emotion and one thought to another. But we are mostly given only the two extreme links of the chain, the beginning and end of the psychological process . . . The peculiarity of Count Tolstoy's gift consists in that he does not restrict himself to the presentation of the results of a psychological process, but is interested in the process itself . . ."

How consciously Tolstoy later developed these tendencies, which Chernyshevski had recognized so early, is shown by the following passage in *Resurrection* : "One of the most widespread superstitions is that every man has his own specific definite qualities : that he is kind, cruel, wise, stupid, energetic, apathetic, and so on. But men are not like that at all. We may say of a man that he is more often kind than cruel, more often wise than stupid, more often energetic than apathetic, or the reverse; but it would not be true to say of one man that he is kind and wise, of another that he is bad and stupid. And yet we always classify people in this way. And that is quite wrong. Men are like rivers : the water is the same in all of them, but every river is narrow and rapid in some places and broader and slower in others, sometimes clear, sometimes troubled, sometimes cold and sometimes warm. It is the same with men. Every man carries in himself the germs of every human quality, but sometimes it is one quality that manifests itself and sometimes another; sometimes a man is quite unlike himself, while still remaining the same man."

A similar opposition to the rigid conception of human character, to the allegedly rigid presentation of characters in older literature, can be very frequently found in the writings of modern naturalists. But when two say the same (or similar) things, they are not the same. The modern naturalists' opposition to rigidity in characterization contained a tendency to do away with the creation of characters altogether. In literature a character cannot be given a face, an outline save in motion, save in active conflict with the outer world, save in action. As long as a character is described only in repose, in some *milieu,* its essential traits can only be stated, but not created. In other words there is no poetic means by which it is possible to distinguish creatively between essential traits and fleeting moods. Hence, if the naturalists protested against the superficial tricks with which a writer attempted in these circumstances to stress permanent characteristics (e.g. by means of constantly recurring expressions or gestures) they were right from their point of view and at any rate consistent. But for this very reason consistent naturalists were forced to let their characters dissolve into an incoherent, chaotic tangle of impermanent moods.

With Tolstoy the case is different. His characters do not, any more than the personages of the naturalists, develop dramatically, as did Balzac's; but their movement through life, their conflicts with the external world nevertheless give them very well-defined outlines. These outlines, however, are by no means as strictly monolinear and clear-cut as those of the characters drawn by the old realists. Tolstoy's plots revolve around the 'extreme possibilities' of the characters, possibilities which never become reality but which come to the surface again and again, thus affording each character many opportunities of expressing their thoughts and emotions. Tolstoy describes the fleeting moods of his characters at least as sensitively and accurately as the most gifted of the newer realists, but nevertheless the figures never dissolve into mere clouds of moods, for they are placed within a precisely circumscribed space, a field of force within which all their moods must oscillate.

Thus Konstantin Levin sometimes leans towards a straightforward reactionary conservatism, while at other times he finds the arguments against private ownership of the land irrefutable. But as these two poles represent the extreme pendulum-swings of the thoughts with which he approaches the problems of his time and as the solution of his life-problem, the compromise that he seeks, lies in the middle between these two extremes, such swings of the pendulum do not turn him into a bundle of moods (in the manner of the newer realists) but mark with accuracy, variety and a wealth of detail the socially inevitable zig-zag path men like Levin must necessarily follow. Tolstoy, as we have already seen, never presents the various manifestations of his characters in isolation from each other, and the relationships between Levin and his brothers, his wife, his friends and other people are very closely linked with his decisions on the most important problems of his life. Thus the swings of the pendulum only enrich his image and far from blurring its outlines, make them all the more clear-cut.

This presentation by means of a certain spread, a latitude for the play of thoughts, moods and emotions, enabled Tolstoy to give a very rich and poetic—because contradictory and indirect—picture of human relationships.

This richness and animation are increased even more by the fact that the latitude Tolstoy allows his characters is not immutable. He shows very carefully how through changes in external circumstances or in the internal growth or deterioration of the characters themselves this latitude can decrease or increase, sometimes even acquire new contents or completely shed old ones. But as Tolstoy always depicts these changes as a continuity, as we are always invited to observe the cause and manner of such changes and as in spite of such changes many of the most important social and individual determinants of the character remain the same, this device further increases the richness of Tolstoy's world and far from blurring the outlines of the characters, traces them even more subtly and intricately.

This method of characterization is an important step forward in the development of realism. Naturally such tendencies were already present in rudimentary form in the old realists. Any character without such oscillation within prescribed limits would always lack flexibility to some extent. What matters here is how important a part this method of presentation played in the creation of characters by various authors. In the writings of the old realists, particularly those who had adopted a dramatic-novelistic manner, the presentation of such a latitude was necessarily merely accessory; on the other hand, the *whole* life of the characters was enacted within such a latitude. But their several movements and hesitations are depicted with dramatic vehemence, suddenness and directness. Remember for instance such a vacillating character as Lucien de Rubempré and recall with what dramatic suddenness, without detailed pendulum-swings, he is converted by Vautrin or decides to commit suicide after his examination by the magistrate.

What is new in Tolstoy is that he made this method the centre around which his characterization revolves. That he did so quite deliberately and that his method was closely linked with his own problems of world-view is shown among other things by the fact that the width and flexibility of the latitude accorded each character are closely connected with the importance of the part played by the character in the whole composition. Episodic figures, particularly those who serve Tolstoy to demonstrate the inhuman rigidity of the society of his time, have comparatively few oscillations of mood. In order that a character may attract the central interest of the writer and reader, its latitude of oscillation must be comparatively great and varied. This applies even to figures whose world-view Tolstoy rejects or criticizes, like Vronski, Karenin or Ivan Ilyich.

The writer's own position is very clearly expressed in the way in which he presents the primary starting-point of these oscillations. Figures whom Tolstoy wants to represent as living human beings are always made to experience a lively interaction between their internal evolution and the external circumstances into which they are placed and with which they must deal. Tolstoy's conception of life has for its natural result that every figure for whom he feels human sympathy, must necessarily take up a problematic attitude to society. It can never accept without a struggle the way of life into which it was born and the tasks imposed on it by circumstances. On the other hand Tolstoy's deepest poetic sympathy is always with the characters who by the social and ideological secession from their original way of life are involved in bitter internal struggles. From Olenin to Nekhlyudov Tolstoy drew a whole gallery of such portraits. The greater the tension arising within them, the more Tolstoy is interested in them, but at the same time (and here Tolstoy reveals himself as the great poet of an important transitional period) he shows the more starkly and palpably, in the oscillations of such characters, the extent to which the Russia of his time was 'turned upside down' even in respect of the smallest, most intimate details of life.

When Tolstoy chooses as a central figure a personage to whom he gives a mainly negative characterization, he makes such figures appear from the start as rigid, straight-lined, and bound by convention even in their vacillations. Then he places them in situations which shake their apparently safe, conventional life-basis, force new problems on them and thus bring motion into the figure. This can be observed very clearly in the figure of Karenin. In spite of his real—although naturally at bottom conventional—love for Anna, her estrangement from him and her adultery with Vronski produces in Karenin even more rigidity, an even more complete transformation into a bureaucratic machine. Not until he stands beside Anna's sick-bed and her profound suffering affects him with physical directness, are the rigid, mechanized, automatically functioning elements of his personality loosened to some extent; in his deeply buried human core something like real life begins to stir. But as this stirring is much too weak to establish new human relations between him and Anna, he soon sinks back into an increased rigidity; the 'human' traits of his later days are mere hypocrisy, a mere religious mask on the face of this internally petrified bureaucrat. The case of Vronski is somewhat different. He is often genuinely dissatisfied with his own mode of life, although this dissatisfaction never opens new perspectives for him, and in him passion unleashes more vigorous human energies. Tolstoy shows with consummate artistry to what extent changes in his external circumstances (retirement from the army, free life abroad) contribute to the loosening-up of Vronski's rigidity. But even here the dominant factors are the conventional barriers imposed by his position in life. His liberated energies cannot carry him beyond a dilettantism which cannot satisfy him for any length of time. When he returns to Russia the inverse process begins at once : his reconversion into a pleasant average aristocrat with perfect manners in whom a great passion is something 'eccentric' and not organically linked with the central interests of his life. The conventional hardening that results does not go so far in Vronski as in Karenin, but it is sufficient to lead inevitably to Anna's tragic catastrophe.

This original and fruitful method of characterization shows that despite all the profound connection with the old realists and all the divergence from the new, Tolstoy yet has certain basic principles in common with the latter. This fact must necessarily be reflected in his style, for a great realist writer cannot close his eyes to social truths, to real changes in the structure of society. Nor can his presentation be concerned only with their content; it must also reflect them in form, even if they are in their inner-most essence inimical to art, even if they contain a threat of des-truction, dissolution, or petrification to the forms of art themselves. The swimming-against-the-current of the great realists is always concrete. They strive to discover, in the concrete material before them, the tendencies which enable them artistically to master and bring to life this same material together with all its anti-artistic traits. Writers whom the ugliness of modern capitalist life inspires with a perfectly justified and understandable horror, but a merely abstract horror, must fall victims to an empty formalism if they take this horror for their starting-point. The forms of great realistic art always come into being as the reflections of the essential traits of reality and their material is the concrete fabric of a certain society in a certain period, even though the main trend of social evolution in it is as inimical to art as is that of fully developed capitalism. Realist literature reflects human beings *in action*. The more vigorously the social and individual character of men finds expression in their deeds, or rather in the mutual interaction of their external circumstances, their emotions and their deeds, the greater the scope of realistic presentation. In classical aesthetics it is often pointed out that powerful, vigorous, active evil-doers and criminals provide far more suitable subjects for literature than insipid, pedestrian mediocrities, those average human beings whose character always manifests itself only in actions which are broken off as soon as begun. But the levelling power of 'finished' capital-ism produces just such mediocrities in ever-increasing numbers. Thus life itself brings forth an obstacle to the development of a great realist literature. But there is a considerable difference be-tween writers who insistently stress this tendency of life in their writings (as most western realists of this period did) and writers who strive to swim against the current, who do not accept the effects of capitalism simply and directly as accomplished facts (or what is worse, go so far as to generalize them and represent them as 'laws of nature') but who depict the *struggle* the final result of which (as a rule, but by no means always) is the coming into being of such prosaic, anti-poetic mediocrity.

Thus behind certain formal and technical similarities between Tolstoy and the newer realists we find real social problems : the problem of the possibility of action for the individual in a developed *bourgeois* society, the problem of the inevitable discrepancy between ideology and reality for all who live in capitalist society, except the class-conscious section of the working class.

The contrast between the imagined and the real is, of course, a very ancient problem in literature. It is the central problem, for instance, of such an immortal book as *Don Quixote*. But what we are concerned with here is the specifically modern form in which this contrast manifests itself—the form which, as disappointment with reality, as disillusionment, has increasingly grown to be· the central problem of the newer realism. True, Balzac had already given one of his major works the title *Lost Illusions,* but in his book the illusions are shattered by social realities in the form of a desperate struggle, a tragic, at times tragicomic, battle with the exigencies of social evolution. The typical novel of disillusionment of the newer realism, Flaubert's *Education Sentimentale,* no longer contains a real struggle. In it an impotent subjectivity faces the meaningless objectivity of the external world. With concealed lyricism the poet takes sides with the impotent dreams of his characters and against the sordid but overwhelming power of social reality. He can, of course, like Flaubert, cover up this attitude with a veil of ironical objectivism. Disappointment and disillusionment as the principal theme of literature is the poetic reflection of the situation in which the best and most honest representatives of the *bourgeois* class find themselves. Reality irresistibly forces upon them the recognition of the senselessness of life in a capitalist society; they see through the falseness, the inner unsubstantiality of *bourgeois* ideology, but are unable to find a solution to this contradiction and remain entangled in the false dilemma of impotent subjectivity and senseless objectivity. The lifelike quality of some such works of art—however problematic they may be from the philosophical and artistic viewpoint—rests on the fact that they express a real social and historical issue, even though by inadequate artistic means.

For Tolstoy, too, the fact that reality is always different from what human beings dream and hope, was a central problem. The Caucasian idyll contradicts the imaginings of Olenin, politics and war those of Bolkonski, love and marriage those of Levin. For Tolstoy, too, it is an axiom that men and women of any value must inevitably be disappointed by life, that for them the discrepancies between ideology and reality are the deepest. The closer a Tolstoyan character approaches stupidity or dishonesty, the narrower is this discrepancy and that is only natural, for stupidity and dishonesty express themselves psychologically above all in the ease with which the thoughts and emotions of fools and scoundrels adapt themselves to the vileness of social reality. Only here and there, in certain periods of Tolstoy's life, can one find episodic figures who, although not portrayed as fools or scoundrels, yet live in emotional and intellectual harmony with their social *milieu* (e.g. old Prince Shcherbatski in *Anna Karenina*).

But disappointment, the fact that reality must differ from the ideas men have about it, has a very different flavour in Tolstoy and in the newer realists, and such disappointments are presented in a totally different manner by Tolstoy and by the modern realistic school. In the first place, for Tolstoy this disappointment is not always a purely negative thing. He very often uses the disappointment of his characters as a means of exposing the subjective narrowness and shallowness of their conception of reality. He shows that reality is in fact different, but immeasurably richer, more multifarious and alive, than their subjective and romantic conception of it; that what reality can give men is something different from what they imagine, but is for that very reason much more than their lame imagination could conceive. This richer reality is always presented by Tolstoy as 'natural' life. Already in his early story *The Cossacks* he caused all romantic conceptions of Olenin about the Caucasus to be shattered by the reality of the rich life of the Caucasian peasants. Olenin is 'disappointed' but this disappointment at the same time enriches him, raises him to a higher level. In a similar way Levin is disappointed in love and marriage; Bezukhov's evolution runs on the same lines.

Here already the social contrast between Tolstoy and the newer realists is clearly visible. The deep connection of Tolstoy's outlook and art with the incipient revolt of the Russian peasantry preserved him from seeing social reality as a dreary desert, as the newer realists did. For the lack of social perspective caused the latter to identify the social realities of their immediate environment with reality in general and to regard the meaninglessness of life in a capitalist society as the metaphysical senselessness of life as such. It is thus that justified criticism of capitalist society degenerated into a despairing misrepresentation of objective reality itself.

But Tolstoy the writer never identified capitalist reality with reality as such. He always saw capitalist society as a world of distortion, as a befouling of human reality proper; he therefore always contrasted it with another, natural and hence human reality. And although his conceptions of this natural, human reality may have been romantically-imaginary or utopian reactionary and his basic attitude, which was to side with the peasantry, gave him a deeper insight into the realities of life, a more just and correct appreciation of this conflict between subjective conception and objective reality.

Hence the disillusionment of Tolstoy's characters is always an exposure of the incompleteness, Utopianism and inconclusiveness of their ideas. This is expressed most clearly whenever Tolstoy contrasts his own Utopian plans of 'making the peasants happy' with reality itself. From *The Morning of a Country Squire* to *Resurrection* and the play *The Light Shineth in the Darkness* Tolstoy has presented this problem in a variety of forms. But the *motif* running through each of them is the shattering of Utopian ideas by the realities of peasant life, the deep and irreconcilable hatred of the peasants for all 'well-intentioned' exploiters and parasites. Here again Tolstoy always shows that the disappointed have only themselves and not reality to blame for their disappointment, that reality is in the right when it contradicts Utopian ideas and that reality expresses a higher and richer truth.

Where Tolstoy appears to be in closest contact with the newer realists is in the portrayal of the life of the exploiters and of the disappointments which necessarily arise among them. But it is precisely here that the difference between Tolstoy and the newer realists is the greatest. Because Tolstoy presents the life of the ruling class as that of exploiters and parasites (although he sees exploitation in the main only in the form of ground-rent) his exposure of the bestiality and senselessness of such a life is not only more profound and correct than that of the newer realists, it is also free from the inflexible, metaphysical quality inherent in the latter. In Tolstoy there is none of the futile jeremiads and empty ironies of the modern realists. His exposure of this reality has its origin in a healthy, vigorous and violent indignation. When his favourite heroes suffer a disappointment in this world, Tolstoy represents them more or less as silly dupes who were unable to see through or tear away even so threadbare a mask. With advancing age this indignation of Tolstoy grows increasingly violent. (An example is the episode between Nekhlyudov and Mariette in *Resurrection*.)

But even in his earlier periods Tolstoy saw nothing fateful or tragic in these typical 'tragedies' of the ruling class. He always thought of these conflicts that they could be overcome with a little common sense and a sound conception of right and wrong. Of course it is part of Tolstoy's philosophy that the ruling class lack this sound conception of right and wrong and can at best acquire it only with great difficulty, after a bitter internal struggle, after hard lessons from life and many disappointments. (E.g. the marriage between Bezukhov and Helen.)

Tolstoy never loses sight of this principle even where the disappointment is of a more fundamental nature and where more serious and intricate conflicts between ideology and reality come to the surface. He harbours a deeply rooted peasant disbelief in the genuine sincerity and consistence of even the 'loftiest' feelings and resolutions of members of the ruling class. When he brings such 'loftiness' into contact and contrast with everyday life and causes it to be shattered by its hard little facts, he seemingly comes very close to the disappointments found in the works of the newer realists. But here again the resemblance is superficial and the basic character the exact opposite. For here again the 'lofty' emotion is every time exposed as futile, weak and not serious, and the real cause of failure is in Tolstoy's eyes not its 'loftiness,' its humanly valuable moral content, but the insignificance of those who harbour it. The 'lofty' feelings harboured by Karenin and Anna in connection with the latter's illness cannot alter the fact that the former is a shrivelled bureaucrat and the latter a blindly infatuated society lady. For all the 'loftiness' of their emotions this tragic highlight must necessarily be followed by the real tragicomedy, i.e. the continuation of their old life, the reversion to the rule of their former, not at all 'lofty,' but quite genuine feelings and the return to their normal level of life.

This perspective, which follows from his acceptance of the peasant point of view, enables Tolstoy to avoid, even in his tragedies of love and marriage, both the trivial pathology and the inflated sham fatality found in the newer realists. Behind every such tragedy of love and marriage — in *Anna Karenina* as in *Kreutzer Sonata* or *The Devil*—the fact that this form of tragedy has its origin in an idle parasitic life is always kept before our eyes.

Thus Tolstoy's hope of the moral regeneration of mankind raises him above the petty narrowness of the newer realists' philosophy. And because he is never concerned primarily with art, but uses art as a means of spreading a gospel for the regeneration of humanity, he is preserved even in his quality of artist from the formless unsubstantiality of the moderns. It is a similar faith, a similar gospelling fervour that makes his contemporary Ibsen superior, even from the artistic viewpoint, to so many other writers of the same period. But we have already seen how great the social difference was between the gospels of Ibsen and Tolstoy. What matters here is not whether the content of these gospels was true or false—Tolstoy preached at least as much reactionary nonsense as Ibsen—what matters is the social movement of which this gospel, for all the falseness of its content, was yet the ideological expression.

Tolstoy's world-view is deeply permeated by reactionary prejudices. But they are indivisibly bound up with that healthy, hopeful and progressive popular movement of which they represent the weak points and defects. Tolstoy's case is not the only case in the literature of the world when a great artist creates immortal masterpieces on the basis of an entirely false philosophy. But in spite of the intricate interaction between a possibly erroneous philosophy and a great realistic creative activity, it is not of course any and every erroneous philosophy which can serve as the foundation for the creation of realistic masterpieces. The illusions and errors of great realist writers can be artistically fruitful only if they are historically necessary illusions and errors bound up with a great social movement. Lenin, the only critic who discovered this connection in Tolstoy, thereby provided the key to Tolstoy's real greatness as a writer. Tolstoy understood little of the nature of capitalism and nothing of the revolutionary movement of the working class, but nevertheless he gave us admirably lifelike and true pictures of Russian society. He could do so because he looked at it from the viewpoint of the revolting peasantry, with all the faults and limits of that movement; but these faults and limits were historically determined and hence could in part become artistically fruitful and in part at least did not hamper the creation of a great artistic world. Lenin said of the peasants before the revolution of 1905 : "In their opposition to serfdom, to the feudal lords and to the state which serves their ends, the peasants still remain a *class*, but a class, not of capitalist society, but of a society based on serfdom." The reactionary limitations and illusions in Tolstoy's world-view stem from this pre-capitalist character of its social basis.

This complicated positive and negative interaction between world-view and creative work in Tolstoy could be traced in every artistic feature throughout his whole *oeuvre*. We wish here only to point out one more feature in which Tolstoy differs sharply from his European contemporaries and by which, in a time of a general decline of the arts, he not only preserved the great realist tradition but carried it worthily on. We are thinking in the first place of the fact that Tolstoy never practised art for art's sake.

For him art was always the communication of certain contents and the artistic form the means of winning over his readers to his views. It was this trait in his art—condemned as tendentious by western aestheticists—which enabled him to save the great tradition of the art of narration. For the great forms of narration were originally plastic presentations of human destinies, and their purpose was to achieve social and moral effects by artistic means. The clear and ordered grouping of events, the gradual uncovering of their causes and origins are always very closely connected with the intentions of the author, which transcend the artistic in the modern, specialized, craft sense of the word.

When the trend of social evolution made the realization of such intentions impossible, when writers were transformed into mere observers of social reality, they necessarily lost this ability of purposefully marshalling the events they narrate. To an increasing degree it came to be the chance interest attaching to certain details which determined the accentuation of the event narrated, rather than the social significance of the event in connection with the general intentions of the author.

By remaining 'old-fashioned' in this respect to the end of his life, Tolstoy was able to preserve a style of narration found only in the very greatest of the old realists. In western Europe it has often been said that after the great crisis in his world-view, Tolstoy's artistic creativeness had declined. It is quite true that the change in his philosophy brought about an essential change in his style—that the naive epic magnificence, the almost Homeric breadth and uninhibitedness of *War and Peace* could not but be lost. It would, however, be a great mistake to underrate the new, splendid, purely artistic qualities of Tolstoy's late works. Even if looking at it merely from the formal-artistic angle, modern western European literature can boast of few stories so perfect in form (in the classical sense) as Tolstoy's *After the Ball*. And in the whole of modern western literature there is not a single novel that could match *Resurrection* in all-embracing epic greatness. Tone, manner and style of Tolstoy's presentation changed very considerably; but in his completed writings the aged Tolstoy remained to his last breath the incomparably greatest artist of his epoch.

8.

It is well known how little Tolstoy's literary work was understood by his contemporaries. The *bourgeois* aestheticists generally stressed only his reactionary traits, representing them as the sole foundation of his art and vulgar-sociology followed in the footsteps of reactionary aesthetics.

Tolstoy's aesthetic views were even more thoroughly misunderstood than his art. His essays on artistic problems were generally interpreted as a rejection of art as such, as a condemnation of every artistic activity, such as Plato had uttered in his time. This misunderstanding is no accident; many points in Tolstoy's critical writings—which we will discuss later—were liable to lead to such misunderstandings. But these misinterpretations have not prevented Tolstoy's writings on art from having a profound effect—on the contrary, they often actually brought it about. For the progressive dissolution of artistic forms under capitalism, the increasing artificiality of the rapidly changing artistic trends and their increasing reluctance to deal with the great problems of mankind, produced in the best representatives of the bourgeois *intelligentsia* a correspondingly increasing dissatisfaction with art in general. Romantic opponents of the culture produced by the capitalist system very often ended up in a complete rejection of art as a useless toy, as a futile occupation serving only for pleasure but contributing nothing to the advancement of the great aims of mankind. Such tendencies could naturally link up with certain aspects of Tolstoy's criticism of art.

Any such conception entirely misinterprets the true meaning of Tolstoy's criticism, the object of which was to oppose the decadent pseudo-art of the present but by no means art as such. On the contrary, Tolstoy always contrasted true, genuine, great and popular art with the sham art of his day.

Tolstoy's criticism was thus directed against modern *bourgeois* art. The starting-point of this criticism is of a magnificent, spontaneously materialist simplicity. Tolstoy asks : for whom and by whom is this art produced. His answer is : for the idlers of the ruling class. The teeming millions of workers do not even know that such an art exists, but even if they did, it would be emotionally inaccessible to them. Tolstoy described more than once with a very dramatic and ironic realism, how the technical subtleties and refinements of this art are produced by men who are simply exploited servants of the ruling class and for whom such activities are a no less humiliating job of work than the satisfying of other needs of the ruling parasites.

But Tolstoy does not stop at merely stating this fact. He proceeds to investigate the mental and spiritual deformations suffered by artists—even gifted and sincere artists—when compelled to serve the needs of an idle minority or when subjected to the ideological influence of its parasitic existence. Tolstoy believed that the great danger threatening art was that it might lose its connection with the great problems of life. In his preface to the Russian translation of Maupassant's works he established these postulates of a genuine artistic attitude to reality:

"These are: first, a correct, i.e. a moral attitude of the author to his theme; secondly, clarity of expression or beauty of form—these two are identical; and thirdly, sincerity, i.e. a sincere love or hate of the thing the artist is presenting."

This essential relation of the artist to his work, which is a result of his relation to social reality, was, according to Tolstoy, increasingly being lost in modern art. Even in Maupassant, of whose gifts as a writer he had a very high opinion, Tolstoy found this false tendency of modern art, which he summed up thus: "it is not only unimportant for a work of art whether the artist had a clear conception of what is right and what is wrong, but on the contrary, an artist should completely disregard all moral considerations, for such a disregarding is an artistic advantage. According to this theory the artist can and should describe the truth, i.e. what is real, what is beautiful and hence pleases him, or even what may serve science as a useful material; but it is no business of the artist to concern himself with what is moral or immoral, right or wrong."

Such an erroneous conception of even very gifted artists Tolstoy attributed to the fact that art had ceased to be the concern of the whole people. In modern times art had come to be a luxury of idle parasites; art had become a strongly specialized occupation and its object was to satisfy this requirement. Tolstoy showed with great acumen how this specialization has an increasingly deteriorating effect on art: empty formal artistry, the prominence of superfluous details that express nothing essential, photographic reproduction of superficial phenomena, loss of understanding of the great problems of life. All these lead to a great impoverishment of art:

"The feelings which arise from the desire of amusement are . . not only limited, but have been well known for a long time and sufficiently expressed . . . The feelings of the mighty and rich, who have had no experience of having to work for a living, are much poorer, much more limited and much more insignificant than the feelings of the working people. The aesthetes and men of our station in life usually assert the contrary. I remember that Goncharov, the author, who was a very shrewd and educated man, but a townsman and aesthete to the marrow, said to me after the publication of Turgenyev's *A Sportsman's Diary* that there was now nothing more left to write about the life of the peasants; the subject was exhausted. In contrast the conflicts and intrigues of the upper classes were an inexhaustible source of themes for the writer."

Tolstoy not only opposed such conceptions and stressed the richness of a life of work and the inner monotony of a parasitic life, but maintained that modern art was much inferior to the really great, really popular art of former days in dealing with the great and decisive problems of life. He also maintained that a wealth of detail was merely a dazzling camouflage of an internal poverty and that the old poets (he adduces as an example the legend of Joseph in the Old Testament) needed no such mass of detail because they were magnificently simple and easy to understand.

"Thus this story is accessible to all men, it has moved men and women of all nations and classes, young and old; it has remained alive to our day and will remain alive for thousands of years after us. But strip the best story-tellers of our time of their details—and what remains? It is therefore impossible to name modern works of literature which really satisfy the postulate of universality. These works are to a great extent spoilt by what is usually termed 'realism,' but what one could much more correctly call 'artistic provincialism.' "

Nothing is easier than to discover weak points in Tolstoy's criticism of modern art. Because he considers that the only right basic attitude to life is the religious one, he attributes the decline of art to the fact that the ruling classes have become irreligious. This reactionary tendency is by no means an isolated slip on the part of Tolstoy—it is on the contrary closely linked with the positive aspects of his aesthetic theory. Tolstoy's appreciation of Shakespeare, Goethe, Beethoven, etc.—his conception that the decadence of art began already with the Renaissance—all this to some extent forms an intellectually coherent systematic whole in which the reactionary side of Tolstoy's world-view finds clear and trenchant expression. It is of course very easy to criticize this aspect of Tolstoy's aesthetic theories, but it would serve no useful purpose to do so as today they are more or less out-of-date and not very important. To dwell on them now would only distract attention from what is important and fruitful in his aesthetical views and from the central problems bequeathed to us by Tolstoy in this sphere.

The most important problem is in our opinion the peasant and plebeian humanism of Tolstoy's aesthetics. This term may at first seem paradoxical, for Tolstoy's judgments, to which we referred above, are in sharp opposition to the best humanist traditions of the eighteenth and nineteenth centuries. With these judgments Tolstoy abjures, not only in superficial symptoms but in the essential core, the traditions of humanism, narrows down its concept and introduces reactionary elements into it. Nevertheless his own aesthetic conceptions are basically linked with the central problems of humanist aesthetics and he was one of the very few thinkers of his time who attempted to keep these traditions alive and develop them further, even though in his own particular way.

What it all amounts to is the defence of human integrity against the deformations which are the necessary concomitants of capitalist civilization. The older *bourgeois* humanists had already found themselves in the paradoxical situation of approving the progressive increase of productive capacity while at the same time deploring as inhuman the division of labour inseparable from capitalism (as Marx showed in the case of Ferguson).

This contradiction, which no *bourgeois* humanist —neither Ferguson nor Schiller—could resolve, is more and more intensified as capitalist economy develops and extends its rule to all phenomena of life, and especially when *bourgeois* ideology enters its apologetic phase and the ideals of humanism become completely estranged from the normal course of life under capitalism. The honest and gifted among modern artists express this estrangement appropriately by regarding art itself as a principle foreign and inimical to life (e.g. Ibsen in his late works). On the eve of the imperialist era this ideology degenerated into a dehumanization of art and philosophy, which vie with each other in extolling the new barbarism (Nietzsche). Imperialist philosophy, finding its fullest development in fascism, has for its central category a concept paradoxically called 'life' which is a compound of every principle antagonistic to life. This concept of life is a declaration of war on human life, on the human spirit, on every value produced by many thousands of years of human evolution.

Tolstoy directs his polemic chiefly against this dehumanization of life, but naturally does so in a manner full of contradictions. In his thinking, Tolstoy was subject to agnosticist influences, tendencies which throw doubt on the validity of human cognition and on human understanding in general (Kant, Schopenhauer, Buddha, etc.). His favourite heroes express such views in an even

more exaggerated form, e.g. Konstantin Levin when he speaks of
the ' knavery ' of reason, etc.

But through all these blunderings there runs still, as the fundamental line of Tolstoy's aesthetic, the orientation of art towards
popularity; towards the great problems of life which because of
their deepness and universality can be understood by all; towards
the old lucidity of form which made Homer or the Bible com-
prehensible to all men. In his Utopian dreams of a future without
parasites, Tolstoy forecasts a future art capable of being learnt
by any worker and which for this reason would in the essentials
of form be superior to the intricate artistry, the irrelevant refinements of the moderns. Looking at art from this angle, Tolstoy
regards it as a mere chaotic muddle in which there is no criterion
for what is right and what is wrong. Sham works of art, because
of their technical excellence, often appear superior to artistically
better, more genuine works of art. No man of letters or aesthete
could find a criterion here, but a peasant with his uncorrupted
taste could easily distinguish the sham work of art from the
genuine. Tolstoy has thus again made Molière's servant-girl the
arbiter of art. This extreme exaggeration of his urge towards a
really superior art once more reveals the deep contradiction underlying his whole conception of art. In the historical sense this contradiction could not be solved in Tolstoy's time and therefore
necessarily remained insoluble for him personally, but at the same
time it contained tendencies soon to bear fruit in the future.

Schiller, in his most interesting essay on *Naive and sentimental
poetry*—the first profound philosophical analysis of the essence of
modern art, brings up this question of Molière's maidservant. He
says :

"Molière, as a naive poet, could rely on his maidservant to tell
him what should remain in and what should be left out of his
comedies. But I would not like to see the same test applied to
Klopstock's *Odes,* to the finest passages in his *Messiah,* in *Paradise
Lost,* in *Nathan the Wise* and many other pieces."

Schiller here wittily expresses the basic contradiction arising
from the problem of the popularity of art in the later *bourgeois*
literature, a contradiction which Tolstoy also saw and which, as
we have seen, he did his best to resolve. Schiller, too, thought that
the simple great art of the 'naive' poets was superior to modern
'sentimental' poetry. But he not only saw the historical necessity
of the emergence of such a more subjective, more problematic,
more complicated art, he also appreciated that this art could also

contribute immortal values to the evolution of mankind. Modern art has with historical necessity receded from the original popularity of art and withdrawn from contact with a great section of the people—Molière's maidservant can no longer act as arbiter for this art—but its greatest representatives have, even on this problematic foundation, produced great works of art, which need not remain unpopular for ever. The non-competence in their case of Molière's maidservant does not diminish the greatness of the works of Goethe and Schiller, Balzac and Stendhal; nor, in spite of the contrary opinion of Tolstoy the aestheticist, of those of Tolstoy himself, even though, here, too, the competence of Molière's maidservant in respect of composition and language is not always and everywhere beyond question.

In the era of the French revolution and the Napoleonic wars Schiller could easily harbour idealistic and exaggerated hopes regarding the future of ' sentimental ' poetry. But at a time when there was a general decline, formal impoverishment and deterioration in *bourgeois* art, the hopelessness of its future must already have been apparent to Tolstoy. In such a situation it was an understandable exaggeration—although of course none the less erroneous—for Tolstoy to extend his adverse judgment on ' sentimental ' art from the present to the past and to reject even its greatest, most genuine products. But in this his very partiality Tolstoy sometimes penetrates deeper to the core of the problems of art than many outstanding thinkers who preceded him and whose judgment was more equitable and impartial, such as Schiller. For Tolstoy the popularity of art is without question the central problem of aesthetics and with bold simplicity he makes the possibility of great artistic forms or their loss dependent on whether the art of the time is linked with the life of the people or detached from it. In the second half of the nineteenth century, when most representatives of popular art either turned to a reactionary romanticism or sank into a narrow and short-sighted provincialism, Tolstoy, as the representative of a peasant revolution in Russia, clamoured for a combination of a genuine great art and popular appeal.

In this connection Tolstoy's peasant, who has a correct judgment on questions of art, appears as a historical link in the chain running from Molière's maidservant to Lenin's cook, who was required to be able to run the government.

The historical significance of this attitude of Tolstoy is not at all lessened by the fact that his concept of popularity, too, reflects the weaknesses of the peasant revolution. These weaknesses manifest themselves chiefly in the fact that Tolstoy interprets the connection of great art and popular quality sometimes far too crudely and literally. reducing far too much the sphere of art to which he concedes the quality of greatness. Lenin's cook, educated by the cultural revolution of Socialism, can overlook a far wider field of the artistic past and see far further and deeper than Tolstoy's peasant.

But these weaknesses of Tolstoy's outlook—which were the weaknesses and deficiencies of a great, historically necessary popular movement—must not be allowed to dim the magnificence of his peasant-plebeian humanism. When in his comedy *The Fruits of Education* he lets the primitive ruses of the simple and intelligent young peasant woman Tanya get the better of her parasitic masters who, by dint of too much education, have grown superstitious, we hear a peal of healthy and triumphant plebeian laughter at the internal hollowness of the ruling class, laughter such as came, on the eve of the French revolution, from the plebeian mouth of a Figaro laughing at the hollowness of aristocratic pretensions.

The conception of humanity in Tolstoy's peasant-plebeian humanism may sometimes have been too narrow and shortsighted, but it nevertheless contains very essential traits of a genuine humanist struggle against the dehumanization of men by capitalism and by all class rule. Tolstoy's humanism demands the integrity of the human personality, its liberation from exploitation, from oppression, from the slavery of capitalist division of labour. It postulates that only a life bound up with creative labour is really consistent with reason. Only a Liberal or pseudo-Socialist vulgarsociologist, who is infatuated with the capitalist form of progress, is capable of seeing only the reactionary aspects of this opposition, however desperate or blindly raging it may appear at times.

Old Hegel, for all that he was a Royal Prussian professor, had a far wider and deeper idea of this problem. He wrote in his *Aesthetic* about the early works of Goethe and Schiller :

"The interest in, and the need for, such a genuine individual totality and live independence will and can never leave us, however desirable and reasonable we may find the nature and evolution of conditions in the developed civil and political life of our time. In this sense we must admire the youthful spirit of Goethe and Schiller in their attempt to regain the lost independence of poetic figures within these existing circumstances of the newer age."

Tolstoy the humanist raised his voice in protest at a time of a much greater decline, a much deeper humiliation of men, than did the classical humanists, and it is for this reason that his protest is more desperate, more elemental and inarticulate, and less subtly modulated than was theirs. But at the same time it is more closely linked with the real protest of the peasants against the inhumanity of the lives they were compelled to lead. Tolstoy's aesthetic, like his art, was a harbinger of the great revolt of the peasants in the revolutions of 1905 and 1917.

9.

Tolstoy saved the traditions of the great realists and carried them on and developed them further in concrete and topical form in an age in which realism had degenerated into naturalism or formalism. Herein lies his greatness as a writer. He saved the idea that great art is indissolubly rooted in the people and must perish if it is torn from its native soil, and that greatness of artistic form is indissolubly linked with the popularity of artistic form and content. Herein lies the undying merit of his aesthetics.

Tolstoy died shortly after the *bourgeois* revolution in Russia and not very long before the great Socialist revolution of October. He is the last great classic of *bourgeois* realism, the last worthy link in the chain that stretches from Cervantes to Balzac. He is a classic of realism, remaining topical to this day, for his content and form can be understood through their own immediate experience of life by great masses of people living today, without the need of historical retrospection. This importance of Tolstoy's realism for the problems of our time, for Socialist realism, his influence over which is still decisive and will remain so for a long time, mirrors the extremely rapid transition from a *bourgeois* to a Socialist revolution which has taken place in Russia.

Very little over thirty years ago a backward, enslaved Tsarist Russia was facing a *bourgeois* revolution. Today it is a Socialist country. In every other country the great flowering of *bourgeois* art is separated by decades or even centuries from the unfolding of the revolutionary movement of the working class and hence the great traditions of art can be restored only by laborious effort on the part of Marxists. In Russia, on the contrary this link has been formed by the revolution itself and hence the literature of Socialist realism can regard as its great classic a writer like Maxim Gorki, who has created perfect examples of Socialist realism and is at the same time immediately and vitally bound up with the great traditions of *bourgeois* realism, above all through the personality and oeuvre of Tolstoy himself.

The existence of this rich and many-sided living connection does not of course imply that Socialist realism should simply take over the Tolstoyan heritage without critical sifting and without developing it further in the Socialist sense. It is precisely the nature of Gorki's realism which shows very clearly how radical and thorough this further evolution must be.

In Gorki's manner of characterization we find many devices for bringing his characters to life which we have described in the preceding as new features in the realism of Tolstoy, as his way of carrying on the realist tradition. But the differences are perhaps even more significant than the similarities. Maxim Gorki, closely bound up with the proletarian revolution, saw boundless possibilities of a further advance of mankind— a perspective necessarily closed to Tolstoy. Hence the inner life of Gorki"'s characters is not limited to so narrow a sphere as of Tolstoy's. It is quite possible for Gorki's characters to break out of the sphere of life into which they were born and shed their inherited and acquired thoughts and emotions without thereby relinquishing their personality and their personal peculiarities; on the contrary, they do so in order to permit their personality to develop more freely, more richly and on a higher level.

In presenting the realizability and actual realization of this possibility, the human—and hence the artistic—significance of the latitude in the inner development of human beings, of which we spoke in connection with Tolstoy, undergoes a considerable change in Gorki. For Tolstoy's characters this latitude limits the circle of their manifestations. But for those of Gorki's characters who are unable to break out of this circle, the limit turns into a tormenting prison wall. Thus in Gorki the basic principle of presentation both of the positive and negative characters is essentially, qualitatively transformed. He has carried on the great realist tradition on the qualitatively different level of Socialist realism.

It cannot be the purpose of this paper to analyze, however sketchily, the multiple threads which connect Tolstoy's realism with Socialist realism. We had perforce to limit ourselves to describe the peculiar position occupied by Tolstoy in the history of nineteenth-century realism, of which he is the last great representative. But in order to give at least an indication of the direction in which lies a fruitful absorption and development of Tolstoy's realism for us, we have pointed out one aspect of Maxim Gorki's immense life-work. The question how Tolstoyan realism fertilized literature in the countries in which there was no rapid transition from *bour-*

geois to proletarian revolution as there was in Tolstoy's own, we propose to discuss in another essay of this series.

1936

CHAPTER SEVEN

The Human Comedy of Pre-Revolutionary Russia

> "It is only when the 'underdogs' no longer *want* the old order and the 'top dog' *can* no longer maintain it, can a revolution be victorious. One could express this truth in other words in this way: a revolution is impossible without a crisis embracing the whole nation, both exploiters and exploited."
>
> LENIN.

GORKI'S OEUVRE straddles the whole period during which the Russian revolutionary crisis was maturing, a process which led to the great October revolution. Gorki is a great writer—and a great writer measured by the standards of the great realistic classics—because he saw and depicted every aspect of this revolutionary crisis. He showed not only the growth of the revolutionary movement among the industrial workers and peasants, but devoted much attention to the portrayal of the *bourgeoisie,* the petty *bourgeoisie,* the intelligentsia, demonstrating in detail why long before the revolution, they could not live in the old way any more and how the insoluble conflicts without such a revolution is impossible, came about in the lives of the 'top dogs.'.

Gorki's creative method is both many-sided and profound. What Marx said of Balzac could be equally applied to him. According to Lafargue Marx said that Balzac not only portrayed the most important types of his time, but 'prophetically created types who existed as yet only in embryonic form under Louis Philippe and did not develop fully until after the death of Louis Philippe, in the reign of Napoleon III.' Gorki is regarded as a great social historian of pre-revolutionary Russia because he grasped the decisive evolutionary tendencies of every section of Russian society, which still remain important in our own epoch of Socialism in Russia, although naturally considerably modified by the effect of a revolution which destroyed the old Russia and gave birth to the new. Gorki's writings were prophetic not only in respect of the types of the various counter-revolutionary struggles, but also in respect of the typical remnants of capitalism which survived the revolution.

Thus it can be said that Gorki poetically recreated the pre-conditions and the pre-history of the great nation-wide crisis of Russian society. It can also be said that very strong historical and social bonds unite the many types and destinies which he describes, and that in this sense (but only in this sense) his *oeuvre* is a connected whole, a 'Human Comedy' of pre-revolutionary Russia. Gorki rarely linked up his writings with each other and although they represent various aspects, and stages of one great process, the characters figuring in the different sections know nothing of each other. This deviation from the Balzacian cycle is no accident. A substantial part of Gorki's work is dedicated to the portrayal of life in the old Russian provinces, with all its barbaric bleakness and isolation. The external world, sometimes even the neighbouring little town, is only a speck on the horizon. A Balzacian linking-up of the various sections by the re-emergence of the same characters in different stories, would be out of keeping with the purpose of presenting this isolation. Only when Gorki later depicts the shaking-up and mixing together of all classes of society by the revolution, does the idea of a cycle become an artistic possibility. (Thus *Yegor Bulichov* and *Dostigayev*, his last great plays, are interconnected).

In the completely closed orbit of a little country town Gorki demonstrates the futility of the first stirrings of the revolution, their isolation from the life of the masses (e.g. the assassination of Tsar Alexander II.); and then shows how this situation is transformed with the birth and growth of the revolutionary working-class movement. In *Klim Samgin* Gorki can already reproduce the ideological echoes of the working-class movement among the petty *bourgeoisie* and the *bourgeois* intelligentsia.

The main theme of Gorki's life-work is that men can no longer live in the way in which they have lived in the past. Gorki began his career as the spokesman of the down-and-outs, but later he came to be a poet of the general class reshuffle and class differentiation which took place in Russia in the last decades preceding the revolution. What he depicted here in the first place was how men came to *develop* into members of a class

This posing of the problem separates Gorki very clearly from the general run of modern *bourgeois* literature and of the vulgar-sociology which is its ideological reflection, and which conceives human beings and the class to which they belong as a mechanical unity. Membership of a class is conceived almost as a biological, certainly as an unchangeable, necessity, a fate that must be accepted. Such writers and vulgar-sociologists marked men with "class brands" as in former times convicts were branded with a hot iron when they were sent to the hulks.

Gorki who had a quite different, even a consciously opposite conception of the nature of class characteristics, said :

'It cannot be disputed that "class characteristics" are the chief, the decisive factor in the development of the "psyche," that they always determine, to a greater or lesser degree, the words and deeds of men. In the harsh tyranny of the capitalist state, men were forced to be the abjectly obedient ants of their ant-hill; doomed to play this part by the consistent pressure of the family, the school, the church and the employers, their instinct of self-preservation urging them to submit to the existing laws and customs; all this is true, but competition inside the ant-hill is so strong, the social chaos in *bourgeois* society is growing so palpably, that the same instinct of self-preservation which makes men the obedient slaves of the capitalists, comes into dramatic conflict with the "class characteristics".'

In this theoretical summing-up of his own literary practice Gorki showed an incomparably deeper understanding of the Marxian conception of the dialectical relationship between the individual and his class (especially in capitalist society) than all the so-called Marxists of "literary science." This is what Marx himself said of this relationship between class and the individual in the capitalist state : 'But in the course of historical development and precisely as a result of the inevitable fact that within the division of labour social relationships take on an independent existence, there appears a division within the life of each individual, in so far as it is personal and in so far as it is determined by some branch of labour and the conditions pertaining to it . . .' The division between the personal individual and the class individual, the accidental nature of the conditions of life for the individual, appears only with the emergence of class, which is itself a product of the *bourgeoisie*. This accidental character is only engendered and developed by competition and the struggle of individuals among themselves. Thus, in imagination, individuals seem more free under the dominance of the *bourgeoisie* than before, because their conditions of life seem accidental; in reality, of course, they are less free, because they are more subjected to the objective compulsion.

Gorki depicts this accidentally, the intricate and contradictory process by which life moulds men into members of a class, i.e., by which the mutual interaction between man and his social surroundings produces personality; how, in this process of personality-making, the traits which make the individual a representative of a class are developed; how they grow, weaken, intersect each other, turn into their opposites, etc.

Most modern writers regard this process not as a process at all, but as a fact accomplished once and for all. Hence they degrade the results of the process into a fatalist acceptance of surroundings, origins, race, etc., unlike Gorki, who constantly stresses the dramatic character of the process, the fact that it is full of conflicts. Like Marx, he sees that these conflicts are sharpest where the life of the individual becomes the object of a clash of class interests, when an individual is faced with a decision involving a class issue; for then it is shown which class characteristics have come to be the dominant ones in the course of the individual's individual development.

This development accordingly moves from conflict to conflict. The outcome of each conflict depends on the individual's previous experience and the nature of the conflict, and is to that extent determined; but by no means in a fatalistic sense. Surprises occur all the time, because in a certain conflict certain qualities come " suddenly " to the surface as a certain individual's most essential qualities. Thus, for instance, a poor orphan, Luka Lunyev (*Three Human Beings*) has, through a chain of accidents, become a merchant. He is very dissatisfied with his life, and searches for " real human beings " who could show him the way to a worthier life. At last he finds such a human being in the person of Medvedeva. But when she reproaches him with " living, as all merchants do, on the unpaid labour of his workers," the class instinct of the merchant " suddenly "—so suddenly that it surprises even himself—asserts itself in Lunyev. We find the same " surprising " dramatic quality—but with opposite results—in the conflict between Ilya Artamonov and his father. The latent conflict (i.e., that Ilya doesn't want to take over the factory) explodes dramatically and leads to a complete rupture when the father reproaches his son : ' We have worked and you want to live without working? You want to play the saint at the expense of the labour of others? '

Such instances are, of course, extreme cases, the explosions of long-latent dramatic tensions. But even conflicts with a lesser explosive tension which apparently comes to nothing, have this internal dramatic character. They mark critical points in the process in which men become conscious of themselves, in which new possibilities of development are opened up or such existing ones finally closed which had for long counted as real possibilities of development only in the imagination of the person concerned. Thus in *Matvey Kozhemyakin* in the course of discussions organized by the old exiled revolutionary, Matvey puts forward a muddled ideology of compromise, which would be tantamount to an ideological amnesty and reconciliation with the exploiters, especially with the merchants. This expression of opinion suddenly explains why Matvey's own attempt to save himself from being suffocated by his environment had remained unsuccessful, and would ever remain so.

It is no accident that in Gorki's writings these conflicts so frequently turn on the relationship between exploiter and exploited and that among Gorki's capitalists it is the merchants who play the most important part; this shows how deeply Gorki understood the specific conditions of his time. The merchants are the central figures in Gorki's world just as the bankers and usurers had been in Balzac's.

In the same way it is no accident that the attitude of the characters to exploitation is so often and so decisively made the core of their human conflicts. The great poetic task devolving upon Gorki was to depict the birth of modern social classes in the Russia of incipient Asiatic capitalism, in a world in which the residue of serfdom had not yet been eliminated from economic life and from the consciousness of the people, while his Western contemporaries dealt with a fully developed capitalism and its already completely ' finished ' classes, a world in which the place and condition of each individual was from the start far more clearly defined than in Gorki's Russia, which was undergoing a violent cataclysm.

In conformity with historical truth, Gorki describes a seething witches' cauldron in which history is brewing the new *classes* of capitalist society out of the old rotten, feudal, and semi-feudal estates. But this does not exhaust the specific quality of the world presented by Gorki. The birth of modern Russian capitalism is at the same time a period of imperialist decay for capitalism elsewhere and also the period in which the preconditions are maturing in Russia for a *bourgeois* revolution which is later to grow into a proletarian revolution. In this historical situation the birth of modern capitalism in Russia was at the same time a process of disintegration and putrefaction. Gorki's great gifts enabled him to make each of his characters represent both these aspects of the process in inseparable connection.

It is for this reason that Gorki devotes so much attention to the modern capitalist, this is why in many of his novels and stories, he portrays several successive generations of capitalists, tracing as accurately as possible the intricate and uneven path of their evolution. In *Foma Gordeyev* he had already introduced the reader to various types of the old-style Russian merchant, differing sharply from each other, not only individually, but also as representatives of the different stages of the development from Asiatic patriarchalism to modern capitalism. This wily Asiatic form of the synthesis of the old and the new exploitation is expressed most pregnantly in the figure of old Mayakin. Gorki shows with the clairvoyance of a genius how Mayakin's son—through the roundabout process of banishment to Siberia—develops into the same type in slightly modernized form. In Mayakov's son-in-law the same ruthless and crafty merchant type appears again in an even more " civilized " incarnation.

The same process is shown in a yet more highly differentiated form in *The House of Artamonov*. In the figure of Pyotr, Gorki brings to life the sloth and conservatism of a part of the old merchant community; in Alexey, on the contrary, he shows the sharp, slippery, crafty adaptability of another section to the requirements of modern capitalism. In the third generation, we find on the one hand the effect of the approaching revolution on the differentiation of the social classes in Ilya Artamonov, who joins the revolutionaries; on the other hand, the mixture of old Russian inertia and imperialist parasitism in Yakov Artamonov.

Gorki paints a broad picture of the social conditions during this development; the chaos, savagery and barbarity of the original accumulation on the eve of a revolution. It is not by accident that all of Gorki's merchant novels contain a number of biographies in which the story of the making of the subject's fortune is told. And all these biographies tell a tale of common theft, brutal robbery and blackmail, forgery and murder. The whole picture shows a close resemblance to the one painted of the original accumulation of capital in England by the great realists of the eighteenth century.

Naturally Gorki laid more stress on portraying the victims than the victimizers. His original starting-point had after all been the portrayal of human beings uprooted and separated from their social group by the development of capitalism. In describing the effects of such things in terms of human destinies, he gives a shocking picture of the brutal, inhuman, Asiatic conditions in which the Russian working class was born and the peasants and artisans transformed into proletarians.

It goes without saying that a writer of Gorki's gifts did not present this dissolution of the old social order as a fatalist acceptance of the loss of the old class standing. Most of his capitalists have themselves originally risen from humble origins. What Gorki shows is that the slightest admixture of decency, conscience or human feeling must prevent any such rise. His Ilya Lunyev gets his " education " by witnessing a murder and being made a semi-accessory to a theft. He thereupon also attempts to " better himself " by murdering and robbing an old moneylender. The rise to capitalist status begins most promisingly, the murder remains undiscovered, but Lunyev nevertheless breaks down because he is humanly incapable of carrying out his schemes; he is not carved out of the hard wood from which a successful capitalist needs to be carved.

Gorki presents this process of disintegration and transformation from every angle. He rightly stresses the dissolution of all the ideologies of old-time Russia, and especially of religion. For neither the revolutionary nor the modern *bourgeois* ideology were born simply and immediately out of the dissolution of the old ideologies. On the contrary; as in every period of disintegration, the process begins with an even greater perplexity of the great masses concerned; the weak sink into apathy or fritter away their strength in short-lived outbursts of senseless revolt, while the heroes of the original accumulation confusedly and yet cunningly adapt their own dishonest interests to both the new and the old ideologies. This is why such a number of religious " prophets " and other swindlers appear in Gorki's writings and why in the dialogues between his characters the question about the truth of the old religion, about the meaning of life, about the path to righteousness plays such an important part.

This ideological confusion reflects the horror, anger and despair felt by the working masses at the atrocities accompanying the social transformation of Russia and at the intertwinement and mingling of the abominations of the old Russia with those of the new. But this horror, anger and despair are at the same time the starting point of revolt. Gorki was originally the poet of the instinctive rebellions of hopeless despair. Later he came into contact with the working-class movement, came to be increasingly bound up with it, and came to understand more and more the road and goal of bolshevism and so his presentation of revolt began to take on a

different aspect. He grows increasingly critical of the heroes of
mere instinctive rebellion and sees the senselessness of such outbursts with ever greater clarity.   Later Gorki said about the
characters in his early writings : ' The Konovalovs are capable of
hero-worship but they themselves are no heroes and very rarely
even " knights-errant for an hour.".'

   Gorki's adherence to the revolutionary working-class movement
manifested itself directly in that the poet now began to depict the
revolutionary struggle of the industrial working class and the poor
peasantry.   Bolshevism enabled Gorki to see in the right light
the aggregate movement of Russian society as a whole and to
assess at their proper value the multiple trends of the oppositional
and revolutionary movements appearing on the scene and directed
against Tsarism.

   Gorki was well aware of the nameless heroism of the old representatives of the Narodnik movement and their gallant, undismayed,
tireless attempts to rouse the torpid masses of peasants and petty
bourgeois to a revolutionary struggle.   But he also saw the confusion in their ideas and their failure and inability to lead the
masses in the right direction. He showed with consummate artistry
the isolation of these heroes among the great mass of the urban and
rural lower middle class who are already desperate but have not yet
awakened to full consciousness of their situation. For all the confusion of their ideas they are yet head and shoulders above this
mass for intelligence and humanity.   When Matvey Kozhemyakin
invites one of these revolutionaries to his house, the latter tells him
that he, the revolutionary, has been to Siberia and is under observation by the police, Matvey says : " I thought so . . . because
you are so clever."   In *Klim Samgin* Gorki later depicted the disintegration of the Narodniki movement and its ever closer assimilation to vulgar Liberalism.

   In this his last, and perhaps most important novel, Gorki paints
a comprehensive picture of the penetration of Marxism into the
Russian intelligentsia, after having shown in *The Mother* the effect
of Marxism on the working-class movement.   It is in the nature of
things that the former should be the more intricate process. Gorki
outlines with great delicacy of touch the social and personal origins
of ' legalist ' Marxism, of the different varieties of Menshevism. He
gives no abstract class analysis, but shows why and how one or the
other form of pseudo-Marxism necessarily came to be the form in
which the personal development of various *bouregois* and *bourgeois*-
intellectual types found expression.   Such personal evolutions are

of course not merely the private business of the individuals concerned. In the end such private aspirations, be it in business, love or friendship, are always shown to be typical manifestations of the developing modern *bourgeoisie* and *bourgeois* intelligentsia of Russia. Gorki also gives a rich and comprehensive picture of the spread of decadent ideologies among the developing *bourgeois* intelligentsia. Maurice Maeterlinck and 'legalist' Marxism get mixed up in the minds of the young generation and provide a remarkable and characteristic parallel to the mixture of residual Asiatic barbarism with modern European decay which he had already shown us in the young generation of the capitalists themselves.

All these trends and tendencies are shown by Gorki to be lurking under the surface of the torpid, apparently motionless swamp of Russian everyday life. This swamp, stirred up for the first time by the revolution of 1905 and drained by the revolution of 1917 and its sequel, leaving only remnants against which Socialist construction is still having to wage a merciless war—this swamp, in Gorki, threatens to engulf all those who are unable to win through to revolutionary truth.

Boredom, relieved only by brutal sex excesses and drinking-bouts (which result in even more hopeless boredom) is the lot of the great masses of the urban and rural lower middle-class.

Most of these accept their aimless and senseless vegetable life— or their comprehensive expulsion from it—as their " fate." This " fate " is the ideology of the indifferent and the weak, with which they seek to justify the stupid aimlessness of their senseless lives.

Gorki ascribes the boredom, the explosions of brutality, the fatalism of these people of the swamp to the fact that they imagine themselves to be living a completely isolated, self-sufficient, purely individual life; they think that they are only victims or at worst parasitic beneficiaries of the social forces at work, but have no room in their consciousness for the common interests of society. In *Matvey Kozhemyakin* Gorki painted a masterly picture of such a 'swamp' in Okurov, a small Russian provincial town. He says about life in Okurov :

' In order to break the tough tentacles of the hopeless boredom in Okurov, which first rouses the beast in man and then, imperceptibly deadening his soul, turns him into a brainless clod—to resist all this a man must strain his mental forces to the utmost and have an unshakable faith in human reason. But a man can win such a faith only by participation in the great life of the world; like the stars in the sky, so must the beacons of all the noble aspirations and hopes that blaze unquenchably all round the earth, ever remain clearly in front of his eyes. Of course it is difficult to see these beacons from Okurov.'

It is one of the finest traits of Gorki's genius that he could discern the connecting principle in apparently widely diverging, even contradictory phenomena. He noticed that the brutally brainless individualism of the old lower middle class persisted unchanged in that section of the younger generation which had acquired a certain new education but had never actively set about changing the old degrading forms of life. In his play *Petty-Bourgeois* Gorki gave a plastic image of this unity between the old and the young and with it the ever-renewed and apparently irresistible power of the old Russian ' swamp.' The incessant and monotonous quarrels between the old and young members of the Bessemenov family express this contradictory unity very clearly. The student sent down from his university, who does not want to take part in a demonstration because he regards it as a "restriction of his personal freedom," is at bottom the same stupid and cowardly petty-*bourgeois* as his father, whose senseless life he will continue amid perpetual bickerings.

2

Gorki looks at this Russian world not as a chronicler, nor as a sociologist, but as a fighting humanist. This means not only that Gorki takes sides, but also that he always depicts the human, the psychological processes, those human tragedies, comedies and tragicomedies, which reflect, in the life of the individual, the social changes that are taking place.

Gorki's humanism manifests itself, above all, in a fierce hatred of apathy and indifference, of every ideology of apathy, of all fatalism. In *Konovalov,* one of his earlier stories, the narrator, who tells the story in the first person, already vainly attempts to convince Konovalov of the irresistible power of circumstance; even this "knight-errant for an hour" refuses to regard his life as determined by a fate from which there is no escape.

In most of his stories Gorki depicts those who are defeated by life. But they are all defeated in an intricate and eventful struggle, the result of which is by no means a foregone conclusion for the individual case. The final outcome is determined rather by a complicated interplay of personality, education, environment, accidental meetings and events. In the outcome of the struggle, however, the class determinants of individual destinies are rendered clearly visible and appear in deep and intricate interconnection with the personal determinants of such individual destinies. But this unity, the merging of social and individual necessities, is always the result of a struggle waged with fluctuating success and is never pre-supposed or taken for granted.

This conception of human destinies, this presentation of human beings enabled Gorki—unlike the modern bourgeois realists—always to show the human values, the human possibilities at first existing and then destroyed in each of his concrete individual cases. But this display of destroyed human values is never due to mere sentimental pity; what Gorki intends is to show up in all their nakedness the mighty social forces which decide the fate of the individual. And with the same inexorable truthfulness he also shows these negative traits in each character which are the immediate occasions of its ruin. Hence Gorki's demonstration of shattered human possibilities is always sharp, hard, polemic, critical, militant. He emphazises especially that the main causes of such destruction of fine and valuable human opportunities lie in a wrong attitude to work and in the self-isolation of such characters in a petty-*bourgeois* individualism.

But however sharply critical Gorki's attitude to his own characters may be—those who perish are nevertheless always fellow human beings to him. Gorki never raises his accusations chiefly against individuals (however negative the traits may be with which he endows them) but always against capitalism and particularly its old-Russian, barbaric, Asiatic variety. Gorki's main accusatory contention is always that Russian capitalism is a mass grave of murdered humanity.

But Gorki is not merely a fighting humanist, he is also a proletarian humanist. However great the grief, hatred and indignation of *bourgeois* humanists may be at the destruction of humanity by capitalism, such indignation must always be tinged either with fatalism or with an abstract morality detached from social circumstance. *Bourgeois* humanists mostly suffer either from a romantic anti-capitalism or certain illusions about 'progress.' Gorki for his part reveals to the reader all the social and individual factors which go to the making of men. When he speaks of 'strength,' 'work,' 'passion,' 'goodness,' etc., he always means socially concrete contents. He never seeks a formal middle course between extremes and is even less willing to extol blindly one or the other extreme. This question is always concrete. Yes, intelligence is naturally preferable to the brainlessness of everyday Russian life. But the question is, intelligence to what end? Is it the brain and vision of a renewer of society or the cunning of a clever rogue? In the same way Gorki deals with the dialectic of goodness, strength, passion, etc. While vigorously championing goodness in contrast to the hard-hearted aloofness of the people drowning in the sticky slime of the petty-*bourgeois swamp,* he sees no less clearly that a certain type of goodness coupled with certain natural leanings, may also be one of the causes of an individual's ruin. Gorki always links up all outstanding human qualities with the great social process of man's struggle for freedom, with the process in the course of which men by their own efforts grow to be more human.

Although Gorki in his presentation of men goes far beyond the bounds of *bourgeois* humanism, his life-work is nevertheless a conservation and further development of the great humanist heritage; above all he is the successor to the great Russian humanists and their revolutionary-humanist clarion-call to the old feudal Russia; he is united with the Russian literary heritage from Pushkin to Tolstoy and Chekhov, and with the great Russian critics by the closest of ties.

His works are a monument bearing witness to the indestructible popularity and vitality of Russian classical literature. Again and again he shows the great stimulating, rousing effect the Russian classics had on their people. (Among the educated classes Gorki often presents literary interests as a mere hobby, snobbery, or self-infection with ideologies of the Western decadents.) One instance, out of a great many, is the influence of Lermontov's *Demon* on the icon-painters, described in Gorki's autobiography.

Such a presentation of the influence of literature is closely linked with Gorki's humanist conception of the general task of literature and illustrates his belief that truly great literature must always be a popular literature. Truly great literature reveals to man the things that make men truly human, reveals to him the great possibilities and faculties that slumber in him and that can be turned into reality by his own actions.

Truly great literature loosens the tongue of the dumb and opens the eyes of the blind. It makes man conscious of himself and of his destinies. And Gorki, the revolutionary humanist, fought above all against the inarticulate, inert, purely instinctive nature of human manifestations in his Russia. He believed that if men once grow really conscious of themselves, their feet are already on the road to the great emancipation of mankind—ultimately, of course, not in each individual case. This is why Gorki presents the dull stolidity

and lack of consciousness even in private life as a dreadful consequence of Tsarist oppression. It is a subtle touch in *The Mother*
when the old working-class woman from whose mind all memories
of her past were erased by ill-treatment, is awakened by her contacts with the revolutionaries to a clear consciousness of all her past
life. As a foil to her, Gorki depicts a number of others, who have
completely lost all remembrance of their own lives, who live from
day to day in a grey daze and stagger from one drinking-bout to
another.

Thus the great mission of true literature is to awaken men to
consciousness of themselves. In order to fulfil this mission it must
have popular appeal. But such popularity does not mean the
blunting of problems or the transformation of literature into propaganda. The popularity of truly great literature should rest on the
fact that it expresses genuine problems on the highest possible level
and digs down to the deepest roots of human suffering, feeling,
thought and action. It is not by accident that poets such as Pushkin and Lermontov are represented as having a great influence on
certain of Gorki's characters. This influence is intended as evidence
for the correctness of his humanist conception of the mission of
literature.

The possibility of such a function of literature is given because in
reality the great objective problems of life do not appear suddenly,
like a bolt from the blue; they are not inventions of some great
genius, but exist in life itself as a chain, the links of which develop
out of each other and are interconnected among themselves. That
the great characters in literature form a continuous series, that a
certain historical tradition can exist in the creation of great typical
characters, is merely the reflection of interconnections existing in
the objective reality of life itself. This link with real life is mirrored
in the critical method of Dobrolyubov and Chernyshevski; the former's review of Goncharov's novel *Oblomov* is a perfect example
of this close link with life. It shows the continuity and within this
continuity the constant evolution of certain problems, in a long line
of characters, from Pushkin's *Onegin* to Goncharov's *Oblomov*.

It is certainly no accident that this both methodologically and
objectively exemplary critique was written about *Oblomov* and not
some other character of fiction. Goncharov's novel shows, with a
typicality rarely surpassed, certain decisively important features of
Russia's specific development, certain specific forms of Russian
backwardness.

Nor is it an accident that Gorki, in his quality of critic and creator of human types, approached the Oblomov problem and its generalization by Dobrolyubov in his own fashion, developing the problem further and generalizing it even more in accordance with the circumstances of his own time. In his tireless struggle against the "Karamazov disease" he gave this analysis of Ivan Karamazov as a new incarnation of the Oblomov type :

'If the reader takes a good look at Ivan Karamazov's wordy effusions, he will see : this is an Oblomov who has turned to nihilism for the sake of bodily comforts and idleness; he will see that Ivan's "rejection of the world" is merely the wordy revolt of a drone and his contention that "man is an evil, savage beast" only the futile chatter of an evil-disposed fellow.'

Gorki thus puts a very wide interpretation on the "Oblomov disease." He shows this disease to be present everywhere where high-sounding words about "lofty" emotions are used to cover up the lack of will or strength required to fight for the transformation of the unsatisfactory world. The line of these Oblomovs depicted by Gorki reaches right down to Klim Samgin.

But Gorki the creator does more than this; he carries the Oblomov line beyond its original limits. He shows a number of characters who, like Goncharov's Oblomov, are ruined precisely by their soft and passive, but pleasing and not valueless humanity; but while in Goncharov's novel these traits are closely linked with Oblomov's parasitic existence as a landowner, Gorki extends the problem to other spheres and shows the dialectic of this passivity and inevitable destruction as it manifests itself in various classes of Russian society. His criticism of petty-*bourgeois* Russia often takes the form of a plebeian version of the Oblomov problem. A clear instance of this is the figure of Yakov in his novel *Three Men.* Yakov says to Ilya Lunev, who wants to rouse him from his passivity : "You are angry, but to no purpose. Just turn this over in your mind : man is made for work and work is made for man . . . Like a wheel—it turns and turns and gets nowhere, and no one knows what it is turning for ? "

The Oblomov disease as presented by Gorki originates in the individualist isolation of men living in the petty-*bourgeois* swamp. The better specimens among them may harbour fine and genuinely human feelings. They are deeply dissatisfied with life in the swamp and make desperate efforts to create a better life for themselves. But all such efforts are frustrated by their feebleness of will and their passivity which are in turn the consequence of their selfish introversion. It was in *Matvey Kozhemayakin* that Gorki gave the most profound and comprehensive picture of the new Oblomov. Matvey's genuinely Oblomovian trait is that he would like to exchange the ugly, repulsive, drunken "idyll" of his parasitic life for a truly human and beautiful, genuine "idyll." He falls in love with a woman revolutionary. "And he imagined a quiet life without need for other people, without a concealed hatred of them and without fear, just the two of them, soul in soul. . . ."

And when he dreams of their life together he always sees it as a monastery or a fortress. Needless to say, not only does this love come to nothing, but Matvey Kozhemyakin's whole life is a failure. But his blood-relationship with Oblomov manifests itself in the sincerity and delicacy of his feelings. A young girl, reading Matvey's diaries when he is already an old man, exclaims : "How lovely! Why, it's just like reading Turgenyev!" The objective continuity of the problem reminds us of Chernyshevski's article on Turgenyev's *A Russian at a Rendezvous*.

This return to the Oblomov problem is obviously an extension and generalization of a burning issue. This is shown not only by Gorki's Oblomov-like characters, but especially by his presentation of the practical man who provides the foil for Oblomov. Goncharov's Stolz is merely a symbol for practical activity in general, and Dobrolyubov saw clearly how feebly rooted he was in the Russian soil of the time, how abstract and Utopian was the presentation of this character. In pointing out the social causes of this abstract quality, Dobrolyubov says ·

"For this reason all we see in Goncharov's novel is that this Stolz is an active sort of fellow, who is always after something, running about, acquiring things, saying that life means doing some work, etc. But what he is doing and how he manages to get things done where all others fail—remains a mystery for us."

In Gorki this abstract activity of the types who serve as counterparts to the Oblomov passivity is clearly differentiated and its concrete dialectic is revealed. The types themselves range from Mayakin and Miron Artamonov on the one hand to the class-conscious heroes of the revolutionary working-class movement on the other. In these new circumstances their struggle decides the fate of Russia. Oblomov, while still an interesting and widespread type, is now of negligible importance in the wider historical sense.

Gorki's original treatment of the Oblomov problem is only one instance among many, all showing how the great traditions of Russian classical literature came to life in his works. Gorki's Socialist realism was the heir to Russian classical literature, just as the revolution of October was the heir to the finest traditions of the past struggles for freedom. It will be one of the most important tasks of our literary history to uncover the numerous threads which link Gorki with the Russian classical literature of the nineteenth century and to show what contribution his new conception of its problems has made towards the development of socialist realism. This would at the same time be the Marxist reformulation of the great tradition as an illustration of which we have mentioned Dobrolyubov's review of Goncharov's *Oblomov*.

3

In Gorki's life-work as in that of many other great modern narrators—one need think only of Rousseau, Goethe or Tolstoy— the autobiographical element plays a very important part. Those great narrators who summed up the essential traits of their epoch in mighty works of literature, had themselves experienced in their own lives the emergence and maturing of the problems of the age. This process of digesting the historical content of an epoch is itself most characteristic for the epoch.

A great narrator regards not only the content of his creative work but its basic manner and style as necessarily determined by the historical realities of the time. How this style was born, why the writer adopted this style and no other, is thus not the private business of the writer, not a mere subjective experience. On the other hand, the ' bad subjectivity' of many modern authors, who simply scatter their ego all over their works, is due to the fact that they are unable to see their own development from the perspective of such a social and historical objectivity. Others (e.g., Flaubert) go so far as to see their own subjectivity merely as a disturbing element interfering with the objectivity of their work. This sort of " austerity " does not, of course, prevent the intrusion of ' bad subjective ' elements into their epic creations.

Gorki's own autobiographical writings follow the tradition of the old classical autobiographies. One might even say that their distinctive characteristic, their *leitmotiv*, is precisely their extraordinary objectivity. This objectivity does not mean that the tone of the narration is impartial. The *tone* of Goethe's autobiographical writings is far more objective than Gorki's. The objectivity consists rather in the content of his autobiography, in the attitude to life expressed in it; it contains very little subjective, personal material.

Gorki shows us his development indirectly, through the circumstances, events, and personal contacts which have influenced it. Only at certain critical points does he sum up his subjective experience of the world as raising his personality to a higher level. But even this is not always a directly subjective summary; the reader is often made to see for himself Gorki's own evolution under the influence of objectively depicted events. Gorki himself gave this account of his autobiographical method : " In my childhood I saw myself as a hive in which many simple, ordinary people deposited, like bees, the honey of their knowledge and thoughts about life, each generously enriching my life with what they had to give. Often this honey was impure and bitter, but all knowledge is still honey."

This objectivity is the most subjective, most personal trait of Gorki's autobiography, for it is here that his profound ties with the life of the working masses, which is the basis of his implacable, militant humanism, finds expression. In the first pages of his autobiography he already reveals these ties very plainly. He says that the story of his childhood appears to him like a " sombre fairy-tale " which he must nevertheless truthfully tell, despite all the horrors it contains. ' Truth takes precedence over pity, and after all I am not speaking about myself, but about that stifling, narrow circle of agonizing experiences in which I lived and in which common Russian folk lived and *still live.*' (My italics. G.L.).

Here the connection between Gorki's objectivity and his militant humanism is clearly visible. This is that ' partiality of the materialist,' about which the young Lenin wrote in his polemic against Struve's sham objectivism. This compound of objectivity and partiality (which is an essential element of proletarian humanism) and its connection with the actual great struggles for the liberation of the workers, is clearly expressed in the autobiography : ' When I recall these leaden abominations of our savage Russian life, I sometimes ask myself " Is it worth while to speak of such things? " And I answer myself with renewed conviction, "Yes, it is worth while ! "'; for this is the tough, vile truth which is still alive to this day. It is a truth which must be known down to its roots, in order that it may be torn out with these its very roots from the memory and soul of men, from our whole hard and shameful life. . . .'

Gorki wrote this in 1913 and added that what is amazing in this life is not the toughness with which its beastly brutalities cling to it, but that ' however thick this layer may be, bright, healthy and creative things can nevertheless break through it; fine, human seeds grow nevertheless, fostering an imperishable hope of our rebirth to a brighter, truly human life.' Thus it is this objectivity itself that provides the means of the real struggle against the powers of darkness.

Gorki knew well enough that it is this objectivity which draws a demarcation line between great and minor literature, between classical literature and the sham subjectivity of his own contemporaries. In an article he wrote in 1908, Gorki said about this difference between old and contemporary literature :

' Characteristic of the old writers is their breadth of conception, the harmony of their world-view, the intensity of their feeling for life; their field of vision encompassed the whole wide world. The ' personality' of a contemporary writer is merely his manner of writing, and the real personality, i.e., the complex of thoughts and feelings, grows ever more elusive, unsubstantial and to tell the truth, miserable. The writer is no longer a mirror of the world, but only a small splinter of it, from which the social backing has worn off, and having lain about in the mire of the city streets, it is no longer able to reflect with its facets the great life of the world; all it mirrors is fragments of street life, little scraps of broken souls."

Gorki's autobiography shows how a true mirror of the world comes into being in our time. It raises afresh the question of the receptivity and sensitivity of the artist, which has been completely twisted from its meaning in the practice of most modern writers. There is a false but deep-seated conviction about, that the essence of receptivity is a passive mirroring of things, that it excludes the possibility of an active approach to life and its problems, that it is the opposite of activity and practice.   This wrong conception derives from modern subjectivity and Gorki rightly saw in it the loss of the " social backing" of that mirror which every writer ought to be.

Such writers experience only themselves. For them receptivity means listening to their own inner sensations, to the experiences of their own ego. Their attention is directed, not towards the outer world, not towards life itself, but towards their own reactions to the outer world and their so-called ' receptivity' is merely a passive contemplation of their own navel. This contrast between Gorki and other contemporary writers is shown perhaps the most vividly in his memories of Leonid Andreyev. Andreyev was a writer of great gifts and was fairly candid in his conversations with Gorki. In one of these candid talks he complained to Gorki that while he, Gorki, was always meeting the most interesting people, he, Andreyev never succeeded in doing anything of the sort. Andreyev did not understand that this was not a matter of good or bad luck, but that it was simply a result of the two writers' different basic approach to life. Andreyev possessed a most vivid imagination and with it a great gift of abstraction entirely lacking in direction. As soon as he met with any manifestation of life, his imagination immediately seized upon it, raised it to a very high degree of abstraction and with that done the phenomenon lost all interest for him. He lacked the patience to listen carefully and grasp the true meaning of the phenomenon, to observe it from every aspect and at every stage of development, compare it painstakingly and methodically with other phenomena and only then give a picture of it, a picture as closely as possible approaching the richness of the section of life it depicted.

But, however paradoxical it may sound, Gorki's patience was a result of his activity, and Andreyev's impatience was a direct result of the fact that he took no active, practical part in the struggles of the time, that he lived a life dedicated to purely literary activities. For the essentials of reality lie deeper and require a patience and receptivity such as Gorki possessed; such traits become visible only in the course of practical activities and can be discerned only by those whose life is focussed on the practical.

The difference between essential and inessential, between what is right and what is merely interesting (even though it may be quite superficial or false) is quite decisive, precisely from the practical point of view. For those who have a passive attitude to life, the boundaries between essential and inessential, between right and wrong, are vague and blurred. It is only in that mutual exchange between the individual and the world which is born out of practice, out of action, that the essential things in the world and in other individuals can be discerned. Only practical participation gives choice and helps to determine the basis of such choice. Only success or failure in social activity can reveal the truly essential things in life.

But activity without receptivity is blind. Only a passionate acceptance of the world such as it is, with all its inexhaustible multiplicity and incessant change, only a passionate desire to learn from the world; only love of reality, even though there are many abominations in it against which one has to struggle and which one hates —a love which is not hopeless because in the same reality one can see a road leading to human goodness—faith in life, and in its movement, through human endeavour towards something better, in spite of all the stupidity and evil manifested every day—only passionate receptivity, provides a foundation for a practical activity of the right kind.

This is optimism without illusions and Gorki possessed it. Illu-

sions veil reality and the lives of those who harbour illusions are
not real lives, but only lives of illusions or of lost illusions. And the
apparent polar opposite of the man of illusions, the sceptic, the dis-
illusioned, experiences just as one-sidedly only his own disappointment and its subjective causes. Modern optimism and pessimism,
modern illusions and disillusions both equally create mere formulas,
even though, as in the case of Andreyev, they may be fantastic and
interesting formulas. Illusions and their loss are equally barriers to
the acceptance and absorption of reality.

But a rich and eventful life is a prerequisite of great literature,
not only in the material sense of a wide experience of life, but also
from the point of view of the depth of the problems presented. A
writer must live a rich life in order to be able to present what is
really typical. It was Richard Hurd, an eighteenth-century English
æstheticist, who expressed this most clearly. In commenting on
the remark made by Aristotle that Sophocles depicted men as they
ought to be, but Euripides as they really were, Hurd wrote :

" . . . . The meaning of which is : Sophocles, from his more
extended commerce with mankind, had enlarged and widened the
narrow, partial conception arising from the contemplation of the
particular character into a complete comprehension of the kind.
Whereas the philosophic Euripides, having been mostly conversant
in the Academy, when he came to look into life, keeping his eyes
too intent on single, really existing personages, sank the kind in
the *individual,* and so painted his characters naturally indeed and
truly with regard to the objects in view, but sometimes without that
general and universally striking likeness which is demanded to the
full exhibition of poetical truth."

One cannot, of course, compare modern writers with Euripides.
By the passage quoted we only wished to touch upon the causes of
the extraordinary poverty of modern literature. We have seen that
the withdrawal from life, which is characteristic of modern writers,
has necessarily produced a position in which they can create only
individual figures; when they are driven to go beyond the merely
individual, they must lose themselves in empty, lifeless abstractions.

Real types can be created only by writers who have an opportunity to make many well-founded comparisons between individuals,
comparisons which are based on rich practical experience and which
are such as to reveal the social and personal causes of affinities
between individuals. The richer the life of the writer, the greater
will be the depth from which he can bring up such affinities; the
wider the compass embracing the unity of the personal and social

elements in the type presented, the more genuine and the more interesting will the character be.

Gorki's autobiography shows us how a rich and eventful life developed in the young Gorki this faculty of creating types by comparing superficially quite different types. In this education of a great writer literature itself, of course, played a very important part. The young Gorki, still in his formation period, already saw that the great vocation of classical literature lay in teaching men to see and express themselves. From the outset Gorki always linked literature with life in his reading. As he read Balzac's *Eugenie Grandet,* he was not only delighted with the magnificent simplicity of the presentation—he immediately compared the old moneylender Grandet with his own grandfather.

But nevertheless literature is only an aid to reality, even though a very important one. What remains decisive is still the richness of life itself, the passionate desire to absorb and reproduce the phenomena of life in all their fullness. Gorki gives very interesting instances of how he began to mould the living men he met into types. I quote only one characteristic example :

" Osip, neat and trim, suddenly appeared to me like the stoker Jacob, who was always indifferent to everything. Sometimes again he reminded me of Peter Vasilyev the proof-reader, sometimes of Peter the cabby; sometimes I thought he had something in common with my grandfather—in one way or another he is like other old men I have known. They were all amazingly interesting old fellows, but I felt somehow that one could not live with them, that it would be difficult and unpleasant. It was as though they ate away your soul and their shrewd talk covered your heart with a layer of brown rust. Was Osip good? No. Was he evil? Not that either. He was shrewd, that much I understood. But while it amazed me by its flexibility, this shrewdness tormented me and in the end I began to feel that he was on all points hostile to me."

Thus Gorki's autobiography shows us how a great poet of our time was born, how a child developed into a mirror of the world. Gorki's objective style emphasizes this character of the book. It shows Maxim Gorki as an important participant in the human comedy of pre-revolutionary Russia and it shows us life as the true teacher of every great poet. Gorki introduces us to this great teacher who formed him and shows us how it was done, how he, Gorki, was taught by life itself to be a man, a fighter and a poet. And it was precisely the experience of its many horrors that turned Gorki into a militant humanist. Tolstoy admired Gorki's goodness

and strength, and told him that after all the things he had been
through he would have every right to be evil.

4.

Like most great story-tellers, Gorki began his career with the
short story; that form which has for its theme a strange, out-of-the-
common, surprising event—an event so conceived that its surprising
aspect gives a both personally and socially characteristic picture of
one or more persons. This nature of the short story makes it a
primeval and ever-popular form of art. Gifted story-tellers among
the people, when they want to tell an audience the story of some
strange and characteristic happening, instinctively adopt a form
that approaches that of the short story. In the same way, young
Gorki, writing admirable short stories at a very early stage in his
career, was not merely following a literary tradition, but obeying an
inborn urge to tell these stories out of his own eventful life, an
urge which literary tradition, the example of other earlier great
writers, merely disciplined and rendered conscious.

On the other hand, all the problematic elements introduced into
the short-story form by the exigencies of contemporary life are also
present already in Gorki's early writings. The more intricate the
conditions of life, the more difficult it is to give an exhaustive
characterization of human beings through a single occurrence in
their lives; all the more so as the accidental element (of which mention was made earlier) in the combination of individual traits with
class traits is a considerable obstacle to the illustration of the socially
typical by the one striking incident on which the short story is
based. Such illustration was still easy in the first period of the
Renaissance; it provided the social basis for the neat perfection of
the short stories of Boccaccio and his contemporaries. In their
beauty there was nothing of the artificial, formalistic, abstract
quality we find in the writings of the modern imitators of the
classical short story.

Owing to the greater intricacy of its material, the modern short
story is of necessity conceived on broader lines than the old : it
embraces a chain of events moving with increasing tension towards
a final event which corresponds to the stylistic *pointe* in the classical
short story. Such a broadening of the short story is naturally not
merely quantitative but involves important new problems of style.

But in spite of these inevitable changes the basic problems of form
relating to the old short story still remain valid for the new. For
if the plot is not vigorously compressed and the characterization

achieved by means of action, the short story dissolves into a millieu-picture, into a reproduction of a mood or into a psychological analysis; and this is exactly what happened to the short story in the hands of the greater part of modern short-story writers.

But since Balzac and Stendhal, the best newer writers have been struggling to give their complicated stories—stories dealing not with one event but with a chain of events, the same sharp and self-suffi-cient form as the old stories possessed. This struggle put the crea-tive imagination of the writer to an increasingly exacting test. For the more intricate the contradictions, the revelation of which forms the *point* of the short story, the more difficult it is to find a plot in which every aspect of such complicated contradictions finds con-crete expression.

The struggle for this form of the short story is a basic element in Gorki's writings, not only in his short stories themselves but in his autobiography and his novels as well. Gorki's writings are crowded with characters in numbers comparable with those of Balzac. Never-theless—or perhaps for this reason—his composition is based, not on characters, but on events. Only his last novels are an exception to this, but elements of his style are still visible in the methods of characterization even here.

As a result of his eventful life, Gorki had such a store of charac-ters and events at his disposal that he could always pick the most suitable to illustrate his point, and could intensify it to an extreme without making it less true to life. He was never forced to adhere to the pattern of the humdrum and average in presenting men and events. And because from the start his intention was to expose the inhuman atrocities of life in old Russia, he could choose the most flagrant cases; the more flagrant the case, the more vividly it demonstrated the horrors possible in the Russia of the time. Gorki's genius manifested itself quite early in the artistry with which he made these flagrant cases appear not only possible, but typical; the inner evolution of his characters, which reveals their typical quali-ties, seems to move towards such a flagrant outcome with fateful necessity. The opposite tendency in Gorki, which forms the counterpart to his exposure of the horrors of Tsarist Russia—i.e., the demonstration that in spite of all abominations, truly human qualities develop and break through—naturally demands a similar presentation of sharply contrasted, flagrant and extraordinary events.

The nineteenth century has on the one hand to some extent as-similated the short story to the novel and on the other hand has developed the novel towards a greater concentration which formerly belonged only to the short story. The first of these movements is a universal characteristic of nineteenth-century literature and only very few great writers have succeeded in preserving the short-story form from dissolution and destruction. The second trend, the evolution of the novel in the direction of greater concentration, marks the struggle of the best writers of the period against the art-destroying conditions introduced into literature by capitalism.

In both respects Gorki follows in the footsteps of the best European writers, but always in his original manner. In his autobiography, and also in a long letter written to Octave Mirbeau, he speaks of the decisive influence Balzac had on his development as a writer. This influence of Balzac is due mainly to the fact that both great writers were at bottom, if not on the surface, faced with the same task : to depict, as a whole, the multiple and intricate contradictions which arise in a period of great social change. It is characteristic of both authors that in their presentation of society, while they strive to show with the greatest possible clarity a process of decay and disintegration, they at the same time, as the great artists they are, try to follow in the footsteps of the classics and depict this decay in an artistically perfect and complete form. It is therefore no accident that in Gorki's first novels we find the same short-story-like concentration as in many novels of Balzac.

But despite this mutual assimilation to one another of the short story and the novel, there still remains a wide gap between them, a gap which all great writers consciously or instinctively respect. The short story, even in its modern wider form, presents a single, stressed individual fate. The workings of social forces appear in it in extreme exaggeration. Convincing evidence of the bare fact that such things are possible at all is sufficient to expose an almost too horrible reality. Let us think of such stories as Gorki's *A Man is Born*. When Gorki wants to show the emergence of humanly valuable forces in this swamp of abominations, he again chooses a similar form of short story (*Yemelyan Pilyai*).

Of course this does not by any means exhaust the thematic range of Gorki's short stories. The short story offers him the possibility of presenting the dialectic of social necessity and individual destiny by means of extreme, particularly interesting cases, and showing the devious, adventurous, sometimes quite fairy-tale-like ways in which the class realities prevail against a stubborn, erring or misguided conscience. Here, too, the short story offers only a limited presentation of certain aspects of a type and not the whole picture of the type in its universal form. But the very possibility of such unusual individual fates illustrates the inevitability of typical situations and renders their understanding easier. We call attention, for instance, to the case of the idle young Oblomov-type dreamer in " Blue Life " who is " rescued " by his class, only to develop into a calculating and surly merchant.

Finally, it is possible in a short story to show certain aspects of great social trends, of vast social complexes, and to show them in a relatively isolated form, letting the movement as a whole provide a general background.

The assimilation to the short-story technique in Gorki's early novels is quite a different matter. Here the typical aspect of the exceptional case must emerge wholly from the chain of events and form the basis for the presentation of an epic totality. Here the unpropitious effect of capitalist conditions hampers the writer incomparably more than in the case of the short story. This difficulty affected all novels of the nineteenth century.

But Gorki in his youth had to face even more serious obstacles than the earlier great novelists of the nineteenth century. For to whatever extent a great writer aims to lay his emphasis, both thematically and ideologically, on the portrayal of the disintegration of a society,—as a narrator he needs a tangible fulcrum for his plot, needs stable connections between characters, who must have common spheres and objectives of action, etc., all in a visible world in which the plot can unfold in epic form. It is well known that capitalism destroys to an increasing extent the " totality of objects "—as Hegel called this postulate of epic poetry. Balzac and Stendhal could still make use of residues left behind by the heroic epoch of *bourgeois* evolution and Tolstoy of remnants of the old semi-feudal patriarchal country life, even though what they depicted was the dissolution of these conditions of life.

But Gorki was on the one hand faced with a far more advanced process of disintegration and restratification, and on the other hand he stressed with far greater accusatory and revolutionary fervour the disintegration of the old form of life and of the old spheres of action. He maintained with passionate polemic force that these old forms of life had lost their living content and had been turned into mere empty shells, cloaks for the bestiality of the old Russia of the Tsars. In order to visualize this contrast quite sharply, one need only compare the descriptions of births, marriages, deaths, etc., in Tolstoy and in Gorki's early works. Gorki scarcely ever describes any such function without some scandalous occurrence in which the stupidity and brutality cloaked by these forms comes to the surface. He often uses such occasions for the final explosion of latent antagonisms. Thus in *Foma Gordeyev,* where a banquet given to celebrate the launching of a new ship serves as the occasion when Foma, driven beyond endurance, flings his hatred and contempt into the face of the capitalists and publicly relates the life-story of each of the guests, with all murders and forgeries and other crimes they have committed. This object-lesson-like critical presentation of the dissolution of the old forms of life is a most important feature of Gorki's whole life-work.

In *Matvey Kozhemyakin* he shows, in the struggle between town and suburb, how the harmless old custom of cheerful and friendly sparring degenerates into a fight of appalling brutality and cruelty; this tendency reaches its culminating point in *Klim Samgin* where Gorki describes the mass panic on the occasion of Nicholas II. coronation in Moscow, when thousands of men, women and children were trampled to death.

Gorki follows this socially inevitable road boldly to its end. But as a result of the events, objects, natural meetings of people and the like, must disappear from his writings—that is, all the things, the typical appearance, typical sequence and typical role in life of which lent the epic poems of the older type their palpable social meaning. Life loses its sensuously perceptible face.

Life crumbles away. We have seen how the old Asiatic form of capitalism turned people into surly and malevolent herrnits and individualists, into beings vegetating like snails in their own cramped shells. This animal-like individualism of the petty-*bourgeois* masses was merely varnished over by the superficial modernization due to developing capitalism. The same boredom, the same vague feeling of futility still ruled their lives, and their dull vegetative existence was relieved only by bouts of bestial excesses.

How is it possible in these circumstances to tell in its continuity a story that matters? How can complete, rich, truly living characters be found in this world?

Every social crisis and reshuffle must increase the accidental quality of individual destinies and especially the consciousness of this accidentality. The more " accidental " the forms of life become, the more difficult it is to put them into poetic form and the more difficult it is to endow them with epic significance. Dostoyevski was already profoundly aware of this problem. At the end of his novel *A Raw Youth* he complained at length of the literary

unsuitability of such an "accidental" family as the one that served
as the subject of the novel. He remarked with an ironical dig at
Tolstoy (without naming him) that only the description of the old
Russian nobility was a good subject for the novelist, for among
them one might "find at least a semblance" of a proper order.
And he lets the writer of the letter draw this conclusion after having read the manuscript : "I must admit that I would not like to
be a novelist depicting a hero coming from an accidental family.
It is a thankless task, without any beautiful forms." Gorki nevertheless undertook this "thankless task." Accidental people, accidental environment, an accidental family—all these things acquire
a realistic meaning, they all stress the disintegration of old Russia.

Like all great writers, Gorki takes this "defect" of his material,
its unsuitability, for presentation, as the starting-point of his creative
task. Only eclectics or epigones run away from the obstacles which
life places in the path of art. Truly great artists have no illusions
about the difficulties arising out of the choice of such socially unsuitable themes. The greatness of the writer's art consists in finding a way to present such unsuitable subjects in truly artistic form
and turn the unfavourable circumstances into carriers and vehicles
of a new, original form born out of this same unsuitable material.

Gorki's starting-point is thus the brutal atomization of Russian
life, its "zoological individualism" as he calls it, its hopeless boredom and apparent immobility. But creator that he is, he directs this
lazy immobility into a continuous series of movements, short bursts
of exertions, desperate explosions, alternating fits of elation and depression. He cuts up the dreary, cloudy mass of boredom into
brief dramatic moments full of internal movement, full of tragedy
and comedy, and creates in his novels a long chain of such small,
but dramatically animated scenes, in which he shows the revolt
of men against their environment, their despair, their relapse into
apathy; in brief, the internal and external destruction of the human personality by the social forces governing life in old Russia.

Even the loneliness of his characters is not a state of mind (as it
always is in the works of the Western writers, whether they extol
or deplore the fact). In Gorki's world loneliness is a prison. Before
Gorki Tolstoy had already depicted the evolution of human beings
not as a movement along a line, but as a movement within a definite, although not mechanically and permanently closed, space; in
other words Tolstoy had already regarded as characteristic of a
man the extreme possibilities between which his development moved
to and fro.

Gorki developed this tendency far beyond the limit reached by Tolstoy and he was far more conscious of the social causes of this " space " than Tolstoy could be. He also regarded the social barriers defining this " space " far more consciously and critically than Tolstoy; he sees in them those same sinister powers against which he had fought passionately all through his life. For this reason, the " space " has in Gorki a far more distinct social character, a social history of its own and is at the same time—far more polemically than in Tolstoy—conceived as a dungeon of the human personality. In this way human loneliness is transformed by Gorki from a condition into a process, into a dramatic happening. Gorki shows how the prison walls which, in spite of their common social origin, are yet very personal walls of solitary confinement, are gradually built up for each individual out of the mutual inter-action of personality and environment.

It is with this in view that Gorki always devoted much attention to the childhood of his heroes, (unlike Balzac who mostly allots a merely episodic role to the early history of his characters) and thus seems to continue the tradition of the older novels, of *Wilhelm Meister's Apprenticeship, Tom Jones* etc. But this similarity is merely seeming. Goethe and Fielding described the childhood of their heroes in order to reveal the genesis of their positive personal qualities, whereas Gorki does so in order to show in tangible vivid form the way in which the particular prison walls surrounding the hero came into being, thus transforming the " space " (which he conceives as a prison wall confining the personality) into a his-torical process. He relates not only the history of the building of the wall, but the unsuccessful attempts to escape and finally the point at which the victim in despair dashes his head to fragments on its stones.

Thus is in Gorki boredom made dramatic, loneliness turned into dialogue, mediocrity poetically animated. Unlike his contempor-aries, Gorki does not ask : what is a mediocrity like— he asks : how does a mediocrity develop, how is a human being distorted into mediocrity? In these his decisive creative problems the sig-nificance of his militant humanism is clearly revealed. Like all honest realists of the capitalist era, Gorki shows how capitalism dismembers the human personality; and in conformity with the con-ditions of old-time Russia, he can show it in a far more atrocious form than the Western realists. But as a militant proletarian hu-manist he regards this dismemberment merely as a transitory historical necessity of a certain period in human evolution and not as an immutable accomplished fact or as a fateful unavoidable destiny. Therefore, while depicting this dismemberment, he is constantly and indignantly up in arms against it. He claims that this dismemberment is the specific historical sin of capitalism. By presenting to our eyes the process of dismemberment, he ceaselessly directs our attention to the image of the whole, the integral, the non-dismembered human being, even though only in the shape of lost possibilities. He is the only writer of his time who presents the fetishized world of capitalism in a manner totally free of fetishism.

This central problem of Gorki's art, these contradictions, this tension, inherent in the life-material he proposes to present, determine his poetic technique. We can here illustrate only a few of the more important traits of this technique : above all the striking brevity of the single scenes out of which he builds up the epic totality of his novels—a result this of the destruction of the "totality of objects."

These scenes, however short, are yet full of sharply pointed inner dramatic tension. Like other great realists, Gorki shows his characters from every aspect, but never by description or analysis, always by means of some action. It follows from the nature of the world depicted by Gorki that such action of his characters can be of only short duration—they are always desperate bursts of effort, followed by a relapse into apathy or bestiality.

Thus, the "defect" of the material he works on compels him to put aside the broad composition of the older narrators; but as a true-born poet he nevertheless does not give up presenting entire human beings in their process of evolution and in action. It is for this purpose that he developed his peculiar style of modelling complete characters by means of a multiplicity of facets, as diamond-cutters display the water of a gem. In a rapid sequence of short scenes he gradually illustrates every one of these facets of his characters. Thus translating into action every possibility latent in a character, such a continuity of short poignant scenes finally adds up to the sum of a human personality destroyed by capitalism and at the same time demonstrates the unity of the individual and the social in such a personality.

Gorki's proletarian humanism enables him to achieve an infallibly true balance and proportion in dealing with this problem. He accuses capitalism of having destroyed the human personality, but he by no means idealizes the blind revolt against this destruction, as Dostoyevski so often does and Dostoyevski's epigones always do.

The correct proportion in depicting the dialectic of social and individual factors is not a formal harmony, but a result of Gorki's correct understanding of the social process which necessarily leads through the abominations of capitalism to a proletarian revolution.

In contradistinction to all his contemporaries, Gorki's short scenes are without exception kept on a very high level. He follows the example of the classics in that he does not permit any naturalist barriers to limit the manner and capacity of expression of his characters. But because of his unparalleled experience and contact with the common people he is able nevertheless to give this higher level of expression a natural form. In other words, the content of the thoughts expressed is on a much higher level than any naturalist "average" would permit; but the situation which gives rise to these thoughts is perfectly true to life and completely typical, and the language in which they are expressed is perfectly in keeping with the social condition and individual character of the person speaking.

Gorki oversteps the naturalist barriers "only" insofar as he presents men and situations on the highest concrete level that is still within the possible scope of the type in question. I mention only one instance of this : old Mayakin comes to see his daughter and finds a notebook and in it a sentence expressing the Hegelian thought that everything that is, is reasonable. The old scoundrel reacts to this sentence with the same passion as old Grandet to a quotation from Bentham. He says : "Hm—everything in the world is reasonable—not badly put, that ! So somebody has found that out ! Yes, very well said indeed . . . And if there were no fools, it would even be quite true. . . . But one always finds fools in places where they don't belong, so one can't say that everything in the world is reasonable ! . . . " In such passages Gorki demonstrates in *statu nascendi* how ideologies come into being and how the men of the present day readily take over from the thoughts of the past what best suits their personal, individual purposes—or, in other words, how ideologies become socially effective.

The raising of such little scenes to levels of this height represents at the same time that general social cohesion which is almost completely lacking in the consciousness of each single individual. The characters in the story believe that they are suffering a merely personal fate and despair in their loneliness, but the reader is brought face to face with all the economic and ideological factors which objectively determine the fate of the individual, even though the latter, in his desperate loneliness, knows nothing of them.

This raising of the level, this method of painting man in his entirety in a world the essence of which is the dismemberment and the destruction of this entirety, was required to turn the stories of *Foma Gordeyev* and *Three People*—although their basic presentation is that of the short story—into genuine novels, i.e. epic totalities. They are, of course, very peculiar, concentrated and poignant novels, novels pervaded by an angry despair, and a humanist protest.

Gorki's increasingly close co-operation with the revolutionary working-class movement, his increasingly complete absorption of Bolshevik theory and last but not least his experience of the first (1905) revolution effected a radical change in his style. It would be difficult to find, within the life-work of a single author, a greater contrast in style that that between *Foma Gordeyev* and *The Mother*. This contrast is born from the soul of the material itself and not as a formalist result of Gorki's own intentions. We call the attention of the reader to the contrast as formulated by Lenin which we have used as an epigraph. In his first short stories and novels Gorki showed that people *could* no longer live in the old way. In *The Mother* he showed how at least the vanguard of the working-class and peasantry was no longer *willing* to live in the old way.

Accordingly, the nature of the human building-components of the novel also undergoes a radical change. Consciousness takes the place of dull despair. Preparations for a revolution and revolutionary action take the place of blind revolt or weary apathy. This new material produced a new style of presentation in *The Mother*. We still see old-time Russia with all its hideous brutality—the picture of this is rendered even more intense by the bestial measures of repression directed by Tsarism against the revolutionary movement of the workers. But the decisive current which here determines the nature and the fate of the characters runs in the opposite direction; Gorki shows the difficult but clear road along which the working-class advances to conquer the dark misery of its life and build a bright, human future for itself.

This liberating influence of the proletarian revolution is presented by Gorki not merely as a hope for the future, but as a present reality which transforms men; proletarian humanism is not merely a distant goal of the revolutionary working-class movement—each step forward in it is at the same time the attainment of this goal in the personal lives of those who take part in the movement. The working-class movement, in plucking men from the unconscious dullness of their lives and turning them into conscious fighters for the emancipation of all mankind, transforms them into harmonious, contented, happy human beings in spite of the hard fate which they have to bear as individuals, in spite of torture, imprisonment and exile.

Thus we find a paradox—surprising harmony in *The Mother* —a harmony born of the material it deals with and hence real in the artistic sense and convincing despite its paradoxicality. The description of the heroic battle fought by the vanguard of the working-class rises to epic heights, and the revolutionary breaking-up of the old forms of life, the revolutionary building-up of the organisations of the working-class gives birth to a new "totality of objects." The strike, the May-day demonstration, the trial, the escape from prison, the funeral of the revolutionary, etc.—all these pictures are painted with the richness and breadth of the true epic. Even the incidents of brutal repression at the demonstration and the funeral are here not a "disturbance," as it would be in the presentation of the disintegration of the old forms of life in novels with *bourgeois* themes, but a great epic struggle, the struggle of light against darkness. With this change in the sphere of action of the characters, the presentation of their single actions also changes. Single scenes, for all the austerity of their presentation, are given a breadth not elsewhere found in Gorki's writings.

The great turning-point which this novel marks in the whole of literature does not consist solely in the fact that Gorki succeeded in creating *positive* heroes and showing by his own original method how men come to be such positive heroes, but also in that Gorki, as the first classic of socialist realism, achieves for the first time in the literature of class society the positive pathos of epic presentation.

This change of style which Bolshevism and the revolution brought about in Gorki's writings, can still be observed in his later novels in which he returned to *bourgeois* themes. Naturally Gorki could not and did not wish to change the basic methods of presentation arising out of the social character of the material he worked on. The *bourgeois* life of old-time Russia and its disintegration did not permit, without violation of the material, any such broadly conceived epic pictures as those found in *The Mother*. The tense, dramatic brevity of single scenes, the facet-like presentation of the characters from every aspect must thus remain the method used.

But the general movement of the later novels has grown broader, quieter, more epic in character. A society is going to its death before our eyes and the author knows that this means a happier future for mankind. The anguish, the searching, the dramatic despair of the early novels disappears and its place is taken by the sovereign calm of the great humanist who sees the path of mankind lying clear before it. This epic calm does not, however, in any way mitigate the sharpness of his protest. On the contrary, his indictment of society is even fiercer and more convincing. But it is no longer a violent diatribe by one who is himself in the thick of the fight; it is the dispassionate pleading of a public prosecutor presenting the case of The People against Capitalism. This attitude determines the epic calm of the style, the high degree of typifying generalization.

The autobiography marks the transition from the style of *The Mother* to the style of the later novels. It shows the contradictory and optimistic process in the course of which Gorki, the great proletarian humanist, rises to the surface out of the hideous depths of Russian provincial life. In a whole gallery of splendid men and women of the people (for instance the wonderful figure of the old grandmother) Gorki depicts the mighty strength of the people, requiring only the leadership given by the working-class and its vanguard in order to be transformed into truly positive human beings in a socialist world.

The first great novel of Gorki's later years, the plebeianized Oblomov, *Matvey Kozhemyakin* we have already discussed in brief. It was followed by the powerful epic painting of the growth and decay of Russian capitalism, in the family chronicle of the Artamonovs. It is no accident that the idea of such a novel, stretching across several generations of capitalists, a novel telling the story of the decadence of capitalism through the medium of the decline of a capitalist family, cropped up at the same time in many countries. Thomas Mann wrote his *Buddenbrooks,* Galsworthy his *Forsyte Saga.* But even the greatest *bourgeois* writers dealt chiefly with the human, intellectual and moral decline of their characters and the decay of capitalism was merely for them a background. Their interest centres around the process of decadence within one family and only the intrinsic truth of the characterization and certain stylistic devices give the whole a symbolic ulterior meaning.

Gorki, too, depicted the personal aspects of this decline and devoted much care to the presentation of the various directions in which hereditary family traits developed. But he shows their live connection with the whole evolution of society in a period of revolutionary crisis far more clearly and richly than can be found in any of the writings of even his greatest contemporaries.   Because Gorki always clearly saw the end of the road, his novels, in spite of the much greater austerity of style, attain a far more generalized typicality and an incomparably greater epic monumentality, than was given to either Thomas Mann or John Galsworthy.

Gorki's last novel, *Klim Samgin,* which we have already mentioned in another connection, has for its theme the history of the *bourgeois* intelligentsia up to the revolution. It is the story of how ideologies were born, transformed and assimilated by the representatives of various sections of the *bourgeoisie* and *bourgeois* intelligentsia in accordance with the requirements of the class struggle.   Gorki here raises to the highest level his method of presenting ideologies in lively interaction with the personal lives of his characters as determined by the course of the class struggle. A separate monograph would be required to do justice to the mastery with which Gorki shows the incursion of Marxian ideas into the *bourgeoisie* and *bourgeois* intelligentsia and the distortion and misrepresentation of these ideas by the representatives of various *bourgeois* pseudo-Marxists.

In *Klim Samgin* Gorki not only gives a historical picture of the evolution of the pre-revolutionary *bourgeois* intelligentsia; he also shows the tendencies which were decisive for the subsequent development of the intelligentsia and their attitude to the dictatorship of the proletariat.

Another problem to be discussed in connection with *Klim Samgin* is the problem of the personality and individualism. In his earlier novels Gorki mostly depicted characters who had originally possessed a live core of personality and in whom this core was trampled upon and crushed by the realities of old-time Russia. In "Klim Samgin" Gorki approaches the problem of personality from a different angle in depicting the inner emptiness of the modern individualistic *bourgeois* intellectual. Although this point is naturally mentioned in other, earlier works of Gorki, it is only in *Klim Samgin* that it is made the focal point of a comprehensive and methodical exposition.

The problem of modern individualism is a general one in the literature of the nineteenth century. It was Ibsen who gave what is perhaps the sharpest criticism of this modern individualism when he makes the ageing Peer Gynt peel an onion and compare each successive layer that comes away with a phase in the evolution of his own personality, until at last he arrives at the conclusion, which greatly shocks him, that all his life and his whole personality is nothing but a heap of peel without any core at all. And what this core-less onion means is shown by Ibsen again with a fine satirical touch in the person of the empty boaster Hjalmar Ekdal in *The Wild Duck*.

Gorki's *Klim Samgin* gives a fine picture of this emptiness of modern individualism. Klim Samgin is a Peer Gynt without imagination, a Hjalmar Ekdal with a far more successful social career than his Ibsenian cousin. His emptiness is the main problem of his life from the very outset; from his infancy he always wants to play the part of an important personage and play-acts himself in and out of a variety of situations with the smoothness of a diplomat. With consummate artistry Gorki places his hero in a great variety of situations and shows with admirable inventiveness how this emptiness, this cautious, diplomatic lack of backbone manifests itself in exactly the same manner in every possible situation in life, from love to politics and business, and how easily this lack of backbone lapses into villainy in critical situations.

On the other hand Gorki shows the whole social environment in which this type is produced and fostered; he also shows how the development of this type is linked with the sharpening of the class struggle between *bourgeoisie* and proletariat. What Ibsen and other Western writers could at best achieve was the correct portrayal of this type as an individual; Gorki makes us feel throughout the novel the approach of the great decisive clash between the classes and shows in a most intricate form, free of all stereotyped or pedantic devices, the connections between the evolution of Klim Samgin's character and this central problem of the epoch. One of the personages in the novel characteristically says to young Klim : " There are only two answers, Samgin, to every question : one is yes and the other no. You seem to want to invent a third. Most people want that, but up to now no one has succeeded in doing so."

By an amazing stroke of genius Gorki here succeeds in incarnating in the completely individual, personal destiny of Klim Samgin the desperate attempt of a considerable section of the Russian intelligentzia to find a " third way " between revolution and counter-revolution, between *bourgeoisie* and proletariat.

The exposure of Klim Samgin's spineless Philistinism completes the picture given by Gorki of pre-revolutionary Russia and makes it into a composition embracing everything essential, into a ' human comedy ' in the Balzacian sense. As the poetic historian of the epoch, as the painter of the tragicomic death of the old order,

Gorki was one of the great gravediggers of capitalism.

But the capitalist world did not die in the October revolution; it must be destroyed bit by bit; it is like the hydra of the legend which grows a new head every time one of its heads is chopped off. Thus Gorki's 'human comedy' is not only an immortal picture of a world that is no more, but a powerful weapon in the struggle against its surviving, harmful remnants. Not for nothing have Lenin and Stalin carried on an incessant struggle against the petty-*bourgeois* world surrounding the working class. This petty-*bourgeois* influence took a variety of forms in the great country of Socialism. But the brutal violence of the kulaks and the refined "culture" of the wreckers had their roots in the same soil of Asiatic capitalism, the merciless exposure of which constituted the greater part of Gorki's life-work. Even today, when a Socialist society has become a reality, it would be a mistake to think that we have nothing further to learn from Gorki. Stalin's warning about the need to overcome the residue of capitalism in the being and consciousness of men reminds us how up-to-date this aspect of Gorki's life-work still is.

Gorki's 'human comedy' differs from that of Balzac in that it does not stop at a complete portrayal of the 'animal kingdom' of philistinism. In Balzac the figure of the heroic Michel Chrestien, the true representative of the revolutionary masses, who fell on the steps of St.-Merry, could be merely an episodic figure in the distance. In Gorki, out of the dissolution of the dreadful darkness of old Russia, there emerges a bright host of revolutionary heroes, who people his stories and who are the true images of the living heroes who really liberated mankind, the heroes of the great October revolution.

CHAPTER EIGHT

Leo Tolstoy and Western European Literature

1.

W E H A V E grown so accustomed to the conception of world literature, to the existence of a relatively large number of writers whose influence reaches far beyond the confines of their own country that we are apt to forget the complicated problems connected with such international influences. The question whether an author is of international stature or not cannot be decided either by speculation or by questionnaires. Such international influences are always contradictory, the more so the more international the influence is. Only in the case of some short-lived fashion can one observe an unanimous, if temporary, enthusiasm; but in the case of great writers criticism and resistance are necessary elements of a fecundating influence. One need only think of the passionate criticisms of Shakespeare, from Voltaire to Shaw and Tolstoy. It is precisely when a writer has grown to be a living influence in the literature of a country not his own, that an intricate tangle of contradictions arise which are hard to unravel.

The influence of a writer in a foreign literature and a foreign culture is in itself a problem. Although the existence of a literature of international scope is an undisputed fact, it is a very complicated fact replete with contradictions. It is neither the sum nor the mean of all national cultures, literatures and great writers, but the living totality of the mutual interactions of their living totalities. However accustomed we are to regard Dante or Cervantes, Walter Scott or Dostoyevski as international figures, it is nevertheless in each case a problem in itself how each of them could have conquered such a place for himself and especially how he could have maintained it. For the ceaseless rebirth of such influence is the essential hallmark of international stature in a writer.

In this respect every national culture is organically and magnificently selfish. Molière's *je prends mon bien où je le trouve* is valid also for the assimilation and rejection of foreign literatures, which are a part of the continuous life-process of all literature. Such organic and healthy assimilation of foreign literatures, which is part of the development of all true writers (through whom great works of literature manifest their influence in other countries than those of their origin) indicates the concrete peculiarity of our problem : a literary work of international effect is always both a native and a stranger in a foreign culture. Chernyshevski, the great Russian critic said that the tendency of Schiller's poems had won rights of citizenship for him in Russia and that therefore Russians regarded Schiller as their own poet, as a participant in their own cultural evolution from the moment his poems were published in the Russian language. Nevertheless Schiller still remains a German poet. But his literary significance undergoes a change in this new sphere of influence, in this new connection; his own national character is sublimated in the union with a new culture in which it becomes effective. No wonder that in these circumstances widely differing appreciations of such phenomena have been expressed. Goethe says : " Wer den Dichter will verstehen, muss in Dichters Lande gehen," while Hebbel argues that " Shakespeare was no more an Englishman than Jesus a Jew." The truth lies, however, not in the middle between these two extremes, but in a synthesis of the two.

This synthesis takes a different form in each case, but nevertheless the story of such influences shows certain definite trends. In the first place these trends are negative : if the attempt is made to adapt a foreign poet completely to the recipient national culture and thus denationalize him completely, no fruitful influence is possible. An instance of this is the treatment of Shakespeare in France from Voltaire to Ducis. No less fruitless is it, on the other hand, to attempt complete assimilation. Ever since the days of Tieck the Germans have tried to acclimatize in Germany the whole of English Elizabethan literature; these attempts, while yielding considerable results in the field of literary history, have had no effect whatever on living German literature, in which Shakespeare alone was and remained a fruitful influence.

It is obvious that these problems cannot be solved either by historico-philosophical generalities, nor by detailed philological research. The latter is of importance for bringing facts to light, but it would be quite useless to try and determine the influence of Dickens on European literature by adding together his influence on various authors, e.g. from Dostoyevski to Raabe. International influences come about by synthesis out of national tendencies and these, again synthetically, arise from the personal evolution of the writers themselves. And everywhere the transition from the particular to the general is not a simple addition, but a jump.

Thus authors of international significance have a twofold influence : on the one hand they carry their national culture into foreign lands, make them known and appreciated there, and turn them into an organic part of the culture which receives them. One can therefore never speak of abstract internationalism, of world literature in general, but only the concrete mutual influence of the literatures of civilized nations on each other. Further, the national character thus accepted in another country is never identical with the real national character (one need only think of the entirely false ideas about " mysterious " Russia in the western countries) nor with the factors which caused the writer to acquire influence in his own country. Sometimes the writer's social and literary background pales or is completely obliterated in the recipient foreign country and this always leads to the formation of a distorted image of him; but at the same time certain essential traits may become more clearly visible in a foreign country than in the writer's own.

It should, however, be stressed once more that the primary determinants of such influences are the literary requirements of the recipient country. All truly great literature, however much of foreign elements it may absorb, keeps to its own organic line of development, determined by the social and historical conditions in the country which gave it birth.

Bernard Shaw has made some very interesting methodological remarks in connection with the history of international influences in literature. He rightly protested against the assertion that his works were derived from Ibsen, Nietzsche, etc., and pointed out that all the ideas for which the critics were trying to find foreign sources, were present in the writings of certain English authors, among others Samuel Butler. Shaw was undoubtedly right when he stated this fact. On the other hand it is to be considered how the native sources of Shaw's art came to be effective. Would Butler, who had remained quite unknown in his lifetime, ever have gained the influence he did gain, had not Scandinavian and Russian literature, had not Ibsen and Tolstoy broken into English culture? Such cases, in which misunderstood or disregarded great authors are, in a manner of speaking, discovered in their own country through the effect of foreign influence, are not as rare as is generally assumed. Vico came to be a live influence in Italy through Hegel and the Hegelians; old German poetry came into its own only after the absorption in Germany of Shakespeare and Ossian, Dante and Calderon.

Shaw's protest thus throws light on a very important problem, provided that it is treated with the requisite methodological caution. For it is certain that a really deep and serious impression cannot be made by any work of foreign literature unless there are no similar tendencies in existence—latently at least—in the country concerned. Such latency increases the fertility of foreign influences, for true influence is always the liberation of latent forces. It is precisely this rousing of latent energies that can make truly great foreign writers function as factors of a national literary development—unlike the superficial influence of passing fashions.

2.

Only if we realize this fact can we arrive at a concrete historical posing of the problem. International literary phenomena come into being only if their effect is constant and is reproduced again on an ever higher plane in each successive generation of writers and readers. It was a brilliant observation of Hegel that every newly arising phenomenon is at first abstract; only as it unfolds does it reveal the concrete totality, the inexhaustible wealth of its inherent possibilities. That this is specially clear in our case follows from the Molièrian principle of the assimilation of foreign literatures. Foreign writers exercise a real influence only when literary developments in the country in question require a stimulus, an impulse indicating some new path, because literature finds itself in some sort of crisis out of which it consciously or unconsciously seeks a way out.

The contacts between need and stimulus are of varying depth and breadth in each case—hence such contacts are sometimes merely episodic, sometimes a lasting association. But the first contact nearly always takes place on a narrow line of acute requirements and is therefore necessarily abstract in relation to the fully developed rich personality of a great writer. The first impression made by great writers in foreign countries is mostly a result of external—and from the point of view of the writer himself often accidental—factors and his influence then grows gradually in width and depth until he gains his full stature.

The international influence of Russian literature and above all of Leo Tolstoy developed in the eighties and nineties of the nineteenth century. (Scandinavian literature and especially Ibsen, developed such international significance at the same time, but for reasons of space we cannot here deal with this). What was the general need which rendered the absorption of these foreign literatures possible? The needs naturally differed in the different western countries, but behind these differences the same social and historical forces were at work and hence we can speak of traits common to them all, although we know that all such generalisations involve a certain coarsening and simplification.

The defeat of the 1848 uprisings in the most important western European countries and in England the collapse of Chartism brought about a profound general ideological depression. This turning-point in historical development is mirrored in literature. This is the epoch of Napoleon III, the emergence of Bismarck's " Bonapartist monarchy," the Prussification of Germany, the great pause in the democratic evolution of England. A universal despairing pessimism descends on the greatest writers and in the tragic figures of Flaubert and Baudelaire this pessimism degenerates into nihilism. That is the one pole and here we find the greatest writers of the period. (The atmosphere of gloom in Dickens' later writings is also a product of this period). The other pole is the compromise with this vile reality; it leads in Germany to an unprecedented triteness of literature, in France to a stiffening of style, to a technically perfect but lifeless routine; and the English " Victorian compromise " has now become the generally accepted characterization of this whole period.

Where decay is greatest, there the desire for regeneration is the strongest. In Germany, once the echoes of the great victory of 1870-71 had died away, the naturalist movement of the eighties made a vigorous attempt to escape from the trite atmosphere of compromise which poisoned German literature after the foundation of the Bismarckian Reich. It is no accident that this attempt at regeneration which did not at first confine itself to literature but strove, however unclearly, to create healthy conditions in all ideological spheres, was at the same time the period in which Tolstoy first grew to be an influence in Germany. The attitude of the German writers of the time to Tolstoy found poignant expression in a poem by Arno Holz :

> " Zola, Ibsen, Leo Tolstoy
> Eine Welt liegt in den Worten,
> Eine die noch nicht verfault
> Eine die noch kerngesund ist !''

In these lines the abstraction mentioned before is quite obvious. We see a general reaction against a literature which had turned away from life and had petrified into tedious conventionalities. For this reason the things Zola, Ibsen and Tolstoy seemed to have in common made a great impression : their adherence to reality, their ruthless, uncompromising reproduction of life as it really is, yet neither impassibly nor cynically, but with the passionate striving to hold a mirror up to the world in order to redeem it by the power of truth.

Of course this view of Tolstoy is an abstraction too, if measured against his real stature. In literature itself Tolstoy's influence manifested itself in a somewhat more concrete form than in the mere theoretical manifestoes of literary schools. Gerhart Hauptmann's first play *Vor Sonnenaufgang* has *The Power of Darkness* for its godfather, but of course only in respect of one aspect of Tolstoy, above all the inexorable ruthlessness of his critical exposure of the ills of society. Hauptmann himself was already aware of certain specific traits in Tolstoy which separated him from Ibsen and particularly from Zola. Hauptmann's stark descriptions of the dark and revolting aspects of modern life have neither the rhetorically decorative monumentality of Zola himself nor do they lose themselves in the labyrinth of low sensual detail we find in Zola's many imitators. Hauptmann's naturalist rendition of reality is far from any vestige of 'impassivity—it is overflowing with pity for the victims of society. Wherever the young Hauptmann rises to a higher poetic plane, he clearly approaches at least one facet of Tolstoy's world.

German naturalism was a rearguard action. The short explosion it represented was possible only because German realism was lagging far behind realism in France and England. For naturalism, in the classical form it took on in the France of 1850-80, was a product of the stifling atmosphere of the second Napoleonic period in European history. The dissatisfaction of the most gifted writers, the writers who looked towards a better future, was therefore directed not only against the narrow outlook and distortions of the literature of compromise but at the same time—often primarily—against the philosophical and artistic barriers opposed by naturalism to the writer. (This feeling became general in Germany, too soon after the spread of naturalism there).

In the beginning and on the surface, the movement against naturalism is of a purely artistic nature; we see attempts to break through or at least to widen the thematic, formal and ideological limits of naturalism; attempts to create a style better suited to the needs of contemporary life. There is no opportunity here of giving even the barest outline of these rapidly changing trends. All we can say here is that Russian literature and especially Tolstoy played an important part in the shaping of these trends, but still an abstract part, still only through those aspects which suited the momentary requirements of the daily struggle between the various schools. Nevertheless, it was a step forward in the recognition of Tolstoy's full personality, in that the naturalist misunderstanding of Tolstoy (in the sense that his powerful realism has anything in common with the slavish copying of reality) faded more and more out of the consciousness of the writers who admired him and the moral and ideological content of his writings began to make itself felt more and more.

We mention only Maeterlinck among the numerous personalities of this transitional epoch. He attempted to show that under the surface of the most commonplace everyday reality great unknown and unfathomable forces were at work and that the real vocation of the drama was to give expression to these forces. He regarded Ibsens's *Ghosts* and Tolstoy's *Power of Darkness* as proof that such contents could be presented in a contemporary form.

Here, too, it is clear that the essence of Tolstoy's philosophy and art was by no means properly understood in any of these impressions made on foreign writers. The example of Maeterlinck illustrates again what we have already said in connection with naturalism : that in the first stages of Tolstoy's impact on the world only a very few limited aspects of his multifarious art were perceived and, for that very reason, even these were abstract and distorted. Tolstoy had, in practice, long been a powerful influence in the world when the true significance of his personality and his art were still very incompletely understood.

This applies to his friends no less than to his enemies, to his adherents no less than to his opponents. About these latter we must make certain observations here, for the opposition to Tolstoy and to the influence of Russian literature in general is highly characteristic for the first, transitional period. There was a general desire to break with the tradition of mid-nineteenth century literature which, especially in France, had developed a deadening formalistic routine. Tolstoy appeared here as the polar opposite of this trend. We propose to deal presently in greater detail with the concrete differences between Tolstoy and his western contemporaries, but before we do so the abstract difference also requires some illustration. The readers of Tolstoy—and in the first place those readers who were themselves writers—felt the tremendous vitality, the vast wealth of reality in Tolstoy's writings, such as was to be found nowhere else at the time; as all this was presented in a form which had little in common with the forms accepted in the western literature of the second half of the nineteenth century, it was inevitable that the juxtaposition of form and formlessness should arise in this connection. This juxtaposition, which completely misses the essence of Tolstoy's art, appears very frequently in both positive and negative form.

In its negative form it is found mostly among writers who attempted to give the ideological and artistic crisis of the time a reactionary twist; who pursued a traditional line not only in their ideological but in their formal tendencies, and who wanted to resolve the crisis—which reached its culminating point in Flaubert's nihilism and his tragic and ascetic struggle for pure form—by ideologically surrendering to all the traditional powers (e.g. in France the church and the monarchy). The adherents of such tendencies in world-view and literature naturally regarded Tolstoy's world as mere chaos and anarchy. Paul Bourget championed this point of view with great vigour, although he was a much too accomplished man of letters not to realize that Tolstoy's ability to make things come alive was comparable only with that of Balzac, Molière or Shakespeare. But his recognition of Tolstoy's qualities was limited to questions of detail; for according to him, Tolstoy was incapable of properly constructing his novels. *War and Peace* and *Anna Karenina,* said Bourget, were reports which could be continued without end, in which events followed each other without gradation, without perspective and without plan, each scene equalling every other in significance.

This fantastically incorrect appreciation of Tolstoy, *un jugement saugrenu* as the French say, is reactionary not only in the aesthetic sense, a defence of the rigidly formalist tradition of the French novel of the time, but rather the aesthetic expression of Bourget's generally reactionary mentality. According to him composition is not a mere literary problem, but a virtue of the spirit. The individual is a function of society : this is for Bourget an axiom, of which in his view Tolstoy was quite ignorant. Naturally enough Bourget made no attempt to prove his thesis by a detailed analysis of Tolstoy's writings. The object of his most violent attacks were Tolstoy's moral and religious writings, especially his direct relationship to the Gospels. " There has never been a religion without a church and there never will be." Christ had given the Gospels not to men but to the Church. Thus Bourget damns

Tolstoy in the name of Catholic bigotry as the Holy Synod in Russia had done in the name of the Greek orthodox church—the only difference is that Bourget extends, by all sorts of sophisms, the anathema on the heretic Tolstoy to the sphere of art as well as of religion. The Bourget case is an exceptionally glaring example of the coincidence of conservative tendencies in the sphere of aesthetics with reactionary political and philosophical views.

But another wrong conception, i.e. that Tolstoy's works were the manifestation of an irresistible natural force which not only burst through all artistic form but basically rejected it, was for a long time much more deeply embedded in the consciousness of Tolstoy's readers, than the openly reactionary interpretations of certain literary groupings. This second conception is narrow and conservative—it raises barriers to the process of regeneration in western literature to which the influence of Tolstoy contributed so much, although it is by no means necessarily conducive to conclusions such as Bourget's, nor to the rejection of Tolstoy's overwhelming impact.

In such circumstances sincere and honest writers cannot but find themselves in an ambiguous position. This ambiguity was expressed by Jules Lemaitre with quite unusual candour. He wanted above all to preserve French men of letters from overestimating the Russians. French writers could select their material better, could construct better, their aversion to showing emotion was due only to delicacy or to the fear of transcending the formal limits of art. Nevertheless Lemaitre admitted that when he read *The Power of Darkness* he was not only impressed but overwhelmed, although he found the form of the play bizarre, the images dark and blurred and the work " lacking all poetic beauty in the true sense." And this strong impression, as Lemaitre ungrudgingly confesses, was made on a writer whose general approach to modern literature was one of a certain *blasé* indifference. But in the case of Tolstoy he felt " as though he were rediscovering the human race; and then one forgives literature, and regains confidence in it, the hope that it will not die in spite of everything . . All that is needed is only to see correctly, to feel deeply, to be a genius . . ."

3.

Such appreciations are a clear expression of the contrast between Tolstoy and the western European literature of his time, even though the expression, as we have seen in the preceding, remains abstract. To render the contrast concrete means not only a deeper and more correct understanding of Tolstoy's art, but the tracing of the road leading to a regeneration of European literature. Such voices were heard comparatively early, but only sporadically; nevertheless, the tendency of development was such as to make these isolated voices gradually grow to be the expression of a consensus of opinion in European literary circles. Here again we must confine ourselves to a few characteristic examples.

Concretization was at first historical and aesthetic. On the one hand the contrast between Tolstoy's art and the style of the Flaubert-Zola period was beginning to be understood. Juxtaposition of these was tantamount to a criticism of the latter and uncovered at the same time the links with the classical past, which if not completely severed, had at least been greatly loosened by the naturalist school and its immediate successors. The enthusiastic pioneers who proclaimed Tolstoy's greatness showed up not only the contrast between him and the writers of the Flaubert-Zola period, but also his deep-seated link with Balzac and the other classics of realism. It is certainly not more a matter of chance that Bourget's rejection of Tolstoy's form is bound up with his monarchist and reactionary views, than that Matthew Arnold's essay on Tolstoy appeared in the same series as his essays on Spinoza, Byron, Heine, and the like. Historical accuracy requires us to state, however, that Flaubert himself was perhaps the first to compare Tolstoy with Shakespeare.

The striving for a correct appreciation of Tolstoy's historical significance necessarily ran parallel not only with the recognition of his great artistic power and the specific nature of his literary form, but also with the search for a new, wider and deeper conception of the novel as a literary form. It is obvious that, regarded from the viewpoint of the traditional French or the Victorian English novel, Tolstoy would of necessity appear formless. It was necessary therefore to go beyond the narrowly conceived aesthetic sphere and pose the question of the human sources, the moral and social foundations of this new art. The deeper men probed into this, the more inevitable was a change of approach.

Matthew Arnold's shrewd common sense raised certain basic problems correctly at a comparatively early date (1887). According to him Tolstoy's greatness consisted in that he would have nothing to do with sham " refined " feelings nor made the slightest concession to low sensuality; he showed the reader many unpleasant things but never anything that might confuse the senses and even less anything that might satisfy those who seek such confusion of the senses.

In this Arnold grasped an important aspect of Tolstoy's art : its normality, its healthiness, the perfect moral equilibrium of an artist who has his heart in the right place and knows exactly what is good and what is evil. But Arnold went even further than this in contrasting Tolstoy with the literature of the time. He quotes Burns' fine phrase about " petrified feelings " and comparing Emma Bovary with Anna Karenina, quite correctly recognizes these "petrified feelings" in the cruelty with which Flaubert treats the characters in his novels.

Havelock Ellis, too, tried to formulate the differences between the old and the newer period in literature. He said that the novel was the moral history of the day, but in a deeper sense than the Goncourts imagined. In Tolstoy he saw such a moral historian of our way of life; and thought that the scope, richness and truth of his art was such as to make him as significant for our time as Balzac or Shakespeare were for theirs. Thus, here again, the recognition that Tolstoy was harking back to the classics, that his art was a new offshoot of the classics, was coupled with a criticism of the naturalists. Havelock Ellis violently attacked Zola's " documentary " style. He says : " What if a novelist has occasionally met me, has noted my appearance and manner of speaking, has studied the furniture of my house and collected a bit of gossip about me? What can he know on this basis about the real tragedies of my life? And it is just these essential tragedies that Tolstoy depicts."

This historical and aesthetic understanding of Tolstoy's art is naturally and constantly on the increase. The newer French critical literature recognizes more and more that the Tolstoyan form is a widening and enrichment of our conception of the novel. Thibaudet, for instance, makes a well-reasoned attack on Bourget's conception of Tolstoy. He says about *War and Peace* that in it Napoleon is represented as having imagined that his campaign against Russia would be played out in the " traditional " five acts, just like all his previous campaigns : march against the capital, a great battle, entry into the capital, conclusion of a peace treaty, triumphal return to Paris. But everything happens quite differently. Napoleon in Moscow is scandalized at Alexander's silence; " this attitude," Thibaudent remarks wittily, " is the same as that of the French novelist who demands that *War and Peace* should follow our ideas of what is classical."

It is interesting and characteristic that the increasing understanding of Tolstoy's artistic conceptions not only revived the great progressive traditions of Western literature, not only renewed and freshened its link with the true classical heritage but also aided the correct understanding of the new and original phenomena which so greatly enriched the literature of the post-Flaubertian period.

Thibaudet is indefatigable in his attacks on Bourget's kind of French traditionalism, on his narrow formalist conception of construction. He sarcastically applies Bourget's standards to so profoundly French a writer as Anatole France and speaks of France's " happy lack of construction " which enables us to open his books at any page and read and enjoy them as we read and enjoy Montaigne or La Bruyére. " Books with construction are read; books without it are read again and again."

The road back to Balzac, Goethe and Shakespeare is thus at the same time the road into the future, the road leading to that rejuvenation of literature which Anatole France, Romain Rolland, Gerhart Hauptmann, Thomas Mann, Bernard Shaw, John Galsworthy brought about at the end of the nineteenth century. Most of these great writers were themselves aware that the assimilation of Tolstoy's moral, social, human and artistic message was an important factor of their own development.

In a letter written to Tolstoy, Shaw mentions the threads connecting Tolstoy's *The Power of Darkness* with his own The *Showing Up of Blanco Posnet*. Here again we find the concrete, probing penetration into the secrets of Tolstoy's artistic method of construction. Let us recall that Jules Lemaître had still thought of *The Power of Darkness* as an elemental outburst of humanity conceived as force of nature; that Maeterlinck saw the virtue of the play in the figure of old Akim, the prophet of Tolstoyan ethics. The sharp eye of the playwright Shaw saw that all the exhortations of the father made no impression whatsoever on the son; but what the god-fearing old father could not achieve, is easy for the old rascal of a soldier who speaks as convincingly as though God's own voice rolled off his tongue. In the scene which shows the two drunken fellows lying side by side in the straw, the elder trying to lift the younger out of his egoism and cowardice by moral argument, Shaw sees a dramatic force never achieved by any scene in any work of the romantics. Shaw says that he drew his Blanco Posnet from these sources of dramatic material which Tolstoy was the first to reveal to novices in the art of the drama.

These remarks, apparently only relating to details of construction, are of the greatest importance. They express what has slowly grown to be generally recognized by prominent writers, serious critics and intelligent readers in the western countries : that what in Tolstoy's works overflows the hitherto accepted narrow forms is not some chaotic, elemental humanism but a different, wider, deeper, more human conception of creative method.

Thus what divides Tolstoy from the decadent trends in modern literature is his opposition not only to a frozen traditional objectivism but also to the subjectivist anarchism of sentiment which is its necessary complementary manifestation. The philosophical and artistic roots of the latter also lie in the inability of the writer to present the phenomena of modern life with adequate artistry; the only difference is that such authors no longer confine themselves to a documentary chronicle of facts but juxtapose their own subjectivity directly and abstractly with such unilluminated facts. Compared with such tendencies, Tolstoy's writings appear mercilessly objective, just as they appeared to be the formless stuff of life itself when compared with the naturalists' lifeless copying of uncomprehended facts or the formal constructions of the traditionalists. It is easy to understand, therefore, that resistance to the novelty of Tolstoy's art should have come from the subjectivist side as well. When we quote Stefan Zweig in this context, as a representative of this school, we want to stress that Zweig of course, had far more understanding of Tolstoy in detail than his polar opposite Bourget. Nevertheless Stefan Zweig criticized the essence of Tolstoy's art no less uncomprehendingly and conservatively than Bourget. He found in Tolstoy a world without dreams, without fancies, without untruths—a terribly empty world, without other light than its inexorable truth, nothing but its clarity, this, too, inexorable. From this he draws the conclusion that Tolstoy's art makes us serious and thoughtful, as does science with its stony light and its cutting objectivity, but never makes us happy.

It was necessary to mention this shade of opinion as well, in describing the opposition to Tolstoy, for only thus can it become clear that Tolstoy's liberating influence, in opening a new way out of the crisis of modern literature, affected all wrong trends existing in the latter and that both German naturalists and French symbolists were deceiving themselves when they looked upon Tolstoy as their own literary forerunner. Tolstoyan realism paints a comprehensive picture of life in all its complexity and movement, —and in this it links up with the legacy left us by the greatest of all, by Shakespeare, by Goethe and by Balzac. Alain, the French

critic and philosopher, writes about this : 'Here there is no more good
or bad, interesting or tedious; everything is part of existence, just
as it is in the real world. No one asks why Karenin has prominent
ears. He just has them.' Alain gives a subtle analysis of Tolstoy's
works from this viewpoint. Here again we must confine ourselves
to a single instance. Alain unconditionally approves the so-called
" lengths " in Tolstoy (and Balzac), for these express the real period
of waiting during which events mature; this waiting therefore is
enjoyed by the reader and makes him feel that Tolstoy's and Balzac's novels always end too soon. Descriptions in the Zola manner
on the contrary interrupt the lapse of time and cause an impatience
which is out of keeping with the nature of the novel. This seemingly quite formal analysis yet throws light into those depths of
constructional methods with which the all-embracing world-view of
great writers gathers in the totality of life in all its movement.
Alain then gives interesting pictures of Tolstoy's world, demonstrating how the intricate dialectic of life is always completely expressed and how at the same time a perfect artistic equilibrium of
conflicting tendencies of life and a wise and equitable social and
moral evaluation of the divergent or conflicting passions of the
characters are produced. We must here unfortunately confine ourselves to a mere mention of the sensitive analysis given by Alain
of the connection between Karenin's ' administrative ' world and
the nature, the human authenticity and the limits of Anna's passion for Vronski.

4.

The scope of Tolstoy's influence on western culture and literature was by no means limited to the successful struggle for a better
understanding of his significance as an artist. It was evident from
the beginning that Tolstoy's stature could not be adequately defined by saying that he was a great writer or by any ever so correct
analysis of his writings. There is a growing conviction that nineteenth-century Russian literature and above all Tolstoy himself, as
its greatest representative, were not only more realistic and profound than the French literature of the Flaubert-Zola period or the
English literature of the Victorian era in England (not to mention
the German literature of this time), but something qualitatively
different. The connection between literature and life was for the
Russians—and here again Tolstoy is the typical literary culminating
point—essentially different from that of the West.

Thomas Mann, in his famous story *Tonio Kröger* expresses
this attitude in trenchant form. The hero of the story is an em-

bodiment of that tragic estrangement of literature from life which made its first poignant appearance in Flaubert's letters, and which was the constantly recurring theme of the ageing Ibsen, reaching its culminating point in his *Epilogue.* Tonio Kröger expounds his despairing, paradoxical conclusions about literature and life to a Russian painter, Lizaveta Ivanovna, and brushes away her consoling words when she warns him not to look into things too closely. She replies : " The purifying, hallowing effect of literature, the destruction of the passions by knowledge and by the word, literature as the means to understanding, to forgiveness and to love, the redeeming power of speech, literature as the noblest manifestation of the human spirit, the man of letters as the perfect man, as the saint—would regarding things in this way mean not looking into them closely enough?" Tonio Kröger's answer contains Thomas Mann's admission that the Tolstoyan period of Russian literature has nothing in common with these tragic (but often merely tragicomic) conflicts of Western civilization. This is what Tonio Kröger says : " You have the right to say this, Lizaveta Ivanovna, because of the works of your poets, because of your adorable Russian literature, which really is that holy literature of which you spoke."

Thomas Mann here struck the chord which determined the melody and rhythm of Tolstoy's powerful impact on the West. The dissatisfaction of the younger generation of writers and readers with the literature of the Flaubertian type is at bottom a revolt against contemporary culture and the new literature is merely the most trenchant expression of this revolt.

Here the longings, searchings and enthusiasm of the new literature link up with Tolstoy's central problems, the problems to which we owe his masterpieces but which were also the cause of his temporary withdrawal from literary activities. Tolstoy's influence on this level is naturally even more contradictory than in the sphere of pure aesthetic. For in Tolstoy's theoretically and propagandistically expressed *Weltanschauung* the limits and deficiencies of his desire to regenerate the world in a peasant-plebeian sense are not counteracted by the perfection of a work of art but are revealed nakedly as limits, barriers, deficiencies and contradictions. Nevertheless nothing could be cheaper and more vulgar than to regard these strivings of Tolstoy merely from the angle of the imperfection of his thinking, its at times paradoxically pedestrian quality and its conservatism,—as so many " practical " Western critics of Tolstoy have done. If we did so, we should be guilty of disregarding or failing to understand one of the most profound (and if correctly understood) the most fruitful criticisms of the culture of our time.

It is scarcely surprising that Western literature did not accept these views of Tolstoy without criticism or opposition, and the best representatives of the West deserve every commendation for having, in spite of their often quite correct rejection of some of Tolstoy's important single assertions, nevertheless penetrated to the fruitful core of his ideas. Where this did not happen, development always ended up in a blind alley—as for instance in the German expressionism of the critical period of the first world war, which accepted Tolstoy's teaching of non-resistance to evil as a dogmatic truth.

Only in critical form was it possible to assimilate Tolstoy's essential opinions and thus absorb his entire personality. Anyone who thought that Tolstoy's criticism of modern art denoted a hostility to art as a whole or a desire to reduce art to the level of children or uneducated peasants (as for instance Upton Sinclair did) has completely missed the essential point.

The fruitful critical assimilation of Tolstoy's world-view typically followed the line taken by Shaw. Shaw agreed with Tolstoy in denying the superiority of Shakespeare's world-view, but rejected Tolstoy's criticism of Shakespeare's art and language. But what is important here is not the rightness or wrongness of these criticisms and anticriticisms. What matters is that Shaw, like Tolstoy, is defending art and culture most ardently precisely when he is attacking their modern distortions with the greatest vigour. The purely academic question of direct influences plays a very subordinate part in this. What is important is that the general atmosphere of Tolstoy's criticism of art is captured when for instance Shaw writes that he likes good music and fine buildings just as Milton or Cromwell or Bunyan did; but if he were to discover that they were being made the instruments of a systematic idolatry of the senses, he would consider it good statecraft to blow up every cathedral in the world with dynamite, organ and all, without paying the slightest attention to the protests of art critics and cultured sensualists.

But even such problems, important as they are, are merely a part of that Tolstoyan atmosphere which we must attempt to grasp. For Tolstoy's whole personality, that of a model of men,—naturally inseparable from Tolstoy as artist and thinker—is constantly growing in stature as a great educator of civilized men, as a mentor, an awakener and a liberator.

This influence of Tolstoy is by no means limited to the sphere of literature in the narrower sense. In many forms, true or false, genuine or distorted, it permeated the mass of the people. When Kipling makes his Tomlinson, the average English *bourgeois,* appear before the tribunal of heaven to give an account of his good and evil deeds, he writes :

> ' And Tomlinson took up his tale and spoke of the good
> in his life,
> " This I have read in a book " he said " and that was told
> to me,
> " And this I have thought that another man thought of a
> prince in Muscovy." '

The ' prince in Muscovy' here already appears as figure in a modern legend.

But this legend, which is merely a distorted vulgar catchword in the mouth of Kipling's sorry hero, grows into a genuine component of the best contents of our lives if the seed sown by Tolstoy falls on the fertile soil of sincere hearts and genuine talent. Jean Richard Bloch wrote a little essay in which he outlined the forces which competed for the decisive influence in the development of his generation. It was the time of the Dreyfus affair. Maurras, representing reaction, proclaimed the slogan *"La politique d'abord* !" Jaurés Guesde and Péguy, representing progress and democracy, proclaimed *"Le social d'abord"* ! In this passionate ideological battle, which demanded immediate internal and external action at that time, Tolstoy's influence began to make itself felt among the most honourable and most gifted representatives of French youth. The slogan of this youth was : " To serve means to serve the good of the people." Bloch tells us. " It was Jaurés, Romain Rolland and Péguy who translated this slogan into French for us, but it was Tolstoy who first uttered it."

The substance of this influence, which Bloch describes in detail was twofold. Of his own generation who found its spiritual leader in Tolstoy, Bloch says : " On the one hand there was a wild revolt, a refusal to bow the knee, explosive crises of libertarianism and on the other hand, increasing together with the force of the personality, the feeling of a duty to one's environment and of being bound up with it." The " service " of which Bloch speaks, is a tendency to overcome individualism, a tendency more mature than any previous attempts; a transcending of the individual which nevertheless does not mean the abdication and dissolution of the personality. This is what Tolstoy helped the young generation to understand with increasing clarity. Their striving was, on the contrary, to avoid the loss and disintegration of the personality and the means to this end was to serve the public interest, ' the good of the people ' with devotion in a truly democratic spirit. That Bloch represents the typical experience of a whole generation must be obvious to anyone who reads Romain Rolland's *Jean Christophe* or Roger Martin du Gard's *Thibauts* with sufficient attention.

Herein lies one of the decisive aspects of the Tolstoyan influence. Shaw formulated his own conception of art in a polemic directed against the sham-modern school. Romain Rolland says the same thing from another angle (apart naturally from the difference in temperament and culture) in his biography of Tolstoy, when he puts the main emphasis on these words of the master : " True art is the expression of our knowledge of the true goodness in all men."

Romain Rolland conceived the Blochian dilemma and its elimination in more general terms than Bloch himself. He saw men, writers, all society facing the tragic choice : " either not to see, or to hate." " Society is always confronted with the dilemma : truth or love. It usually decides to sacrifice both truth and love." In this attitude to the problems of modern society and culture, Tolstoy has shown the western intelligentsia the way they must follow. Romain Rolland, too, in his attempt to clarify the nature of the realism of Tolstoy, turned against the realism of Flaubert. But for him the aesthetical conflict is turned into a conflict of cultural philosophy and policy. " The light of the sun is not enough, what is needed is the light of the heart. Tolstoy's realism is incarnated in each of his characters and because he regards them all with the same eyes, he finds something lovable in every one of them, and can make us feel the ties which fraternally unite us with them. By his love he reaches down to the very roots of life."

To attain a clear vision of the truth by means of love, a love embracing all mankind—such was the task Tolstoy set the writers of Western Europe. It was in the struggle to overcome the contradictions formulated by Romain Rolland that the great writers of the new literature were tempered to true greatness. Of course, this contradiction had arisen only in the conditions of modern *bourgeois* society, but because it was not a figment of the brain, no mere "inner experience " but an objective contradiction inherent in the present age, it had been the cause of the frustration and ultimate infertility of many, often very gifted, writers.

This contradiction and its Tolstoyan elimination naturally manifest themselves in different ways in the works of different authors. Gerhard Hauptmann once said about the critical attitude of nineteenth-century poets : " Every poet had become a critic. The whole of German literature was all criticism. The same applies to Russian and French literature. . . But what raised Tolstoy above all others and made him a saint of the past century, was his irresistible urge to help; this urge he expressed with a pathos which shook the world and silenced all opposition. This fact is paramount . . . Tolstoy has become a symbol of reconciliation, an idea before which all opposition is mute, although his single judgments are mostly wrong . . . "

Thomas Mann, attempting to assimilate Tolstoy's entire personality, draws a profoundly thought-out parallel between him and Goethe. Although well aware of Goethe's limitations, he regards him as the central figure of all that is progressive in German culture and struggles passionately to clear him of the dross of reactionary legends, and recognize and present him as the champion of the humanist liberation of the Germans. An important element of this parallel—of the wealth of thought of which we cannot give even the barest outline here—is that both Goethe and Tolstoy, despite all their social, national and personal differences, were earthbound like Antaeus, men of a primeval, earthly ability of palpable presentation of plasticity, in contrast to such classic representatives of the purely spiritual as Schiller and Dostoyevski. On the other hand, both of them had grown far beyond mere authorship. Thomas Mann interestingly defines this tendency, common to them both, as teaching and self-portrayal, both these spheres being closely connected with each other. The confession, the autobiographical story, does not mean for either of them a confinement to their own ego, but on the contrary a demonstration of the great universal streams of life, bound up with such phases of the writers' own lives as reflect them most vividly, thus once more overcoming the contradictions attaching to modern individualism.

This brief glance at Thomas Mann's important book brings us back to the second crucial point in Jean Richard Bloch's Tolstoyan creed. It is significant—and we hope that after all that has been said before, this will no longer appear paradoxical—that the more correctly the true core of Tolstoy's *oeuvre* is recognised in a Western country, the more closer he appears linked with the central figures of the recipient nation's own culture. Thus, in Bloch and Rolland, Tolstoy appears as the successor to Rousseau; in Thomas Mann, as a companion to Goethe; and when Bernard Shaw comments on Tolstoy's aesthetic from the angle of his own philosophy of art, he mentions the name of Milton.

Links thus established reach further, however, than merely the sphere of culture. Let us remember that Shaw mentions Cromwell as well as Milton; that in Bloch's essay Montaigne's revolutionary Republican friend Etienne de La Boétie is made to appear beside Rousseau; and that Romain Rolland attempts to found a true theatre of the people and begins his great cycle of plays about the French revolution at the time when Tolstoy's impact on him is the strongest.

These affinities are as little accidental as the links with Shakespeare and Balzac, of which mention was made in the preceding. They show that the deeper the understanding of Tolstoy's oeuvre, the closer the link with the great progressive traditions of the recipient country and with those of the democratic revolution. (Goethe, too, was not merely a contemporary of the French revolution, but a poetic mirror of it and his alleged total rejection of it was a myth propagated by the reactionaries.) Where there is such a deeper understanding, the retrograde traits in one or the other of Tolstoy's opinions melt away and as the passionate urge forward which is the essence of his being is revealed, he joins in fraternal union the band of great progressive figures of each nation and aids the peoples to preserve, deepen and regenerate their own progressive traditions. Only thus could Tolstoy come to be the integral property of all who love freedom.

5.

The road from Tolstoy's first appearance on the scene, as the godfather of German naturalism or French symbolism, to such a deeper comprehension was naturally long. Nevertheless it would be a mistake—today more than ever—to regard as final the image of Tolstoy which the west has evolved up to the present. As we have already said, a true cultural assimilation can never remain static—unless there is constant reproduction on a higher plane and in greater depth, the borrowed cultural asset must dwindle and fade away. This applies, of course, to all fecundating influences in all national cultures, be these influences foreign or home-bred.

This general truth is doubly valid in times of stress and crisis. The concrete character of the present world-cataclysm and Tolstoy's concrete nature make extremely probable a further, even deeper conception of his being, an even better understanding of his essential core.

For the present life-and-death struggle between freedom and slavery, betwen a humane civilization and a diabolic barbarism, has widened the gulf between progress and obscurantism in the minds of very many people in the west and has shown the terrible dangers of any—even purely ideological—dallying with an ever-alert, ever-militant reaction. On the other hand the heroic struggle of the Soviet peoples, their successful resistance to Hitler's military might, their glorious counter-attack against the fascist invaders, have directed the attention of the whole civilized world more than ever before towards the regenerated, free Russian people. Many more people than ever before are desirous of understanding more fully the moral and spiritual, social and historical sources of the now so powerfully manifested, irresistible strength of the Soviet people.

The inner dialectic of both tendencies will necessarily lead to a more adequate and complete understanding of Tolstoy. Up to now it was not easy for many people to break through the veil which reactionary prejudice and legend had woven around his image. It is almost a miracle that in such conditions a conception even as correct as the one outlined in the preceding, could have been evolved. The best-known western interpreters of Russian culture and literature were often unequivocal reactionaries, who could not and would not see the bonds which united Tolstoy with the great progressive and revolutionary movements of his country. It suffices to mention Merezhkovski who was for long the most influential interpreter of Tolstoy and Dostoyevski for much of the western intelligentsia. For this reason it often happens that those who wished to acquaint themselves with the national background of the great writer through independent study, were confronted by an imaginary, non-existent " mysterious Russia " or at best were lured astray by very unimportant phenomena, such as the Russian religious sects. That in such most unpropitious ideological conditions, at least the leading western writers could yet develop in their minds an essentially progressive image of Tolstoy bears witness not only to the high quality of their intellectual and artistic culture but also to the strength of their democratic instincts.

Lately, however, interest has been increasingly focussed on the real Russia, the country of a liberated nation fighting heroically for its freedom, and on the history of this liberation. Once research is directed towards this question, a riddle which had greatly puzzled all true interpreters of Tolstoy, the question why Russia had remained free of that ideological depression, which found its most magnificent and typical artistic expression in Flaubert, appears in a new, concrete social and historical light. Then it becomes manifest that while in the west the defeat of the movements of 1848 broke the back of the revolutionary movement for a very long time the Russian people had never ceased to fight for its liberation from the rising of the Decembrists in 1825 to the final victory in the great October revolution of 1917. It underwent many bitter periods of repression and oppression, but the fighters never laid down their arms. Particularly the period in which Tolstoy's personality was basically formed—a period of deepest depression in the West—was in Russia the period of a magnificent flowering of progressive and revolutionary energies, the time not only of Tolstoy and Dostoyevski, but of Chernyshevski, Dobrolyubov, Saltykov-Shchedrin, to name only the greatest.

This period and the last-named authors are as good as unknown in the west. Yet only if Tolstoy is not regarded merely as a companion to Dostoyevski, only if his connection with the revolutionary democracy of his time, with Chernyshevski, Dobrolyubov and Saltykov-Shchedrin is clearly understood, and the threads revealed which lead from here to Lenin, Stalin and Gorki, and if in the light of these discoveries Pushkin and Lermontov, Gogol and Bielinski are recognized as their precursors, can a truly adequate picture of the real Tolstoy be formed.

Such necessary corrections and adjustments by no means compromise the results attained up to now in the assimilation of Tolstoy; they merely raise them to a higher level. For we hope to have shown in the preceding pages that certain prominent interpreters of Tolstoy in the west had already advanced a long way on this road, even though they had often done so only instinctively and not consciously, in the historical sense of the word.

Often not consciously, but not always. Romain Rolland, for instance, clearly understood why Tolstoy had struggled so long with his plan for a novel dealing with the Decembrists and why the evolution of Pierre Bezukhov, or the dreams of young Nikolai Bolkonski all tended towards the Decembrist idea. A better knowledge of the true history of the Russian people will therefore merely have to transform these mostly latent tendencies into active and conscious ones. The Tolstoy-image of the west is on the eve of a further transformation, a deeper, better, more adequate understanding based on the knowledge of the history of the Russian people. Such an adequate understanding of Tolstoy will link his figure even more closely with the trends and ideologies which had ever been and ever shall be the eternal fountainheads of the regeneration of the spirit of freedom.

CHAPTER NINE

The Liberator

I N   H I S   funeral oration at Gorki's grave Molotov said : " After
the death of Lenin, Gorki's death is the heaviest blow suffered by
our country and the whole human race." The greatest writer of
our time is dead. We shall miss not only the works which his still
fresh vigour would have given us, but this great man himself, a
man who was the living sum of all real values of the past, the
trustee for the heritage of socialist realism, the tangible proof for
us and for international public opinion that a proletarian revolution, victorious socialism, brings a tremendous flowering of culture.
The whole world mourns the passing of this great man, but the
greatest loss is that of the Soviet writers. We stand orphaned.
Our teacher, our master, our mentor is dead and with him we have
lost the living conscience of Soviet literature.

If we now attempt to define what Maxim Gorki, the writer, the
teacher and the man has meant for us—and the answer to this
question cannot be given at the first attempt—we are not faced
with merely a literary task. The task is political in the best, most
topical sense of the word. It involves the defining of the duties
of writers in the present stage of development, the time of the
irresistible advance of the Stakhanov movement, the time of victorious proletarian democracy, the time of the elimination of class
distinctions, the incipient elimination of the social division between
urban and rural, manual and intellectual labour.

What has Gorki been for us writers ? We say : he was our
model, our master, our mentor. But all these words are inaccurate
approximations of his significance. If we try to give a somewhat
closer definition, it might be appropriate to quote what Goethe said
in the year of his death about his relation to the younger writers :
"Unser Meister ist derjenige unter dessen Anleitung wir uns in
einer Kunst fortwährend üben und welcher uns, wie wir nach und
nach zur Fertigkeit gelangen, stufenweise die Grundsätze mitteilt
nach welchen handelnd wir das ersehnte Ziel am sichersten errei-
chen. In solchem Sinne war ich *Meister* von niemand. Wenn ich

aber aussprechen soll was ich 'den Deutschen überhaupt, besonders den jungen Dichtern geworden bin, so darf ich mich wohl ihren *Befreier* nennen . . ."

Goethe summarizes this liberating influence by saying that what he taught the young poets was above all to make their lives richer and more earnest. " Poetischer Gehalt ist aber Gehalt des eigenen Lebens " he says in the resumé. The language and technique of German poetry was already on a high level at this time. Poetic expression no longer presented any insuperable difficulties. On the contrary there was a danger of empty technical excellence, the danger of mistaking the technical mastery of literary form for true poetry. The danger, the servitude from which Goethe claimed to have liberated the young poets was the illusion that mastery of the formal is already good poetry, and that contents somehow appear in such stuff of their own accord; the ' liberation ' consisted in pointing out to them the decisive part played by the contents of the poet's own life. He tells the young poets in humorously wise lines :

> " Jüngling, merke dir in Zeiten
> Wo sich Geist und Sinn erhöht,
> Dass die Muse zu *begleiten*
> Doch zu *leiten* nicht versteht."

Goethe the liberator thus proclaimed that the culture of life is the foundation of artistic and literary culture.

It would be ridiculous, of course, to take the parallel which here offers itself all too literally. We all know the fundamental differences between the times of the aged Goethe and our own, and everyone is sufficiently acquainted with the essential diversity of the tasks facing literature in the two epochs.

But despite all such differences, Goethe's basic ideas are of the greatest importance for us precisely at the present moment. After an article in *Pravda* had squarely posed the problem of our art and literature and made naturalism and formalism in them a controversial issue, a long discussion took place in the Association of Soviet Writers. Unfortunately, Maxim Gorki could not be present in person, but he did give his point of view about it with his characteristic candour in an article in which he wrote :

" As this debate did not originate within the Association itself, but was suggested from the outside, the doubt may arise whether the matter would go beyond mere words?"

This critical remark is characteristic of the liberating role played by Gorki in our literature. He saw that life itself was posing with ever-increasing urgency the problem of the elimination of any residues of capitalism in the Soviet Union; he also saw that a considerable section of Soviet writers regarded this fundamental, vital question from the narrow angle of the literary craft alone.

What is literary culture? Above all it is awareness of human greatness, the ability to see human greatness everywhere where it truly manifests itself in life, even though in hidden, imperfect forms as yet incapable of clear expression. It is the ability to discover the growth of humanity and to experience it with inner understanding; the ability to recognize in their first manifestations new things, things pregnant with the future.

In his great speech at the first congress of the All-Union Association of Soviet Writers, Gorki criticized our literature chiefly from this angle. He said : "We are very poor observers of reality," and then, by means of apparently insignificant remarks, he proceeded to show how the concrete growth of the new type of man, the transformation of our whole reality, even of our landscape, has often eluded the eye of our writers; that many of our writers have not yet a sufficient feeling for what is new and great in our reality.

Gorki grew to be the greatest writer of his time because he had won for himself this literary culture, based on a culture of life, in the most unfavourable circumstances of Asiatic capitalism and Tsarist oppression. In this connection it is worth reading what he says in his memoirs about Leonid Andreyev, whom he twice accuses of having distorted and minimized great phenomena of life for the sake of subjective literary prejudices. Gorki says there : " Certain things in our reality, i.e. the quite rare and positive things, must be represented exactly as they are and in no other way." And later : " I still cannot agree that such rare manifestations of ideal human feelings may be arbitrarily distorted by a poet for the sake of some favourite dogma."

This respect for greatness in human life is the foundation on which Gorki's literary culture rests; it is at the same time the source of his inexorable hatred of every form of barbarism. The accent is on the word *every*. Gorki hated the " primeval " barbarism of old-time Russia with a fanatical hatred. Few such fierce enemies of stupidity and cruelty as Gorki can be found in the entire literature of the world. He hated with a clairvoyant hatred the increasingly barbaric cruelty of monopoly capitalism. What is your attitude to an imperialist war? What is your attitude to Fascism?—such were the basic questions which determined his attitude to other writers.

But his all-embracing vision exposed the refined and sublimated forms of barbarism with the same clairvoyant hatred. In his speech at the writer's congress he said about Dostoyevski : " Dostoyevski has been called a seeker for truth. If he did seek it, he found it in the brutal animal instincts of men and he found it, not in order to fight it, but in order to justify and excuse it." His discerning eye saw the unifying principle behind the various forms taken by imperialist barbarism, and cared little whether it manifested itself in the unconcealed bestiality of Fascist outrages or appeared in " spiritually " sublimated alluring literary form; he always saw in them their common principle : the glorification of the animal in man, the contempt for human greatness and for everything that makes men men, everything that in the course of an infinitely long evolution had turned them from brutes and semi-brutes into human beings.

He deeply felt the truth of Engels' views on the part played by labour in this process of evolution and the inseparable connection between labour and human greatness and, on the opposite pole, between parasitism and barbarism. In the same speech from which we have quoted the passage about Dostoyevski, he repeatedly stressed the importance of folk-lore for the writer of that unwritten poetry of the working people, which had created the prototypes of the greatest heroes of literature and legend, figures like Herakles, Prometheus and Faust.

This intimate union of the deepest problems and highest perfection of form in literature with their folk origins can be realised consciously and without contradictions only in a Socialist society. The literature of a class society could by its very nature never really and completely assimilate the tremendous stimuli radiated by the poetry of the people. In exceptionally favourable circumstances (e.g. in the Renaissance) the peculiar genius of a few outstanding creative spirits such as Shakespeare, Cervantes or Rabelais had sporadically enabled at least a part of this treasure to be preserved in the eternal form of a literature of the highest order. The contradictory nature of literary evolution in a class society manifests itself among others in the fact that in certain circumstances the only possible really progressive path may require a turning away from the popular element (as Bielinski and Chernyshevski have shown in the case of Lomonosov) and that on the other hand, the poetry of the people may itself be reduced to a narrow, shallow provincialism.

These contradictions can be eliminated only by the liberation of all latent, suppressed and dislocated energies of the working people in a great proletarian revolution. Only a victorious proletarian revolution affords the *possibility* of mining these treasures, making use of these energies and raising literature and art to hitherto unprecedented heights. But even in the Soviet Union the surviving remnants of capitalism oppose serious obstacles to the *realization* of such possibilities. As long as writers have no clear conception of the true human greatness manifested in the poetry of the people, as long as they do not understand the artistic superiority a genuine bond which the poetry of the people gives to literature, preoccupation with the poetry of the people and the elements and tendencies conducive to a true popularity of literature remain mere folkloristic speciality with little or no influence on the general evolution of literature.

Maxim Gorki always brought the problem of the popular element in literature into close relation with the heritage of the past. For only if the popular element in poetry is made the focal point of all historical and aesthetic consideration of literature, can the real historical roots of the latter be traced. Gorki himself had very decided views on this point. He said in the speech repeatedly quoted already : " There is every reason to hope that when Marxists will have written a history of culture, we shall see that the part played by the *bourgeoisie* in the creation of culture has been greatly overestimated, especially in the sphere of literature ... " Gorki here applies to the sphere of culture what Marx and Engels, Lenin and Stalin have said before him about the part played by the *bourgeoisie* in the history of *bourgeois* revolutions : that the tasks of the *bourgeois* revolutions were always carried out really radically by the plebeian democratic elements *against the will* of the *bourgeoisie*. It is such fetishist insistence on the alleged leading role of the *bourgeoisie* in the *bourgeois* revolutions that has led to the contemptible capitulation of the reformists to the reactionary *bourgeoisie* and been at the root of the theoretical collapse of Plekhanov's conceptions. In contrast, the original development of this Marxist conception by Lenin, the tactics of a " democratic dictatorship of the proletariat and peasantry " which Lenin very clearly formulated as the completion of the *bourgeois* revolution against the will of the *bourgeoisie,* rendered possible the transition of the *bourgeois* revolution into a proletarian revolution and prepared the way for the victory of the latter in October 1917.

The overestimation of the creative role of the *bourgeoisie* is a remnant— much propagated by the reformists—of earlier *bour-*

geois apologetics and falsifications of history. A French writer held views similar to those of Gorki on this point. He said : ' A literature can never derive and renew its strength save from the foundations, from the soil, from the people. Literature is like Antaeus who lost his strength and virtue when his feet left mother earth,—as the Grecian legend tells us with such profound significance. What imbued our French literature—which needed it so badly—with a new vital strength in the eighteenth century, was not Montesquieu, not even Voltaire, for all their genius; no, it was the *roturiers,* the plebeians. It was Jean Jacques, it was Diderot."

The correct husbanding of this heritage is exemplified by Gorki, in whose *œuvre* the highest aims of artistic creation are organically rooted in the production of a true revolutionary popularity and nevertheless closely linked with the traditions of the great masterpieces of world literature.

A really profound conception of reality : such is the common foundation of artistic excellence and popularity of literature.   In his story *Konovalov,* for instance, Gorki shows how a true presentation of the genuine problems of life exercises an overwhelming influence on men of the people, to the point of changing their lives, and how such a serious effect of literature on the people can arise only from the depths of the writer's own conception of life.

With this conception of what is " popular " Gorki does away with the sham dilemma haunting the literature of the decaying *bourgeoisie* : the dilemma of the " ivory tower " on the one hand and propagandistic writing on the other. Gorki rejects a formalist withdrawal from life as decidedly as he does all " practical " limitations of literature. As a writer Gorki has always been topical and he has never set a demarcation line between his work as a writer and his work as a revolutionary journalist and propagandist.   On the contrary, his greatest masterpieces always sprang from his work as a journalist : *Foma Gordeyev* from his early struggle against capitalism when a reporter on the staff of a provincial newspaper; *The Mother* from journalistic activities during the first revolution; and *Klim Samgin* from his struggle against the wreckers of the victorious proletarian revolution.

But here again the lesson we have to learn from Gorki is to understand the real, vital bond between Gorki and the world around him. His journalistic experience helped him to get a close-up of life, of its motive forces, its dominant types and its typical conflicts and to participate, himself a fighter, in the struggles that were going on.   The wide knowledge of the world which he thus acquired and the deeply poetic forming of the rich content of his life finally enabled Gorki to discern and to put into literary form those basic and decisive human motives and those reflections of reality which are not always immediately visible on the surface. That is why he mostly approaches his problems from a certain distance, that is why he reaches so far into the past to put before us the genesis of the main types of our own time. The future historian of our revolution, the investigator of the difficulties which had to be overcome before a socialist society could be created, will say of Gorki's *œuvre* what Engels said of Balzac: "...even about economic details I have learnt more from them than from all the books of all the professional historians, economists and statisticians of the time.." By means of such a concrete historical conception of social phenomena, Gorki was able to overcome the modern pseudo-dilemma of ivory tower or propaganda pamphlet. For both of these—although with opposite signs and different subjective intentions—are equally unhistorical and both remain equally confined to the directly visible surface of life.

Culture signifies a broad and deep knowledge of life and its purpose is to give man real mastery over life. Gorki's life-history differs from that of most contemporary authors precisely by the width and depth of his interests and by the intensity with which he worked from his early youth to his death at the widening and deepening of his culture. Gorki has never been merely a writer in the narrow modern sense of the word, i.e. a person who produces books on the basis of an innate gift, specializes for such production and "observes" reality merely as the material for future books. Gorki grew to be a great writer because he incessantly and successfully fought against the distorting effect on the writer, of capitalist division of labour. This struggle itself incessantly enriched his experience of life, and his stature as an artist grew from book to book. The danger of the exhaustion of one's gift—a typical danger threatening the authors "specialized" through capitalist division of labour—did not exist for him.

Gorki never fails to emphasize most decidedly how great the importance of work in itself was for the development of his gifts and for his performance as a writer. He says for instance about a conversation he had with Leonid Andreyev: "I reassured him, told him that I did not consider myself an Arab steed but only a heavy carthorse and that I knew very well that my success was due less to my natural gifts than to my diligence and ability to work hard." In this sharply polemic form this is a preposterous exaggeration and certainly not Gorki's serious opinion of himself. But however exaggerated it may be, there is a core of truth in it. Gorki never considered the essence of poetic talent to be a playful, inventive imagination, a formal perfection of style or any other modern hallmark of " genius." He regarded himself as a result of his own work, performed on his own person.

That should not, of course, prevent us from trying to discover the secret of his innate unique genius, which we believe is to be found at a point quite different from the one where it is customary to seek such secrets, in him or in other great writers. Leo Tolstoy, who naturally enough was both foreign and averse to Gorki's world of thought from it, said this of him : " I cannot understand your mind . . . but you have a wise heart, . . yes, a wise heart."

A wise heart : that is perhaps the best description ever given of Maxim Gorki. The occasion on which the remark was made is so characteristic both of Tolstoy and of Gorki that it deserves to be mentioned here, especially as it permits the drawing of further conclusions regarding Gorki as an artist. Gorki was telling Tolstoy a story about his own youth. He had been working as odd-job-man and gardener in the house of a general's widow; she was a former prostitute, was always drunk and incessantly persecuted several young women living in the house. One day she met the girls in the garden and began to scold them in the most obscene terms. The girls wanted escape, but the general's wife barred their way and went on with her cursing. Gorki tried to intervene, at first with fair words, but in vain. At last he seized the old lady by the shoulders and pulled her away from the gate. The drunken harridan cursed even more, and accused Gorki of immoral relations with one of the girls. Finally " she quickly tore open her dressing-gown, pulled up her shift and shouted : ' I am better than any of these rats !'. At last I lost my temper, turned her with her back to me and hit her on the bottom end of her back, until she quickly jumped through the gate and ran away .. " And although the general's widow tried to get him to stay, Gorki immediately left her service.

Apparently just a coarse, somewhat obscene incident of Gorki's life as a tramp. But it is interesting to note Tolstoy's reaction to this story. First he went off into a fit of laughter and when he had somewhat recovered from it, he said : " It was most magnanimous of you to hit her only like that. Every other man would have hit her over the head .. " After a pause he said : " You are a funny chap ! Don't take it amiss, but you *are* a very funny chap !

It is amazing how good you still are, although you would be perfectly justified in being bad. You are strong, that is a good thing . . ." And as his final conclusion he made the remark, already quoted, about Gorki's " wise heart."

The simplicity and coarseness of this anecdote affords a suitable opportunity for demonstrating certain aspects of Gorki's character which are important from the human and literary point of view. The first of these is what Tolstoy expressed so neatly : his generosity, his instinctive moderation even in his angry spontaneous reaction to the cruelty and obscenity of the general's widow. Without a moment's reflection he immediately punishes and shames her but not more than is absolutely necessary, not an inch further; he never allows himself to be dragged down, even for an instant, into her atmosphere of beastliness and filth. Nevertheless he reacts to coarseness with coarseness. But—again instinctively—he gives the scene which begins with obscenity, a humoristic twist, thereby humanly and artistically counteracting this obscenity. For all the coarseness of the whole anecdote, it yet expresses Gorki's manliness, inner purity and delicacy no less distinctly than all his other manifestations and all his writings. He had a wise heart.

This wisdom of the heart is of the greatest artistic importance. Modern art suffers, among other things, from another pseudo-dilemma : the contrast of " delicacy " and " grossness ", falling all the time into one or the other of these false extremes. Like every other problem in art, it springs from life itself. The modern author faces the constantly increasing bestiality of life without being able to do anything about it. He either surrenders to this bestiality and depicts it in its naked, senseless, animal grossness or else he escapes from it into a sphere in which his withdrawal from life and all its brutality can be made superficially credible : he escapes into an empty "refinement."

The coarseness of the old writers had nothing to do with this dilemma. In the coarse scenes we find in Shakespeare, Cervantes or Rabelais many wild human passions explode brutally enough, for without depicting such passions no picture of life can be complete; but these passions are relegated to their proper place in the picture of the world presented to us by great poets and writers. The poet whose culture is genuine, the poet who masters life with his reason and his feeling, must come to grips with its negative as well as its positive forces; he derives artistic enjoyment from the struggle between the two, because his knowledge of men and his faith in their fundamental goodness causes him never to doubt their final victory over their animal instincts. But the modern writer is helpless in the face of the bestiality of the times.

Not so Gorki : he had a "wise heart." In the struggle between humanizing forces and the brute bestiality engendered in class society he never lost sight of the way out; more than that, he never ceased to fight for this way out, which is Socialism. The pathos of this struggle enabled him to find an artistic equilibrium where his contemporaries saw only the disharmony of their two false extremes. Gorki's art knows nothing of the modern false extremes of an "intimate" art on the one pole and a pseudo-monumentality divorced from reality on the other. He does not meticulously copy nature nor distort reality for the sake of an artificial stylization. He has a wise heart and hence wise senses which can bring to the surface from the depths of reality its essential traits. And because everything he sees and forms is humanly momentous, he can present seemingly uninteresting scenes of everyday life without losing his true monumentality and becoming "intimate"; he can depict the coarsest things in men in all their blatancy without so much as a shadow of modern grossness falling on his writing and without his having to resort to a false monumentality.

In the course of his long, eventful and laborious life, Gorki raised to an ever higher plane this innate feeling for what is human and humanly genuine. The connection with the revolutionary working-class movement, the experience of the struggle and victory of the working-class developed his culture and his art to ever greater perfection. He is the first great master of Socialist realism, for he demonstrated concretely, in his work as an artist, that the contradictions of *bourgeois* art can be overcome in Socialist practice.

INDEX OF AUTHORITIES

275